Adventure Guide

Vietnam, Laos & Cambodia

Janet Arrowood

HUNTER

HUNTER PUBLISHING, INC,
130 Campus Drive, Edison, NJ 08818
☎ 732-225-1900; 800-255-0343; fax 732-417-1744
www.hunterpublishing.com

Ulysses Travel Publications
4176 Saint-Denis, Montréal, Québec
Canada H2W 2M5
☎ 514-843-9882, ext. 2232; fax 514-843-9448

Windsor Books
The Boundary, Wheatley Road, Garsington
Oxford, OX44 9EJ England
☎ 01865-361122; fax 01865-361133

ISBN 1-58843-520-2
© 2006 Hunter Publishing, Inc.
Manufactured in the United States of America

This and other Hunter travel guides are also available as e-books through Amazon.com, NetLibrary.com, EBSCO and other digital partners. For more information, e-mail us at comments@hunterpublishing.com.

Cover photo: *Bronze elephant sculpture at the entry to the National Museum of Arts, Phnom Penh, Cambodia* (© Kevin Lang/Alamy)
Spine photo: *Dragon, Southern Laos temple* (© Janet Arrowood)
All interior color photos © Janet Arrowood, unless otherwise indicated.

Maps by Kim André, © 2006 Hunter Publishing, Inc.
Index by Nancy Wolff

1 2 3 4

Contents

Introduction   **1**
  The Recent Past   2
  The Land   3
  Why Come Here?   4
  Cautions & Advice   6
  Customs, Immigration & Visas   12
    Vietnamese Embassies in   12
      Great Britain   12
      Australia   12
      Canada   12
      United States   12
    Foreign Embassies in Vietnam   13
    Cambodian Embassies in   13
      United States   13
      France   14
      Australia   14
    Foreign Embassies in Cambodia   14
    Laotian Embassies in   14
      Australia   14
      United States   **15**
    Foreign Embassies in Laos   15
    Visas   15
    Immigration & Customs   16
    Departure Taxes   17
  Electrical Appliances   17
  Opening Hours   18
  Money Matters   18
  Laundry   19
  Booking Tours   19
  Health Considerations   23
  Getting There   30
  Getting Around   30
  The Weather   31
  What to Pack   31
    What to Wear/Take on the Flight   32
    What to Pack   33
  Selecting Your Accommodations   35
  Dining Out   38
  Overview – Vietnam   39
    About the Country   39
    Fast Facts   40
    Touring   41
      Suggested Itineraries   44

Highlights   46
History   47
Customs & Culture   51
Geography & Land   51
Climate   52
Flora & Fauna   52
Government & Economy   52
Lifestyles   53
Food Basics   55
Clothing & Costumes   56
Visas Requirements   56
Getting There   56
Overview – Laos   57
Fast Facts   59
Touring   60
   Suggested Itineraries   60
   Highlights   61
Customs & Culture   63
Basic History   64
Visas Requirements   67
Getting There   68
Religion   71
Arts & Crafts   72
Museums   73
Lifestyles   73
Food   74
Clothing & Costumes   75
Overview – Cambodia   75
The Democratic Republic of Kampuchea   75
Fast Facts   77
Touring   78
   Suggested Itineraries   78
   Highlights   79
History   81
Food   84
People, Culture & Customs   85
   Dance   86
   The People   87
   Religion   88
   Language   89
The Sex Trade   89
The Adoption Racket   90
Visa Requirements   90
Getting There   90
Getting Around by Air   91
The Vietnam War   92

Vietnam **97**
  Introduction 97
    The Country at a Glance 97
    Getting There & Around 100
    Weather & When to Visit 103
      The South 104
      The Central Highlands 105
      The Central Coast 105
      Hanoi & The North 106
      What to Take 107
    Hotel Basics 108
  Hanoi 108
    History 108
    Arrival 109
    Where to Stay 111
      Old Quarter 112
      French Quarter 113
    Where to Eat 114
      Old Quarter 115
      French Quarter 115
      Markets & Supermarkets 116
    Nightlife 117
      Bars & Clubs 117
    Shopping 117
    Tours & Travels 119
    Getting Around & Away 120
      Short Haul 120
      Long Haul 121
    What to See & Do 121
      Central Hanoi 121
        Ho An Kiem Lake 122
        The French Quarter 122
        The Old Quarter 123
        The West Side 124
      Outside the Central Area 125
    Useful Information 125
      Airlines 125
      Embassies & Consulates 126
      Internet/Communications 126
      Medical Facilities 126
    Day-Trips from Hanoi 127
      Halong Bay 127
      Sapa & the Mountains (then off to China) 127
        Where to Stay 128
        Where to Eat 129
        What to Do & See 129

Lao Cai 130
The Red River Estuary & Delta 130
Leaving Hanoi 131
Hué 131
History 131
Getting There & Away 132
Getting Around 132
Where to Stay 133
Pre-Booked/Pre-Paid Hotel Options 133
General Hotel Options 133
Where to Eat 134
Nightlife 134
Shopping 135
Tours & Travels 135
What to See & Do 135
The Citadel 135
The Flag Tower 135
The Imperial City 135
Museums 137
Phu Cat 138
Nearby Sights 138
The Royal Tombs or Mausoleums 138
Useful Information 139
Airlines 139
Internet/Communications 139
Medical Facilities 139
Danang 139
History 139
Getting There & Away 140
Getting Around 140
Where to Stay 140
Pre-Booked/Pre-Pay Options 140
General Hotel Options 141
Where to Eat 142
Nightlife 142
Shopping 142
Tours & Travels 142
What to See & Do 142
The Cham Museum 143
The Coa Dai Temple 143
Day-Trips from Danang 143
The Beaches 143
Marble Mountains 143
Bach Ma National Park 143
Useful Information 144
Airlines 144

Embassies & Consulates   144
Internet/Communications   144
Medical Facilities   144
Hoi An   145
History   145
Getting There & Away   145
Getting Around   145
Where to Stay   146
Pre-Book/Pre-Pay Options   146
General Hotel Options   146
Where to Eat   147
Nightlife   147
Shopping   147
Tours & Travels   148
What to See & Do   148
The Old City   148
Assembly Halls   149
Merchants' Houses (Shophouses)   149
Museums   150
The Market   150
Day-Trips from Hoi An   150
My Son   150
Useful Information   151
Airlines   151
Embassies & Consulates   151
Internet/Communications   151
Nha Trang   152
History   152
Getting There & Away   152
Where to Stay   152
Pre-Book/Pre-Pay Options   152
General Options   154
Where to Eat   154
Nightlife   155
Shopping   155
Adventures on Water   155
Tours & Travels   155
Getting Around   156
What to See & Do   156
Islands   157
Useful Information   157
Airlines   157
Embassies & Consulates   157
Internet/Communications   157
Medical Facilities   157
Dalat & the Southern Highlands   158

History 158
Getting There & Away 158
Getting Around 159
Where to Stay 159
    Pre-Book/Pre-Pay Options 160
    General Hotel Options 160
Where to Eat 161
Nightlife 161
Shopping 161
Tours & Travels 162
What to See & Do 162
Day-Trips from Dalat 163
Useful Information 163
    Airlines 163
    Embassies & Consulates 164
    Golf/Tennis 164
    Internet/Communications 164
    Medical Facilities 164
Ho Chi Minh City (HCMC/Saigon) 164
History 164
Getting There & Away 165
Where to Stay 167
    Pre-Booked/Pre-Paid Hotel Options 167
    General Hotel Options 169
    Pham Ngu Lao Area 169
    Dong Khoi Area 170
Where to Eat 170
    Dong Khoi Area 170
    Pham Ngu Lao (the backpacker area) 171
Nightlife 171
Shopping 171
Tours & Travels 172
Getting Around 172
What to See & Do 173
    The Dong Khoi Area 173
    The Cathedral 173
    The Old General Post Office 173
    Lam Son Square 173
    The Nguyen Hué Area 174
    The Ho Chi Minh City Museum 174
    Along the River 174
    Ben Thanh Market Area 174
    Le Duan Boulevard to the Botanical Gardens 175
    The Botanical Gardens & Zoo 175
    The History Museum 175
    The Reunification Palace & Surrounding Area 175

North of Dien Bien Phu Area | 175
Day-Trips from Ho Chi Minh City | 176
Useful Information | 176
  Airlines | 176
  Embassies/Consulates | 176
  Internet/Communications | 177
  Medical Facilities | 177
The Mekong Delta | 177
  History | 177
  Getting There & Away | 177
  Where to Stay | 178
    My Tho | 178
    Ben Tre | 178
    Vinh Long | 179
    Can Tho | 179
  Where to Eat | 179
    My Tho | 179
    Ben Tre | 179
    Vinh Long | 179
    Can Tho | 179
  Nightlife | 179
  Shopping | 180
  Tours & Travels | 180
  Getting Around | 180
  What to See & Do | 181
    Ben Tre | 181
    Can Tho | 181
  Useful Information | 181
    Airlines | 181
    Embassies & Consulates | 182
    Internet/Communications | 182
    Medical Facilities | 182
Vietnam Adventure Travel | 182
  Mekong Delta | 182
    Mekong Delta by Bike | 182
  Red River Delta | 183
  Sa Pa (Sapa) Trekking | 183
  Mount Sapa | 184
  Suggested Walking Itineraries | 185
  Suggested Biking Itineraries | 186
  Motorcycle Touring | 188

Laos | **189**
Introduction | 189
  The Country at a Glance | 189
  History | 193
    The Early Years | 193

The Mongol Influence	194
The Lan Xang Kingdom – Modern Laos	194
The Split of the Lan Xang Kingdom	195
The 19th Century	195
World War II	196
After the War	196
Under the Pathet Lao	197
Climate	198
Physical Adventures	198
Cultural Adventures	201
Getting There & Around	201
The Weather & When to Visit	203
What to See & Do	203
Vientiane	204
History	204
Where to Stay	204
Pre-Paid/Pre-Booked Hotel Options	206
General Hotel Options	206
Where to Eat	207
Nightlife	208
Shopping	208
Tours & Travels	209
Getting Around & Away	209
What to See & Do	212
The Wats	212
Monuments	213
Day-Trips from Vientiane	213
River Trips	213
Hiking, Cycling & Walking	214
Cars & Motor Scooters	214
Useful Information	214
Airlines	214
Banks/Money Exchange	215
Embassies/Consulates	215
Internet/Communications	215
Medical Facilities	216
Vang Vieng	216
History	216
Where to Stay	216
Where to Eat	217
Nightlife	217
Shopping	217
Tours & Travels	217
Getting Around & Away	217
What to See & Do	218
Useful Information	218

Airlines	218
Banks/Money Exchange	218
Embassies/Consulates	218
Internet/Communications	218
Medical	218
Bokeo	219
History	219
Where to Stay	219
Where to Eat	219
What to See & Do	219
Xiengkhuang (Xieng Khoung)	220
Where to Stay	220
Where to Eat	220
Getting Around & Away	220
What to See & Do	220
Day-Trips from Xiengkhuang	221
Useful Information	222
Airlines	222
Banks/Money Exchange	222
Embassies/Consulates	222
Internet/Communications	222
Medical	222
Savannakhet	222
History	222
Where to Stay	223
Where to Eat	223
Nightlife	223
Shopping	223
Tours & Travels	223
Getting Around & Away	223
What to See & Do	225
Useful Information	225
Airlines	225
Banks/Money Exchange	225
Embassies/Consulates	225
Internet/Communications	225
Medical	225
Champasak	226
History	226
Where to Stay	226
Pre-Book/Prepay Hotel Options	226
General Hotel Options	227
Where to Eat	228
Getting There & Around	228
What to See & Do	229
Champasak Temple Complex	229

Wat Phu   229
Day-Trips from Champasak   230
Useful Information   231
Pakse (Pakxe)   231
  Places to Stay   231
  Places to Eat   232
  Nightlife   232
  Shopping   232
  Tours & Travels   232
  Getting There & Around   232
  Useful Information   234
    Airlines   234
    Banks/Money Exchange   234
    Embassies/Consulates   234
    Internet/Communications   234
    Medical   234
Northern Laos   234
  Luang Prabang   235
    History   235
    Getting There & Away   238
    Getting Around   241
    What to See & Do   241
      The "Must See" Wats   242
      Wats Along Phothisarath   242
      The National Museum   244
      Suggested Walking Tour   244
    Where to Stay   244
      Pre-Book/Prepay Hotel Options   245
      General Hotel Options   245
    Where to Eat   246
    Nightlife   247
    Shopping   247
    Tours & Travels   248
    Day-Trips from Luang Prabang   248
      Pak Ou Caves – Upstream   249
      Khouang-Sy Waterfalls – Downstream   249
      Caving   250
      River Trips   250
      Cycling   250
      Walking & Hiking   251
    Useful Information   251
      Airlines   251
      Banks/Money Exchange   251
      Embassies/Consulates   251
      Internet/Communications   251
      Medical   252

Adventures in Northern Laos   252
    Hiking & Trekking   252
    Elephant Rides   256
    Mountain Biking   258
    Rafting, Boating, Canoeing & Kayaking   258
    Tubing   259
    Venturing Farther into Luang Prabang Province   259
        Tour Operators & Arrangers   260
    Trekking   261
        On the Mekong River   261

Cambodia   **263**
    The Country at a Glance   263
    History   263
        Prehistory/Early Kingdoms   264
        The Indianized Kingdom of Funan   264
        The Chenla State   264
        What Caused the Angkor Empire's Rise?   265
        Why Did the Angkor Civilization Fall?   265
        Highlights of the Angkor Kings   267
    Weather & When to Visit   276
    Phnom Penh   277
        Where to Stay   279
            Central   280
            Sisowath Quay   281
        Where to Eat   282
            Central   282
            Sisowath Quay Area   283
        What to See & Do   283
            The Royal Palace   284
            The Silver Pagoda   285
            The National Museum of Cambodia   286
            The Riverside   286
            Wat Phnom   286
            The Victory Monument   287
            South of the Center of Town   287
        Day Trips from Phnom Penh   287
            Oudong   287
            Choueng Ek – The Killing Fields   288
            Kirirom National Park   288
            Mekong River Cruises   288
            Transportation in Town   289
            Hiking, Cycling & Walking   289
            Cars, Scooters & Cyclos   289
            Buses & Taxis   289
        Useful Information   289
            Airlines   289

Embassies & Consulates 290
Internet/Communications 290
Medical Facilities 290
Siem Reap/Angkor Wat 290
Getting There 291
By Air/From the Airport 291
Overland 291
Where to Stay 292
Pre-Paid/Pre-Booked Options 292
General Hotel Options 293
Where to Eat 293
Near the River 293
Near the Old Market 294
Entertainment 294
Markets & Shopping 294
Tours & Travels 294
What to See & Do 294
The Angkor Complex 294
Seeing the Temples 296
Around the Area 306
Outlying Temples 307
Transportation in Town 308
Hiking, Cycling & Walking 308
Useful Information 308
Airlines 308
Embassies & Consulates 308
Internet/Communications 308
Medical Facilities 308
Battambang 309
Getting There 309
Where to Stay 310
Where to Eat 310
Sihanoukville 310
Getting There & Away 310
Where to Stay 310
Ochental Beach 310
Victory Beach 310
Where to Eat 311
Entertainment 311
What to Do & See 311
Local Transportation 312
Bokor Hill Station – Kampot 312
Getting There & Away 312
Where to Stay 313
Where to Eat 313

Books & Websites   313

Index   315

Maps
Vietnam, Laos & Cambodia   inside front cover
Vietnam
  Vietnam Regions   51
  Vietnam   100
  Hanoi   111
  Sapa   130
  Central Hué   137
  Hoi An   148
  Nha Trang·   154
  Ho Chi Minh City (Saigon)   169
  Mekong Delta   179
Laos
  Laos   58
  Vientiane   205
  Luang Prabang   236
Cambodia
  Cambodia   75
  Phnom Penh   278
  Temples of Angkor   303

Introduction

Why visit this part of the world? It is relatively safe, untrammeled by tourists, and still gives a taste of the "old" Southeast Asia and French Colonial empire. There are tremendous waterfalls, impressive rivers, huge lakes, wildlife, elephant rides, jungles, wonderful people, and fabulous food. The costs are a fraction of those "at home" and the experience will last a lifetime. Once you've

In this Chapter

- The Recent Past   2
- The Land   3
- Why Come Here?   4
- Cautions & Advice   6
- Customs, Immigration & Visas   12
- Electrical Appliances   17
- Money Matters   18
- Booking Tours   19
- Health   23
- Getting There   30
- Getting Around   30
- The Weather   31
- What to Pack   31
- Selecting Accommodations   35
- Dining Out   38
- Overview - Vietnam   39
- Overview - Laos   57
- Overview - Cambodia   75
- The Vietnam War   92

been, the region will call you back again and again. Adventure awaits.

Note: The earthquake and accompanying tsunami of December 2004 did not directly affect any of the countries covered in this book. At the same time, the difficulty getting relief supplies to the affected countries shows how poor the infrastructure in this part of the world can be. Many of the tips in this book are intended to make your trip easier.

RESPONSIBLE TRAVEL

As more people visit this beautiful and largely unspoiled region it is very important to be a responsible, environmentally aware traveler. True eco-tourism hasn't arrived here yet. Adventure and active travel are beginning to catch on, and even to boom in Vietnam and parts of Laos, but the infrastructure and services are lagging behind the expectations of many travelers. Remember, the people here have to stay when we leave, and they live with the attitudes, damage, and goodwill we bring and leave behind. Please recycle your water bottles, pick up your trash, save water and electricity. Resources are scarce, precious, and expensive.

■ The Recent Past

For much of the past 150 years the region encompassing Laos, Vietnam, and Cambodia was referred to as French Indochina/Cochinchina. Indeed, the French occupation, stretching from about 1850 to the early 1950s, has left a mark on these three countries that adds to their cultural, historical, architectural, and gastronomic appeal. At the same time, they have been severely impacted by internal and external wars, the imposition of communism/socialism, and the absence, for many decades, of any sort of tourism.

It is only in the past 10-15 years that tourists have returned to discover the unique attractions and almost pristine beauty of the region. In fact, it has been mostly during the past five years that significant tourist infrastructure has been developed, with tourists returning in substantial numbers. For the first time in 30 years you can now fly directly into the region (Hanoi and Ho Chi Minh City) on an American-flagged airline – United Airlines – as well as on many Asian and European carriers (Air France, Lufthansa, Singapore, Thai, among others).

Eco-tourism in the area is in its infancy. Cultural and adventure travel are only at the toddler stage. Still, changes are happening at a near-lightning pace, so you are in for a real treat. The people are warm and welcoming; the temples are spectacular; the museums are fascinating; the opportunities to explore and experience unique cultures are almost limitless; and the variety of action-packed and light adventure opportunities is boundless.

The area has been repeatedly invaded, influenced, or controlled by peoples from China, Thailand, France, the United States, Burma, India, and many other countries. Their influences can be readily seen in the art, language, customs, culture, and landscape of each country.

In recent years, communism/socialism (and a degree of isolationism) have been the prevailing cultural influence in Laos and Vietnam, but the hard-core versions that were initially imported are being softened to allow for free enterprise, foreign investment, and the blossoming of small businesses. In Cambodia there are still lingering effects of the Pol Pot regime, but things are changing and improving.

Although there are many superficial similarities between the three countries, each is really quite different. Within countries, different areas feel different, too.

The northern part of Vietnam has the longest history of communism/socialism, and it shows in subtle and not-so-subtle ways. The government's reach is long, but 30 fewer years of communist rule makes for a noticeable difference between the North and the South.

In Cambodia, the smaller towns feel more welcoming and less restrictive than does Phnom Penh, but the energy level in Phnom Penh is so much higher.

In Laos, the biggest distinction is between the city and village dwellers. As Vientiane grows, and the non-Governmental Organizations (NGOs) extend their influence, the laid-back atmosphere will continue to fade. For example, Vientiane (Laos) used to be a small backwater serving as a national capital, but the ASEAN (Association of Southeast Asian Nations) summit in November 2004 has started to change all that.

■ The Land

The more traveled parts of Cambodia are relatively flat and almost water-logged. The short stretch of coast is quite beautiful and rarely visited.

Vietnam is extremely rugged across most of its land area, except right along the coast, and even that area is far from flat. The exception is the Mekong Delta, which is flat, almost boggy in places, and hot.

Laos is rugged, with a few flat valleys, especially along the rivers, and there's no coastline.

■ Why Come Here?

In Southeast Asia there is a sense of the new and unknown. The dollar is still worth something. True adventure and ancient cultures are getting harder to find. The world is being overrun with CNN, BBC, DVDs, CDs, fancy electronic devices, and other modern "conveniences." The poorest house in the most southerly reaches of Laos may have a generator and a huge satellite dish, while a frightening number of children die before their fifth birthday and the local hospital is not much more than a shack with a few beds, fewer staff, poor sanitation, and almost no supplies.

The people across Southeast Asia are warm and welcoming. They are becoming more experienced in dealing with Western travelers and their needs and desires. The food is good, and prices are phenomenally low. You won't find many five-star hotels outside Hanoi and Saigon (HCMC, or Ho Chi Minh City), but there are lots of mom-and-pop places with air-conditioning, hot water, private bathrooms, satellite TV, decent beds, buffet breakfasts, and a genuinely welcoming attitude. You can travel amazingly cheaply and, with a few precautions, stay healthy, happy, involved, and active. And the scenery is spectacular. The region offers something for all types of travelers.

For the Adventure-Seeker

- ☐ Tubing or rafting on peaceful or raging rivers
- ☐ Canoeing on historic lakes
- ☐ Kayaking in the South China Sea
- ☐ Hiking or trekking over gentle or rugged terrain for a day, a week, or a month
- ☐ Snorkeling or scuba diving in near-pristine waters with fantastic fish and coral
- ☐ Biking the length of Vietnam or Laos
- ☐ Mountain biking virgin terrain
- ☐ Riding an elephant

□ Cycling lazily around the Laotian Mekong Islands

□ Hot springs

□ Viewing some of the largest waterfalls in the world

□ Golfing in exotic locations

□ Power boating along the Mekong, or floating down it

□ Boating to almost untouched islands

□ Volunteering to help some of the poorest people in the world

□ Watching elephants being trained to haul teak logs and tourists

For the Culture-Vulture

□ Visit temples, UNESCO World Heritage Sites, ancient monuments, and cities with remnants of Colonial history and architecture

□ Explore museums with displays from cultures that are thousands of years old

□ Visit wats (temples) painted and gilded in fantastic colors

□ Watch the monks of all ages going about in saffron, red, and yellow robes

□ Stay in, and tour, exotic villas

□ Walk through ancient outdoor universities

□ Trek to hill tribe areas and see how much of the world lives, while collecting wonderful ethnic art

□ Visit the former royal palaces

□ Wander through local and crafts markets

□ Shop until you drop

The list of activities and sights is nearly endless and constantly growing. By the time this book is published, you may be able to go parasailing, hang-gliding, water-skiing, and more. There are golf courses opening, and more museums being restored every year.

Eco-tourism is in its infancy, so your opportunities to see and help preserve some of world's last double- and triple-canopy jungle and old-growth mahogany and teak forests are out there. You can even golf in Vietnam (bring your own clubs!) or mountain bike in Laos (bring your own helmet!).

Although the focus of this guide is an active, outdoor-oriented trip with lots of cultural activities and shopping, if you have a bit more time and really want to see the country and make an impact, consider working as a volunteer. There are hundreds of organizations that can coordinate almost anything you want to do. Maybe you'll want to teach English, or help bring a water line into a remote village, or participate in an archeological dig. I have a friend who spent three weeks teaching English in the Mekong Delta and said it was the most wonderful, educational, and rewarding experience of her life. Try an Internet search for "International Volunteer Opportunities" or visit a website such as www.globalvolunteers.org or www.iesc.org.

■ Cautions & Advice

E-mail and the Internet are wonderful inventions. Access across Southeast Asia is easy, cheap, and fast. Take advantage of them to smooth your trip arrangements and hold copies of key documents.

You can set up a Yahoo, MSN, Hotmail, or similar e-mail account and use it to:

- ☐ E-mail yourself and others scanned copies of your passport information, visa pages, paper tickets, and other hardcopy documents.
- ☐ E-mail yourself and others lists of your credit/debit card numbers and contact numbers.
- ☐ List your other emergency contact information.
- ☐ Hold copies of your itinerary, e-tickets, and hotel/travel vouchers.

On the Roads

Overall, Southeast Asia is a safe, traveler-friendly destination. The drivers, however, are a different story!

In Laos there have been occasional incidents of highway banditry in the vicinity of Vang Vieng (on the road from Luang Prabang to Vientiane). The same applies in parts of Vietnam, especially Ho Chi Minh City. Phnom Penh is another high-risk area.

It is always a good idea to travel with others, rather than walking or riding (on a scooter) alone, and to make sure someone knows your itinerary. You might consider e-mailing your agenda to yourself and several people back home before leaving a city to travel along the highways.

You can rent motor scooters, but they are not always in good shape, and helmets are scarce. The roads can also be incredibly twisting and in poor repair. It is now possible to rent a car but prices are high – plan on $50-$100 per day. I spoke with people who rented cars in Laos and they said the driving was not bad since there are so few cars in the country. But watch out for the maniacal drivers behind the wheels of buses and heavy trucks!

Watch Your Shoes

Most guesthouses and temples (and some shops and museums) expect you to take off your shoes. Unfortunately, shoes, especially brand name athletic shoes, have a tendency to go missing. The cost of a pair of Nikes is more than many people make in a month, so the temptation can be high. It is very hard to find satisfactory replacement shoes that fit non-Asian feet.

I highly recommend taking your shoes to your room or carrying them in your pack at the temples. Wear socks, too, or carry a pair for the times you have to "lose the shoes." The floors are not necessarily as clean as you might like, and ground-in dirt is hard to remove. The dirt tends to be gritty, gluey, and reddish.

Don't Drink the Water

Assume that only bottled water is safe to drink. Make sure the bottle is opened in front of you. If it comes to the table opened, send it back.

Many places serve "ozonated" or irradiated water in bottles. As long as this is opened in front of you it is as safe as, and much cheaper than, bottled brand-name water.

Keep in mind that you should avoid tap water in all its forms – on unpeeled or uncooked/undercooked vegetables and fruits, brushing your teeth, ice, smoothies, and so forth. Many places do buy their ice from local companies that make it from purified water, so use your judgment here. The local people don't intend to make you sick, but they can drink local water and you shouldn't. In fact, most locals don't drink the tap water, either!

Drugs

One word – DON'T. Drugs can get you in trouble so fast your head will spin. They are completely and totally and unequivocally illegal. Sometimes the authorities look the other way; sometimes they don't.

Be especially careful of friendly locals on the trip from Luang Prabang to Vang Vieng; the same goes for locals and other travelers in Vang Vieng. These "friendly" people may invite you to a party where drugs are present, or they may plant drugs on your person or in your belongings, then inform the local police or threaten you to extort money.

Phnom Penh is another area where you need to be careful of the friendly locals and the local police. Many Westerners have been set-up and had to pay exorbitant "fines" to get out of the situation. The police are not always your friends. In poor countries the officials, including those in law enforcement, are often on the take.

Southeast Asian jails are not pleasant places, and the sentences are long and harsh. There is a book called *Forget You Have A Daughter*, by Sandra Gregory. I recommend you read it before you try something that could land you in a Southeast Asian jail.

Robbery

 Thievery is not a major problem in Southeast Asia, but it does happen. These are countries of very poor people, and to them a tourist looks rich, even in beat-up sneakers, a T-shirt, and jeans. Keep your passport, tickets, credit cards, cash, and traveler's checks in a safe place. If you are traveling with someone else, consider having them carry a copy of all your stuff, and vice versa.

I prefer a neck pouch – women can put on the pouch, then put on their bra, and tuck the pouch into the waist of their skirt or pants. It's almost impossible to snatch that way. Men should consider the neck pouch and tuck it tightly into their pants and cinch their belt snugly. Money belts are too easy to steal. A traveler's tip to consider. Have a "throwaway" money pouch or purse with your "walking around" money for the day, a few American dollars and an expired credit card. If someone insists on relieving you of your valuables you can throw this on the ground and ease away when the thief goes to retrieve it.

> **A Suggestion:** Walk around wearing your money pouch for a few days before you leave home so you get used to it. Don't make the traveler's number-one mistake – patting your money pouch or wallet to see if it's still there. That is like shouting, "Here's the important stuff – come and get it!" If you prefer to carry a fanny pack, go to a travel store and get one with wire inside so it can't be easily slashed off your waist or slashed open, and wear the pouch in the front, not behind.

Increasingly, thieves operate on scooters. They ride double, and the passenger leans over and grabs or slashes anything hanging loose. Their favorite targets are daypacks, fanny packs, cameras, and camera bags. If they've seen you patting a pocket, they'll slash that area with a knife. Stay well back from the curb, and hold loose items close to your body. This is a big problem in HCMC and Phnom Penh, and it's beginning to happen in Hanoi and smaller Vietnamese cities. Laos is still relatively safe, except for the road trip from Luang Prabang to Vientiane.

ATMs

There are lots of scams involving hooks, glue, double-stick tape, and other means to snag your card inside the ATM. There are "surfers" who will watch to get your PIN and then, when you can't get your card out of the machine, they wait for you to leave and remove your card (with tweezers in most cases), use your PIN, and have a great time while the money lasts. There are also people who crowd you and then grab some or all of your money when the ATM spits it out, or they assault you as you walk away. Try to have a friend stand guard while you use your card and secure your cash. Several credit card companies (such as American Express) and many American and Canadian banks are now offering "pre-loaded" bank cards. You get several cards that have been pre-loaded with a certain dollar amount. They work like ATM and credit/debit cards, but the total available limit is relatively low so if they are lost or stolen the damage to your finances in minimized. You can lose only the balance remaining on the card. By taking several cards you can reduce your loss exposure tremendously. See the *Useful Information* sections throughout this guide for more.

Passport, Credit Cards, Valuables

 Leave a copy of everything with someone who will accept a collect call from you. This means your passport, any visas you obtained before leaving, your ticket (even e-tickets), your credit cards (front and back to include the phone number in case of theft), your traveler's checks serial numbers, and anything else of value that can be copied. Make sure you have a copy of the first page and any visa pages in your passport, keep these copies separate from the actual documents, and give your travel partner(s) copies, too. Always take enough pictures for visas (assume two per visa). Then have another two photos so you can use them, with a copy of your passport, should you need a replacement.

Don't let your credit card out of your sight. If the vendor insists on taking it to another room, refuse. The only possible exception is four- or five-star hotels, restaurants, travel agencies, and the like. Even then, follow your instincts! There have been many instances of waiters and shop clerks having a hand-held device that can read your credit card's magnetic strip (this is called "skimming"), then creating a duplicate card and having a grand old time shopping and spending *your* money. An alternative is to get "pre-loaded" debit cards, as mentioned above.

It is a good idea to let your credit card company (and bank) know where you are going and what kind of charges you plan to make. These companies monitor your purchases and if they see something that appears way out of line they will try to reach you. If they can't reach you immediately, they will cancel your card. Then you are in a really tough spot.

Vouchers

If you book hotels and many flights from outside Southeast Asia you can almost always pre-pay and get vouchers. This reduces the amount of cash and traveler's checks you have to carry. It also gives you an "address" if needed for visas, sending cash, or getting replacement credit/ATM cards or tickets sent. In addition, if the worst happens and you lose your cards and cash and traveler's checks, or get seriously ill, you have a place to go.

Make sure to bring copies of your vouchers. This is very important since the agent or website you used may have actually booked through a third party. If you can't show the name of the actual booking entity you may find you don't have a room or seat. A friend and I learned this in Burma. I had copies of the vouchers from our booking agent in Thailand. It turns out they had used a third party and that was the name under which our reservation was made – not our names, and not our agent's name. Had I not brought the vouchers we would have been out of luck.

Jewelry

Don't wear chains, earrings, or expensive jewelry. You will be a target for thieves, many of whom will rip the items through your ears or off your neck or wrist. Most people can't tell the good from the cheap, either, so if it looks remotely expensive, leave it at home (even if it only cost a few dollars). Having an earring ripped out of your ear is painful, and more so if it cost only $15!

■ Customs, Immigration & Visas

Here is some general information for some countries. Note that embassies and consulates move surprisingly often. Their websites are a valuable source of information. I recommend a Google (or similar) search before you leave to make sure you have current addresses and telephone numbers for the embassies and consulates relative to your nationality and destinations.

Vietnamese Embassies in

Great Britain
12-14 Victoria Road, London W8 5RD
☎ 0870 005 6985
Fax 020 7937 6108
Visa Section:
☎ 0870 005 6985
www.vietnam.embassyhomepage.com

Australia
Embassy of the Socialist Republic of Vietnam
6 Timbarra Crescent, O'Malley, ACT 2606
☎ 2-62866059/62901549
Fax 2-62864534/62902908
vembassy@webone.com.au
www.vietnamembassy.org.au

Canada
Embassy of the Socialist Republic
of Vietnam in Canada
470 Wilbrod Street
Ottawa, Ontario K1N 6M8
☎ (613) 236-0772; (613) 232-1957, (613) 236-2688
Fax (613) 236-2704
vietem@istar.ca; www.vietnamembassy-canada.ca

United States
Embassy of Vietnam
1233 20th St., NW, #400
Washington, DC 20036
☎ (202) 861-0737
Fax (202) 861-0917
info@vietnamembassy-usa.org
www.vietnamembassy-usa.org/embassy

Foreign Embassies in Vietnam
United Kingdom
British Embassy
Central Building
4th floor
31 Hai Ba Trung
Hanoi
☎ (4) 936 0500

Canada
31 Hung Vuong
Hanoi, Vietnam
☎ (4) 734 5000
Fax (4) 734 5049
hanoi@dfait-maeci.gc.ca

Australia
8 Dao Tan Street
Ba Dinh District
Hanoi, Vietnam
☎ (4) 831 7755
Fax (4) 831 7711

United States
7 Lang Ha Street
Ba Dinh District
Hanoi, Vietnam
☎ (4) 772 1500
Fax (4) 772 1510

Cambodian Embassies in
United States
Royal Embassy of Cambodia
4530 16th Street NW
Washington DC 20011
☎ (202) 726-7742
Fax (202) 726-8381
cambodia@embassy.org

France

Royal Embassy of Cambodia
4 rue Adolphe Yvon
75116 Paris, France
☎ (1) 45 03 47 20
Fax (1) 45 03 47 40

Australia

The Royal Embassy of Cambodia
5 Canterbury Crescent
Deakin, ACT 2600, Australia
☎ 2 6273 1259 or +61 2 6273 1154
Fax 2 6273 1053
CambodianEmbassy@ozemail.com.au

Foreign Embassies in Cambodia

Australia

Villa11, R V Senei Vannavaut Oum (St. 254)
Daun Penh District
Phnom Penh, Cambodia
☎ 855 23 213 470
Fax 855 23 213 413
australian.embassy.cambodia@dfat.gov.au

United States

16, Street 228 (between streets 51 and 63)
Phnom Penh, Cambodia
☎ 855 23 216 436/216 438
Fax 855 23 216 437

Laotian Embassies in

Australia

1 Dalman Crescent, O' Malley
Canberra, ACT 2606
☎ (6) 2864595, (6) 2866933
Fax (6) 2901910

United States
2222 S Street NW
Washington, DC 20008
☎ (202) 332-6416/17
Fax (202) 332 4923

Foreign Embassies in Laos

Australia
Rue J. Nehru, Quartier Phone Xay
PO Box 292, Vientiane Laos
IDD Code 856-21
☎ (856-21) 413600
Fax (856-21) 413601

United States
Box 114, Rue Bartholonie
Vientiane, Laos PDR
(Mailing: Box V, APO AP 96546, Vientiane)
☎ 212-581/2/5
Fax 212-584

United Kingdom
PO Box 6626
Vientiane, Laos
☎ 413606
Fax 413607
btolaos@loxinfo.co.th

Visas

Westerners need visas for all three countries. Currently you can get visas upon arrival in the main Cambodian airports (Siem Reap/Angkor Wat and Phnom Penh) and most main entry points into Laos (the airports and the Friendship Bridge). Vietnam does not issue visas upon arrival.

You can obtain all your visas before you leave home, or do so en route (at an Asian gateway such as Hong Kong, Tokyo, or Bangkok).

Visa costs vary based on your nationality and how fast you want the visa. Expect to spend about US$30-$40 for Laotian and Cambodian visas (plus postage) and about US$40-$50 for a Vietnamese visa. If you want the visa sooner than five to seven business days (plus mailing time), expect to pay another $30-$40 per visa. If you use a visa-handling service, they add another $20 per visa.

My preference has always been to collect onward visas in the country I visit just beforehand. For example, I usually get the Vietnamese visa in Bangkok (and it is faster, cheaper than at home, and payable in Thai Baht), then get the Laotian visa either on arrival or in Hanoi, and then get the Cambodian visa either on arrival or in Laos. Note that the Laotian visa and Cambodian visa are usually payable in US dollars or, if acquired in Thailand, in Thai Baht.

Immigration & Customs

All three countries require arriving visitors (and passengers on internal flights) to go through some form of immigration and customs. It will help if you are reasonably dressed and very polite. These are not Western countries and they do not always appreciate our sense of fun or humor.

The allowable items vary by country and change constantly. If the item(s) you want to bring in has a serial number, note it in your passport. A digital photo of items that are electronic might be a good record to have (e-mail it to yourself before you leave home). Generally speaking, you can bring a laptop computer and peripherals, a still (digital and/or SLR-type) camera and film/discs, a video camera, a cell phone, and similar devices, and you don't have to declare them. You can also bring in cigarettes (about 200), a liter of alcohol, and similar luxury goods. Check with each country's official website before you enter – the allowances and rules are always changing.

> **Tip:** The customs forms are confusing. Many places (even Thailand) have posted signs saying you can bring only a few hundred dollars of personal items and must declare all electronics. This is not really the case. When in doubt, ask the customs officials if something should be declared.

Most Asian countries have you fill out two forms – an arrival form (for immigration and customs) and a departure card. Some places staple the departure card onto your passport – others don't. **Don't lose the departure card!** Without it, you will have a very hard time getting out of the country.

 Don't overstay your visa. Most of these countries will renew your visa once. However, if you overstay, the cost is $5-$10 per day (or more) and you can actually be jailed.

Departure Taxes

These taxes are a fact of life in most of Asia.

If you enter through Thailand and leave the airport, you have to pay a Thai Baht 500 (about US$13) departure tax. This must be paid in Baht – no other currency is accepted.

Most countries charge about US$10 as a departure tax, but this may change if the dollar continues to weaken. In addition, Laos charges a few thousand Kip (under US$1) for internal flights.

■ Electrical Appliances

 The voltage is 220-240 volts, 50 hertz. I have found the voltage to be on the high side, so even 220-volt appliances may run hot. Most outlets take both the US/Canadian-style flat pins and the European/Asian-style round pins. This does not mean your North American appliances will work. They won't – they will fry. The exceptions are devices with switches for 120 to 240 voltage, and those with power supplies. Always check the fine print to make sure the voltage accommodated goes to 240, not just 220.

Power is erratic, so a portable surge suppressor is a good idea for laptops and cell phones. Don't leave something plugged in and charging when you are gone. If the power goes out, immediately unplug the devices so they are not plugged in when the power surges back on.

■ Opening Hours

 Shops in Southeast Asia are generally open from 8 am to 8 pm or later, especially outside shopping centers and hotels. They are often open seven days a week, even on local holidays.

Offices and businesses are generally open Monday to Friday from 8 am to 5 or 6 pm. They may close at noon for lunch, but this is pretty unusual.

Restaurants keep long hours – generally from 8 am (or earlier if they serve breakfast) to 10 or 11 pm, seven days a week. Note that Muslim-operated restaurants will often close on Friday/Saturday, and don't usually serve liquor.

■ Money Matters

 Banks are easy to locate, but moneychangers offer much better exchange rates so you are not likely to go into a bank at all. Beware of unofficial money-changers, such as the women who hang out at the south end of Hoan Kiem Lake in Hanoi – they will rip you off.

ATMs are pretty scarce in most of northern Vietnam, and all of Laos and Cambodia. In HCMC there seems to be an ATM at every corner. Hanoi has a few (generally at the ANZ banks) and more are sprouting every month.

In southern Vietnam, there are ATMs around the larger towns. Most banks can change money, but whether they will is another story. The airport exchanges are hit and miss.

One of the better places to change money is at a hotel. Most post their rates for US dollars.

Dollars are still the preferred currency, but you may be able to exchange euros now. Laos is an exception and most places there require payment in the local currency, known as Kip.

CURRENCY TIP

Many countries in Asia prefer or even require US dollars. Make sure the dollars you bring are:

- Not worn
- Clean, with no writing or stains
- No older than 10 years

Currency Conversion	
Vietnam	US$1 = 14,891 Vietnam Dong (VND)
Laos	US$1 = 10,842 Lao Kip (LAK)
Cambodia	US$1 = 4,262 Cambodian Riel (KHR)

■ Laundry

Most hotels will handle this for a few dollars per kg/2.2 lbs.

■ Booking Tours

Please remember you are traveling in a developing nation, not a modernized one full of concern for your safety and convenience. As long as you keep this in mind, and apply a hefty dose of common sense to everything you consider doing, travel "off the beaten path" can be fun and the experience of a lifetime.

If you are going to book a tour (either at home or when you arrive) here are the steps I recommend.

Step 1

Ask other travelers in your physical condition, age, and budget range what they did (or plan to do), why, and what they liked and disliked about the experience. Other travelers are often the best, and most reliable, source of up-to-date information about any destination. After all, they've just "been there, done that" (or decided *not* to 'do that'!).

Find out if they made all their own arrangements, had a hotel or travel agent do it for them, pre-arranged their activities before arrival, and what the experience was like. Ask them what they would do differently and why. Ask them what sights they wish they had seen and which ones they would cheerfully skip. If they used websites, get the addresses.

❖ Questions to Ask

☐ How large was the tour group?

☐ How organized were the guide and the travel company?

☐ Were there unplanned deviations from the scheduled itinerary?

- [ ] What did the trip cost?
- [ ] What did the fees cover?
- [ ] What did the fees *not* cover?
- [ ] How was the food?
- [ ] Any unexpected or intolerable aspects to the trip?
- [ ] Did they feel they received their money's worth?
- [ ] Would they do the trip again?
- [ ] What was the name of the guide or trip leader?
- [ ] How good was the English spoken by the guide and the people who handled the booking?
- [ ] How good was the guide's local and historical knowledge?
- [ ] Was a money-back guarantee offered?
- [ ] Who arranged for visas and park entrance or similar fees?
- [ ] Was the appropriate safety equipment available and in good condition (helmets, life jackets)?
- [ ] Did they feel safe?
- [ ] Were mosquito nets and linens provided?
- [ ] Were cots and/or sleeping bags and mosquito nets provided for camping trips?
- [ ] Was too much activity packed into each day?
- [ ] How was the transportation?
- [ ] Was enough time allowed to explore markets, temples, museums, and so forth?
- [ ] Was the shopping limited to roadside places filled with tour buses?

You can probably think of dozens of other questions now, and you'll have even more as you travel.

Step 2

Surf the Web for more information, using sites such as Google, Yahoo or MSN.

I am not a big organized-tour or pre-booking person. But I do have some favorite websites for making advance arrangements. My top four sites are:

- [ ] Whatever airline you favor.

□ www.cheaptickets.com, for discount fares in Southeast Asia.

□ www.sunfar.co.th, for general reservations, tours, airline tickets, and hard-to-arrange activities. The owner, Winston Wu, lived in San Francisco for many years and speaks and writes fluent English. The company has relationships with all the top Southeast Asian tour and travel companies and airlines. They handled a recent trip to Burma for me and I couldn't have been more pleased. I saved about 30% over other companies and all the work was done for me.

□ www.asia-hotels.com, if you want to make your own hotel arrangements ahead of time. They have some amazing rates, especially for big city and airport hotels.

Include the Department of Health and Human Services, the State Department, and other Federal government sites in your search. These are good sites for basic, but often not truly current, information. State Department warnings are frequently out-of-date, and tend to paint a much grimmer picture of a situation than is warranted. If you are traveling in small groups and not flaunting your "American-ness," or "British-ness," or other nationality, you are usually well under the radar screen of any troublemakers. Targets for these groups tend to be larger, well-heeled groups of tourists. Nonetheless, there are unexpected blow-ups anywhere, and one of the most problematic places is the stretch of highway from a bit south of Luang Prabang to Vientiane (generally from Van Vieng and south).

Step 3

Let your in-country embassy and/or consulate know you are there and what your approximate itinerary and departure dates are. Embassies and consulates can be a good source of warnings and current information about the country.

As your itinerary is established, e-mail, and/or fax, and/or telephone the details to someone who can intervene on your behalf. Make sure you store all the details online (in your Yahoo or similar account) so you can access the information remotely.

If you haven't already done so, fax (or scan and e-mail) a copy of your passport to someone in your home country. You should carry several copies of your passport, as well as a few extra photos for visas and passport replacement. You might even have a digital passport photo on a CD, and scan and include the inside pages of your passport and any visa pages on this CD. The same applies to your credit card and ATM card numbers.

> **Tip:** Many travelers to Southeast Asia enter the region via Hong Kong or Bangkok. These two cities are excellent places to take care of "housekeeping" details you may have overlooked or not had time to do before you left home. You can find all the modern conveniences in either place. You can collect visas, get passport-sized photos, scan and e-mail documents, make onward flight, tour, or hotel arrangements. If you've never been to Southeast Asia, these gateway cities make for a good first step.

Step 4

Make sure you have all the necessary inoculations and preventive medications/sprays. If you will not be able to get boiled water, take a purifying system and use it. Don't forget a small, but complete, first aid kit.

> **Tip:** The recent earthquake and tsunami only serve to emphasize the importance of a first aid kit and water purification system. Southeast Asia is prone to typhoons (hurricanes) and other natural disasters. While the chances of anything bad happening are very slim, it never hurts to be prepared.

If you are going to be at elevations above 2,000 meters (6,600 feet), take time to acclimate and avoid alcohol. Consider getting a prescription for Diamox to help with altitude adjustment.

Step 5

Be very careful carrying cash, traveler's checks, bank cards or debit cards. One solution is to buy several "pre-loaded" debit cards. They have PINs and work just like a cash advance, but they look and function like credit cards. If someone gets hold of the card and PIN, you are at risk for only the value remaining on the card, and if the issuer is VISA or MasterCard, you are probably on the hook for $50 or less. Even better, these cards aren't much use to identity thieves since they are not true credit cards.

Step 6

Book the trip. Make sure the agent you deal with is really the one running the trip, or interview the consolidating company if the agent doesn't run the actual trip. Insist on physically inspecting all the equipment and choosing the items you want. If the trip includes whitewater rafting or kayaking, and you want a helmet, make sure they are included and do not appear to have been damaged. The same applies for bicycle, scooter, and motorbike helmets.

Use a credit card to pay. That way you have some recourse when you get home if the trip was not as promised. Save all the trip documentation.

Step 7

Have reasonable expectations. Don't over pack – you may not have porters and there are not elevators and escalators where you'll be going. But there aren't many convenience stores, either! Enjoy – it's the experience of a lifetime.

■ Health Considerations

Across Southeast Asia there are lots of illnesses you could worry about. Some of them are preventable, and some are not.

Don't go into rivers and lakes unless you know the water is safe and you have had the right immunizations – more on those in a bit. Avoid mosquitoes and other insects with a passion. If you are surrounded by people who are sneezing and coughing, go somewhere else or wear a surgical mask. Wash your hands frequently. Don't drink the water. Don't brush your teeth in the water. Don't rinse your contacts in the water. If you can't peel it or it isn't well-cooked, don't eat it. You get the picture. I have spent a lot of time in Asia and the only time I got a stomach illness was when I had a salad at a five-star hotel in Malaysia. You never know.

Preventive Measures

The air is often polluted, with heavy concentrations of particulates, pollens, and molds you have not been exposed to. You may have allergies for the first time ever, or sinus problems (I always do over there), or itchy eyes, or a running nose. I am a great believer in over-the-counter allergy-sinus medication (such as Coricidin or something similar) as a preventive and coping measure. If you can keep your sinus and nasal passages clear, you are far less likely to get the sinus infection or "Asian crud" (blocked sinuses, running nose, cough, and plugged ears) that can plague you for weeks after your return. You'll sleep better, too.

Expensive antibiotics such as Amoxycillin are available over-the-counter (OTC) and inexpensively in most parts of Asia. If you have fever, chills, severe aches, or other symptoms consistent with a bacterial illness, you might resort to a course of antibiotics. Only you and your regular physician know your tolerance for antibiotics, so use extreme care when purchasing and taking OTC medications. Fortunately, most high-end medications are produced in English-speaking countries so the names and dosages are written in English. You can almost always find an English-speaking (and possibly English-educated) doctor or other medical professional, even in the smallest towns.

I highly recommend researching any medication online before taking it. If possible, e-mail your doctor at home and get his or her input and suggestions before you take anything. Nonetheless, there may come a time when you have no choice but to take antibiotics, anti-malarials, anti virals, or anti-parasitical medications. Use common sense.

Author's Note: During my most recent trip to Vietnam I experienced a terrible headache, sinus infection, fever, aches, and chills. I went to the Women's Hospital in Ho Chi Minh City (HCMC). I consulted with a nurse and she escorted me to a pharmacy a few doors away. After explaining my symptoms to the pharmacist, I was given a week's worth of Amoxycillin and a bunch of other stuff, neatly packaged into twice-a-day packages. Total cost: $15. I didn't know what most of it was, so I did a Google search to determine possible side-effects and cautions (such as "take with food" or "avoid alcohol") and then e-mailed my regular doctor for advice. The antibiotics did the trick.

Of course, you shouldn't take too much over the counter (or prescription) medication. Different medications interact with one another in strange and often dangerous ways. Herbal supplements and sun exposure and OTC medications can cancel one another or prescription medications out. Or they can enhance an effect. Always consult a pharmacist and your local doctor with a complete list of everything you are or will be taking, even if it's just a multi-vitamin, anti-malarial, and aspirin.

Malaria & Anti-Malarials

Mosquitoes in Southeast Asia are becoming increasingly resistant to anti-malarials. I spoke at great length with a Thai doctor at the Chiang Mai medical facility (where they specialize in malaria research and treatment) and he voiced several concerns.

First, the more frequently people take medication, the quicker the mosquitoes become resistent.

Second, the treatment for malaria is usually heavier doses of the same stuff you're taking to prevent it.

Third, what you take to prevent malaria can damage your liver and other internal parts.

Fourth, the treatment doesn't always work (the numbers I have seen suggest 70% effectiveness).

To further compound matters, many people think they can stop taking the medication as soon as they're out of a malarial area. Since the incubation period for malaria is weeks, this is not the case.

Note that the Centers for Disease Control (www.cdc.gov) recommend taking anti-malarials in most of Southeast Asia. It's your call, but I highly recommend talking with a public health specialist before you make your choice. Anti-malarial medications have to be started several weeks before you leave. Taking the wrong medication or not taking it long enough may be worse than not taking it at all.

Mosquito-Borne Illnesses

 Mosquitoes are a problem in any humid, sub-tropical to tropical area, and that's where you'll be on this trip. In addition to malaria, there are Japanese encephalitis and dengue (breakbone) fever to consider. You can get an immunization for encephalitis (a great idea), but not for dengue. The best prevention for all three of these is a combination of DEET repellent and covering up, plus a mosquito net at night.

> **Tip:** A word of advice about mosquito netting
> – make sure there are no mosquitoes sharing
> it with you when you close yourself in!

Dengue mosquitoes tend to bite during the day, so if anyone tells you not to worry about daytime bites (malarial mosquitoes bite at dusk and dawn), don't believe them. Bring or buy mosquito coils to use when you're sitting outside – in open boats, at restaurants.

> **Tip:** An interesting precaution is to buy clothing that is impregnated with mosquito-repellent. Many sporting goods stores carry this type of clothing. You can also get clothing coated with sunscreen – another good idea.

Specific Immunizations

Hepatitis

Hepatitis A is an immunization I wouldn't leave home without. Hepatitis B immunizations (and the newer C and other options) are more of a personal (and lifestyle) choice. If there is a chance you might have a sexual encounter, you might want to get the other hepatitis immunizations. The same goes for any possible encounters with needles (drug or medicinal). If you have any concern about needing to use Asian medical facilities, the other hepatitis shots might be a good idea. Ask your doctor and the public health officials in your area. The jury is still out on how long any hepatitis shot lasts, but the working number seems to be at least 10 years after you've had the initial series.

What Other Immunizations Should You Consider?

Tetanus, Diphtheria, Pertussis (DPT). This is essential, even at home. Once every 10 years and you're reasonably covered for tetanus, diphtheria, and pertussis. If the vaccine is in short supply, as has been the case in recent years, call around to various county health services and tell them you are going to remote areas of Asia and really need the shot. Someone will help you out.

Polio. Another big concern in Asia. If you have had a certain number of polio boosters you may not need another, but ask your doctor or public health service.

Typhoid. Some people are allergic to variations of this vaccine. (I have a terrible reaction to the injected version, but I can handle the newer oral version.) The cure for typhoid is antibiotics, so if you don't get the immunization (once every three years), and you do contract typhoid, you are probably curable. However, there seems to be an upswing in typhoid cases that are not responding to traditional antibiotics, so an immunization is probably a good idea. This is not an easily avoided disease since it is food- and/or water-borne.

Meningitis. This is a nasty illness – I had the viral version of it coming out of India. It's like the worst case of flu imaginable (and that's just the viral kind). The bacterial version is a very serious illness. You might be able to take preventive antibiotics, but you need to get the facts and talk to your doctor. There are immunizations for some viral meningitis strains, but there are so many strains that the shot you get may or may not work. Viral meningitis is caught from people who have or are carrying it. Washing your hands helps, but if people around you are sneezing and coughing, getting away from them is your best option.

Japanese Encephalitis. Another nasty, but easily preventable illness. Get the immunization. It should last for 10 years.

Cholera. The immunizations for this one are very ineffective and rarely recommended unless you are going to an area with an active outbreak. Don't drink the water!

Yellow Fever. This immunization is good for 10 years. You don't normally need it unless you are coming from an area where there is an active outbreak. Make sure to bring your proof of immunization, especially if you have been in Africa or South America recently. If you can't prove you've had the immunization, you will be turned away at the border entry. In Southeast Asia, yellow fever has not been a problem for many years.

Pneumonia & Influenza. These are two immunizations most Americans can readily get if they are considered at risk (over 60, in poor health, etc.). If you are considered at risk and have not had these shots, you probably want to get them before going anywhere, not just to Southeast Asia. As always, consult with appropriate medical personnel before getting, or choosing not to get, any immunization.

> **Tip:** Record all your immunizations in an official shot record. If you are coming from an affected area, this yellow international shot record is the only thing the authorities will accept.

Antibiotics

Antibiotics are available OTC in Asia. If you have chosen not to take anti-malarials and believe you have contracted the disease, seek out an English-speaking doctor who can diagnose you and recommend the correct treatment. By having the information written in the local language, you can be assured of getting the right medication. The same applies if you decide you want to get anti-malarials once you're over there (they will likely be much cheaper).

Medical Facilities

Try to get to Hanoi, HCMC, or Thailand if you need serious care. Pharmacies will dispense almost anything (such as antibiotics) without a prescription. Make sure you know what you are taking and that it is not expired.

Minimizing Jet-Lag

Get enough rest. When you take the dry air and cramped conditions of an airline flight, the long waiting times before boarding and between flights, the hours on the plane, and the time change (almost halfway around the world), you're going to start out tired. You'll probably have problems sleeping once you're there, too. There are lots of tips out there for dealing with jet lag. If something has worked for you, do it again. If this is your first time flying across eight to 12 time zones, here's what works for me:

Don't drink alcohol the night before. Get a good night's sleep. Don't get to the airport any earlier than you absolutely have to. Try to book flights that leave at less crowded times of the day. Allow about two hours for each connection. If you can sleep on the plane, fine – it passes the time but doesn't do much for preventing jet-lag for me. Get a bulkhead or exit row seat if at all possible. I prefer windows because if I'm on the aisle I get climbed on and over and bumped by carts and people in the aisles. Go easy on the alcohol, and skip the fatty portions of the meals (such as the cheesecake dessert). I think eating a reasonable amount of food, especially just before arrival, helps reset my internal clock. Wear earplugs the entire flight. Noise-canceling headphones are also good.

When I reach my destination, I believe it is important to go to sleep at as close to my normal time (but in the new time zone) as possible. That usually means going right to bed since most Asian flights arrive between 6 pm and midnight. When I wake up, I get up and read (since it's usually about 4 am local time), and fall back asleep for an hour or two. Then I get on with it as if I'm in the time zone I belong in. After four days or so, I actually feel human again.

■ Getting There

 Shop around – there are often great deals if you are flexible in your routing. Check websites for the airlines you prefer, plus sites such as **www.orbitz.com**, **www.expedia.com**, and **www.cheaptickets.com** (my preferred non-airline site).

I recently checked the United Airlines website for Denver-Bangkok flights and found round-trip fares for as low as $800. The routing is Denver-San Francisco or Denver-LA or Denver-Seattle, then on to Tokyo and Bangkok. For travel to Vietnam, Denver-HCMC flights were as low as $900-$1,000. The routing is via San Francisco, LA or Seattle, then on to Tokyo or Hong Kong, then on to Saigon (HCMC) or Hanoi.

Laos is served by one or two major European or Asian airlines, but only in and out of Vientiane. Your two main choices are **Vietnam Airlines** and **Lao Aviation**. Vietnam Airlines has more options but the last leg is usually a codeshare with Lao Aviation (except into Vientiane). Laos is land-locked, so you can't get there by cruise ship.

If you work with a travel specialist, or are familiar with the intricacies of the airline websites, you can book a split ticket and go into one gateway city and out of another. The cost should be similar to going in and out of the same city.

> **Tip:** The airport in Tokyo has shower facilities in the airline clubs (free for members and Business/First Class/Elite travelers) and public facilities as well. If you have at least 90 minutes on the ground in the Tokyo (Narita) airport, I highly recommend using the shower facilities. You'll feel 1,000% better. The public facilities cost about $5, and you can use a credit card. You get a little "care" kit with soap, shower gel, a razor, and a few other niceties like a toothbrush.

■ Getting Around

Most US and major European airlines no longer require reconfirmation of flights, although doing so is a good idea.

Asian airlines are different. There is a high demand for seats, so if you fail to reconfirm at least 72 hours before your flight – you should actually do so at least 72 hours before and again the day before – you may not have a seat. Flights between adjacent countries in Southeast Asia and within countries are overbooked and frequently canceled or rescheduled. In fact, flights often leave earlier than originally scheduled, so you could be there on-time and still miss your flight. Asian airlines depart the minute the plane is full. If you are not there, but someone else is standing by, they will get your seat so the plane can leave. Then you have the hassle of getting a refund and rebooking your flight. If you can, pay by credit card on government-owned carriers – dealing with your credit card company is easier than with most Southeast Asian airlines.

■ The Weather

All three countries have monsoonal climates. That means there is a dry season and a wet season. In addition, there are hot and cool portions in each dry season. In a country as long as Vietnam, with its extended coastline, there are different monsoons in different parts of the country, so planning is essential if you don't like mosquitoes and mud. See each country for specific information.

■ What to Pack

You've heard it before – pack what you think you'll need and then take out half the items. Easier said than done!

> **Tip:** With all the airline issues – thievery, computer glitches, sick-outs, strikes, bankruptcy, and so on – it is far better to make like a Sherpa and take only what you can carry with you. No waits for bags, no lost luggage, no stolen items…

While Vietnam, Laos, and Cambodia are Third World countries, they are not without most of the things we take for granted. Laundry service is cheap, fast, and good. Clothes to fit Westerners are readily available in markets and shops. Custom tailors are fast and of top quality. You could come back with a whole new wardrobe and buy a suitcase there to carry everything.

Some things are just excess weight to schlep around. Your 110 volt appliances aren't going to work. They will plug into the walls, but the voltage will toast most North American appliances. The exceptions are electrical items that include a power supply – laptops and some battery chargers come to mind. Before you plug anything in, even with a power supply, read the fine print.

Many North American cell phones won't work in Asia. It's not a coverage issue; it has to do with the internal workings of your phone. You generally need a multi-band GSM capability. Ask your cell phone provider to explain what you'll need to stay connected in Asia, and make sure your charger will work before you lug your phone with you. Make sure you know the per-minute charges before you dial or answer a call – the cost may shock you.

Some things are cheaper than at home and easily obtained in Asia. Antibiotics and anti-malarials are available OTC in almost any pharmacy.

Some items aren't readily available or are not of an acceptable brand or quality. Feminine hygiene products and contraceptives come to mind. Ditto contact lenses, cleaning and sterilizing supplies, and many non-prescription medications. If you are bringing sporting equipment, especially bicycles or other products with moving parts, a repair kit is a good idea. Shoes are hard to find – we have big feet.

Following is a suggested packing list for two to four weeks in all but the coldest areas.

What to Wear/Take on the Flight

- ☐ Long pants (with Lycra)
- ☐ Socks, walking shoes
- ☐ Long-sleeved cotton shirt

Above: Karst rock formations, Ha Long Bay, Vietnam

Below: Hill tribeswoman, on the road to Sapa, Vietnam

Looking across the hills, outside Sapa

Above: Early morning mist above Sapa

Below: Tourist village outside Sapa

The hills just above Sapa

- Windbreaker
- Daypack and money pouch (I prefer the neck pouch), pouch/wallet for "walking around money"
- ATM card, credit card, passport/visa, cash, traveler's checks, copies of all documents, tickets
- Books, pens, guidebook, magazines, addresses, candy, cough drops, tissues, towelettes
- Medications, prescriptions, Coricidin or similar, aspirin, first aid kit
- Electronics (cell phone, digital camera, laptop...)
- Camera (and film if needed), transfer device, extra cards
- DVDs and computer power cord
- CD player and CDs
- Eyeshade and earplugs

What to Pack

- 1 skirt and/or long pants
- 1 long-sleeved cotton shirt
- 2 shorts (walking)
- 4-5 T-shirts
- 5-7 sets of underwear
- 1 pair sandals
- Swimsuit/cover-up
- 5-7 pairs of socks
- Lotion, sunscreen
- Cosmetics
- Shampoo, comb, soap, razors, etc.
- DEET spray – at least 25% strength
- Hair dryer (switchable voltage)
- Waterproof bags for electronics
- Plastic bag for dirty clothes
- Umbrella, poncho
- Sleepwear
- Earplugs (extra)
- Vitamins and prescriptions

- □ Aspirin
- □ Cotton sweater
- □ Flashlight
- □ Chargers for electronics
- □ Extra batteries (lots)
- □ Hand towel (you may not like the looks of the seats on buses)
- □ Silk sleeping sheet
- □ Mosquito netting and coils if you are going to stay in lower-end hotels or hostels, especially in the river deltas or during the rainy season

Less really is more. The items listed above should fit into a carry-on bag and your "personal item," and then you can skip airport luggage lines and have your luggage arrive when you do. I like to put my laptop in a daypack – it is less obvious and easy to carry around. My windbreaker fits in there, too.

I've never had a problem getting things washed. Laundry service is fast and of excellent quality. For a few dollars you can have someone else wash and dry the entire contents of your carry-on bag.

Now that there are so many Western travelers in Southeast Asia, stores and open-air markets carry clothes that fit almost anyone. These are the same clothes I pay a lot of money for at home, so I often supplement or even replace my wardrobe while I'm traveling. You can also get clothes made for bargain prices – in just a few days – and that fit like a glove.

I often take older clothes since a few weeks using Asian transport makes me want to burn some of the things I wore. That's okay – getting rid of old clothes gives me room for a few more souvenirs!

The postal services from Asia are a bit expensive and very slow, but still pretty reliable. If you're going to make a few purchases that won't fit in your bags, or have some clothes made, consider mailing them home. If you need a heavier sweater for a few days, buy one in the market and either give it to someone who needs it or mail it home.

Once you've settled on the items to take, do a packing "dry-run." Think about your reason for taking each item. No one is going to care what you wear as long as it's clean, modest, and not ragged. Southeast Asia is filled with stairs instead of elevators. You'll be carrying your bags far more than in Europe, Australia, or North America. You'll be walking in the streets, dodging motor scooters, and cramming yourself and your stuff into smaller places than you're used to. Bigger isn't better – and it can be darned inconvenient!

A few things to speed your trip:

> **Tip:** You can't protect your checked baggage from being rifled by TSA inspectors, but you can make it harder for the airline baggage handlers to get in and help themselves to your stuff. Buy and use a TSA-approved lock. I recommend the ones that have a tab that switches from green to red when the lock is opened.

Don't put film or valuables in your checked bags. That includes house and car keys, jewelry, electronics, eye glasses, medications, and other items of value.

On your return trip, try to take your new clothes and souvenirs with you in your carry-on bag. That makes the customs declaration easier to fill out and leaves would-be thieves with access to your travel-stained clothes rather than your new stuff.

■ Selecting Your Accommodations

Prices

Hotels in Southeast Asia are much less expensive than their Western counterparts. There are many online booking services that can get you four- and five-star hotels for less than half the published rates. I often use www.asia-hotels.com and have always been pleased with their rates, responsiveness, and service.

If you arrive in Bangkok (the most common gateway) or Hong Kong, you are likely to arrive very late at night after about 24 hours in transit. You will probably be exhausted, so having a hotel to go to – one that meets you at the arrivals hall with your name on a sign and a van waiting outside – borders on sheer heaven. It is very worthwhile to book a hotel close to the airport. In Bangkok I use **Asia Airport**, **Comfort Inn**

HOTEL PRICE CHART	
Rates are per room based on double occupancy.	
$	Under $12
$$	$12-$25
$$$	$26-$40
$$$$	$40-$80
$$$$$	Over $80

and Suites (both about US$30-$45) or the **Miracle Grand Conference Hotel** (US$65-$70). This price includes airport transfers both ways and all taxes and service, but not breakfast. It takes about 10-15 minutes to/from the airport.

> **Note:** The pick-up sign may have your name or just the name of the hotel, the Asia Airport and Comfort Inn are to the right as you leave customs and the Miracle Grand people usually wait to the left.

Walk-in prices are about double the online booking prices, and they do take credit cards. The Comfort Inn is noisy and less flexible with check-out times than the Asia Airport. The Asia Airport doesn't have a restaurant to speak of, but there are a few options in the shopping center below. The Miracle Grand actually includes a buffet breakfast in its price and the rooms are very nice and quiet.

> **Tip:** When you are looking for hotels in Southeast Asia, I recommend using a website such as **www.asia-hotels.com** and prepaying with a credit card. This avoids unpleasant surprises such as sudden price increases or no availability. In addition, the pre-booked and pre-paid hotel prices almost always include all taxes and service charges, and often include breakfast and airport transfers. However, pre-booking or prepaying does limit your flexibility to change your plans. Therefore the ac-

tual hotel information in each country section of this guide has two sets of listings – hotels that are best booked online ahead of time, and other hotels that you might try to book directly or upon arrival. There is some overlap in these two categories.

Location

Another note – getting around the various cities and towns is cheap and easy using local transport. Therefore I don't generally recommend choosing a hotel based on its exact area. It's far better to look for features and price, and get around by taxi or other means. Maps that try to show hotel locations are usually hard to read and imprecise.

Quality

Hotels across the three countries are fairly similar, although standards are a bit higher in Vietnam. Western-quality hotels are easy to find in the popular destinations, but they can be quite pricey. The higher-end hotels charge excessive amounts for use of the Internet – as an example, a five-star hotel in Siem Reap charges an hourly rate of $10 or so, plus fees for every byte you send or receive; local hotels and places in town are just as fast and charge less than $3 per hour.

Higher-end hotels have their own restaurants in most cases – in fact, many packaged tours include three meals a day at the hotel's restaurant if you want to hide from the people and the country. Budget hotels may offer breakfast, but that's often in in the restaurant area. Prices should include all taxes and service charges, but in the $$$$ and $$$$$ categories this may not be the case.

> **Tip:** Most hotels charge the same amount for double or single occupancy. Some hotels have actual single rooms, but they are few and far between. The less expensive hotels and guesthouses often provide a continental breakfast, even if they don't have a restaurant – but you may have to ask and negotiate the cost if it's not included in the room rate. Note that tax

and service can add 15-20% to the room cost, so make sure they are included in the quoted rate. Tipping is not expected, except in the top hotels, but small amounts are often appreciated in the local restaurants, unless your bill clearly indicates the service charge was included.

The beds tend to be much harder than Westerners are used to, so if that's a problem you might consider taking an inflatable mattress such as one used to float in a swimming pool. Your back and neck will thank you.

■ Dining Out

Prices

 Restaurant meals tend to be quite reasonable and of excellent quality almost anywhere – even from the corner noodle shops. Make sure the place and the staff look clean and have a high turnover of

RESTAURANT PRICES	
$	Under $2
$$	$2-$5
$$$	$6-$10
$$$$	$11-$20
$$$$$	Over $20

diners, and then take a bit of care with what you eat – no raw foods, at least until you've been there awhile, and stick to the bottled, purified water. This applies even at the swankiest restaurants – the staff is hired from the local populace and they get the food and water from the same markets as the noodle shops do.

Restaurant prices vary widely, but for less than $5 you can usually get a complete meal in smaller, local restaurants. At the same time, you can go to the top international restaurants and pay what you would at home for a meal, or maybe even more.

Tipping is not expected, and some people view it as an insult, especially in the northern part of Vietnam. Still, the gesture is often welcome, but the amounts should be small – 5-10%.

■ Overview - Vietnam

For most people, Vietnam (its official name is the People's Republic of Vietnam) is a country defined by French colonialism, followed by years of war with the French and then the Americans. If you ask them, the Vietnamese will quickly tell you they didn't fight the "Vietnam War," they fought the "War of American Aggression" (and won when Saigon fell). Since then the country has been developing rapidly despite the strictures of communism and the destruction left by the War. The government began loosening the restrictions on free enterprise and travel in the late 1980s and this continued through the 1990s. Today Vietnam is a country experiencing sustained economic growth of 7% or more per year.

> **Note:** Place names vary so I have shown the two most common spellings for most places. I have also usually referred to the Vietnamese-American war as the "War" to avoid political issues.

About the Country

The conquest of Vietnam by France began in 1858 and was completed by 1884. It became part of French Indochina in 1887. Vietnam declared its Independence after World War II, but the French continued to rule until 1954 when they were defeated by communist forces under Ho Chi Minh. The communists then took control of the North. US economic and military aid to South Vietnam grew through the 1960s in an attempt to bolster the government. This effort failed, and US armed forces were withdrawn, following a cease-fire agreement in 1973. Two years later, North Vietnamese forces overran the South. For more than two decades the country experienced little economic growth because of leadership policies. Since 2001, Vietnamese authorities have committed to economic liberalization and enacted structural reforms to modernize the economy, encourage the growth of small businesses, and produce more competitive, export-driven industries. The country continues to experience protests from the

Montagnard ethnic minority population of the Central Highlands over loss of land to Vietnamese settlers.

Vietnam is a poor, densely-populated country. It is slowly recovering from the ravages of war, the loss of financial support from the old Soviet Bloc, and the rigidities of a centrally-planned economy. Substantial progress was achieved from 1986 to 1996 (from an extremely low starting point). Growth averaged around 9% per year from 1993 to 1997. The 1997 Asian financial crisis highlighted the problems in the Vietnamese economy but, rather than prompting reform, it reaffirmed the government's belief that shifting to a market-oriented economy would lead to disaster. GDP growth of 8.5% in 1997 fell to 6% in 1998 and 5% in 1999. Growth then rose to 6%-7% from 2000-2002.

Fast Facts

Country Name:
Socialist Republic of Vietnam (official long form); Vietnam (official short form); Cong Hoa Xa Hoi Chu Nghia Viet Nam (local long form); Viet Nam (local short form).

Abbreviation: SRV.

Government Type: Communist state.

Capital: Hanoi.

Location: Southeastern Asia, bordering the Gulf of Thailand, Gulf of Tonkin, and South China Sea, alongside China, Laos, and Cambodia.

Area: 329,560 sq km/128,528 sq miles; land 325,360 sq km/126,890 sq miles; water 4,200 sq km/1,638 sq miles.

Comparative Size: Slightly larger than New Mexico.

Climate: Tropical in south; monsoonal in north with hot, rainy season (mid-May to mid-September) and warm, dry season (mid-October to mid-March).

Terrain: Low, flat delta in south and north; central highlands; hilly, mountainous in far north and northwest.

Elevation: Lowest point, South China Sea – 0 m/0 feet; highest point, Fan Si Pan – 3,144 m/10,312 feet.

Environmental Issues: Logging and slash-and-burn agricultural practices contribute to deforestation and soil degradation; water pollution and over-fishing threaten marine life populations; groundwater contamination limits potable water supply; growing urban industrialization and population migration are rapidly degrading environment in Hanoi and Ho Chi Minh City.

Natural Resources: Phosphates, coal, manganese, bauxite, chromate, offshore oil and gas deposits, forests, hydropower.

Population: 82,689,518.

Ethnic Groups: Vietnamese 85%-90%, plus Chinese, Hmong, Thai, Khmer, Cham, mountain groups.

Religions: Buddhist, Hoa Hao, Cao Dai, Christian (predominantly Roman Catholic, some Protestant), indigenous beliefs, Muslim.

Languages: Vietnamese (official), English (increasingly favored as a second language), some French, Chinese, and Khmer; mountain area languages (Mon-Khmer and Malayo-Polynesian).

Currency: Dong (VND).

Exchange Rate: 14,891 Dong = US$1.

Visa: Required of most Western nationalities. **Not** available upon arrival at major entry points, it must be obtained in advance. Cost is about US$40-$50, plus three passport photos. Allow five days for normal delivery (plus mailing time if you apply by mail). Express delivery is about two or three days and costs $20 more.

Major Holidays

January 1 . . . . New Year's Day
January 29-31 . . . Têt, Lunar New Year (changes each year)
April 30 . . . . Liberation of Saigon
May 1 . . . . May Day
September 2 . . . . National Day

Touring

Vietnam is increasingly gearing up for tourism, and its infrastructure is expanding, although not fast enough to meet the demands of the increasing numbers of international visitors. Still, travel standards are higher here than in the rest of the region.

Vietnam Airlines is expanding and improving its fleet to include Boeing 777s and Airbus 320s. Air France flies here from Bangkok, Japan Airlines flies in from several cities, and other Asian airlines also fly here. American and United Airlines should have extended their routes from Tokyo and/or Hong Kong to Hanoi and HCMC by the time you read this. Quantas makes the trip from Australia.

The roads in Vietnam are far better surfaced, marked, and maintained than in Laos or Cambodia – many roads are black-topped (sealed) as opposed to their dirt counterparts in many areas of Southeast Asia. A variety of tourist cafés run their own fleets of transit vans and modern air-conditioned buses, so travel around the country is relatively fast, comfortable, and easy.

Vietnam has a decent north-south train route. You can go north to the Chinese border, continue to Beijing, connect to the long-haul trains across China, and eventually to the Trans-Siberian Express across Russia and back to Europe. It is also possible (but slow) to take the train to Phnom Penh in Cambodia, and down to the coast, but not into Laos or Thailand. Prices are quite high, though; flying is a cheaper alternative.

Going from north to south (a journey of over 1,600 km or 1,000 miles), Vietnam is a feast for the senses, if a bit overwhelming in its sheer length and diversity. You should absolutely spend time in **Sapa (Sa Pa)** and vicinity, hiking, trekking, visiting hill tribes (the Montagnards) and get up to the **Chinese border** to watch the trading hubbub. **Hanoi** is filled with delightful remnants of the French Colonial past – mansions, museums, the Opera, and more – as well as one of the oldest universities in the world. **Hoan (Ho An) Lake** is a magical playground for tourists and locals alike, once you get past the "postcard and travel book" touts. Rent a bicycle if you dare and really explore the Old City and French Quarter.

Heading east to the coast, you don't want to miss the old quarter in **Haiphong (Hai Phong)**, once the most heavily-mined harbor in the world, or the opportunity to explore **Halong (Ha Long) Bay** and its many islands, limestone outcroppings, and caves. You can get as remote as you want, even leaving electricity behind on a few islands. For swimming, sea kayaking, snorkeling, or just hanging out on a boat or island – Halong Bay is the place in the North.

Skipping down the coast you pass through the former DMZ (demilitarized zone) and come to the **Marble Mountains** and one of several tunnel complexes used in the War. From here it's on to Da Nang (Danang), Hoi An, and Hué.

Hoi An sits on a river estuary, and has been an important trading post with China and other neighbors for centuries. There is a large ethnic Chinese population and many people still live and work in the quaint, painted shophouses built by their ancestors. There are numerous craft villages nearby – great for exploring on foot or by bicycle. You might even rent a boat and motor or paddle up the river. It's only about 40 km/24 miles to some impressive Cham ruins.

Hué is the old imperial capital, and has been largely reconstructed. The citadel (the old Forbidden City) is beautiful at sunrise or sunset. The imperial temples south of the city along the Perfume River are worth a visit, and a bicycle is the way to do it.

Farther down the coast is the beach resort (and wartime rest and recreation) resort of **Nha Trang**. Known to travelers from all over the world for its laid-back beach lifestyle, Nha Trang is also a great place to charter a boat or take a tour to some of the nearby islands, go snorkeling or scuba diving, or even fishing. The surrounding villages are easily explored on a bicycle.

Heading inland there's **Dalat (Da Lat)** – my personal favorite. Set in mountains at about 1,500 meters/5,000 feet of elevation, Da Lat is a pleasant retreat from the beaches and flat coastal areas. There are monasteries nearby, and hill tribes to trek to. The city is dominated by a large lake where you can rent paddleboats and canoes. It's also a university town, so students will want to practice their English with you. Buy them a coffee and prepare for a great learning experience.

Then it's off to **Ho Chi Minh City**, called HCMC by most people, and remembered as Saigon by many. The city is a bit more compact and less frenetic than Hanoi (although more populous), and there are many remnants of the long French presence. As with the rest of the country, the baguettes, coffee, and pastries are not to be missed. The Opera and old Post Office are worth a look, too.

Finally, don't miss the **Mekong River Delta**. After meandering its way from China, through the Golden Triangle (Laos, Burma, Thailand), spending a long time flowing most of the length of Laos, and going through a bit of Cambodia, the Mekong finishes with a flourish by creating a huge, fertile delta in the far south of Vietnam. Life is slower-paced, the land is incredibly green, and it's only four hours by hydrofoil or bus from HCMC.

> **Tip:** Several US airlines have started flying to Vietnam again. None of the flights is non-stop; they go through Tokyo or Osaka in Japan, or Hong Kong. So far United and American Airlines fly into both Hanoi and Ho Chi Minh City (Saigon). Don't forget the day you lose when you cross the International Dateline (you get it back on your return!). You are looking at about 24 hours in transit no matter which airline/city/routing combinations you chose. It's a bit longer from the East Coast and a bit shorter from the West Coast.

Suggested Itineraries

10 days – A Taste of North or South: This is the bare minimum since you need two days just to get there and one to get back. If you fly into Bangkok or Hong Kong you may lose another day waiting for connections onward, especially coming from North America. With seven days "on the ground" you're going to need to fly, or take overnight trains. You'll also want to book private or very small group tours to fit your limited time schedule. Group tours don't necessarily leave every day.

1. Fly into Hanoi. Spend the first day in Hanoi, exploring Old Hanoi and the French Quarter, and do a bit of shopping. Take some time to see the outdoor university and one of the many museums. Set up a two-day trip to **Halong Bay** and Cat Ba Island. You'll get to hike up to a cave, and take a walk around

Cat Ba Island. If it's summer, you might rent a bike and cycle the perimeter of the island before it gets dark. Return to Hanoi and take the night train on a private tour (three days, four nights) to **Sapa**. Spend the first and last nights of your trip on the train (1st class sleeper) and then you'll have two days of guided trekking (12-km/seven-mile and 17-km/10-mile trips) with the third day in Sapa to explore. These trips can be arranged at almost any guest house or hotel in Hanoi. Return to Hanoi in the early morning of the seventh day, and fly back to your gateway Asian city the same day.

2. Fly in to **HCMC**. Spend the first day in HCMC, exploring the remnants of Colonial glory – especially the Opera and the Old Post Office – and arrange your onward travel. Take the hydrofoil to **Can Tho**, and spend two peaceful days peddling around the Delta. Take the hydrofoil back to HCMC, spend the night, then fly to **Hué** – the old Imperial City. Rent a bicycle or hire a taxi and visit some of the tombs of the Ming Emperors just south of the city. The next day, visit the **Forbidden City**, and that evening take a bus to **Hoi An**. Spend two days around Hoi An, exploring the old Chinese shophouses, and then hike to some of the nearby craft villages. The next day, take an organized tour to the **Cham** site, about 40 km/24 miles west of Hoi An. If you want to get some tailor-made silk clothes, make a tailor your first stop on arrival in Hoi An and your last stop on the way to the train or airport (in Danang). Fly from Danang or take the night train back to HCMC, then continue to your original Asian gateway city.

Two Weeks – Add a Bit of Spice: With four extra days, you could do the North or South itinerary above and then fly to the other main city (Hanoi or HCMC).

1. If you do the northern route, you could do the itinerary in Option 1, then fly to HCMC, spend a day there and two days in the Mekong Delta, then fly back to your Asian gateway city. Or you could fly to Hué, spend two days, then fly to HCMC and spend a day before beginning the journey home.

2. If you do the southern route, you could do the itinerary in Option 2, then fly to Hanoi, and take a three-night, two-day trip to Sapa, then a day tour of Hanoi before starting home.

Alternatively, you could take the two-day, one-night trip to Halong Bay, then visit Hanoi for two days and then head home.

To really see and explore and do things, you need to spend at least three weeks...

Highlights

The coast of Vietnam is ideal for exploring in a sea kayak, darting in and out of hidden coves and bays. The relatively untraveled roads lend themselves to long or short bicycle trips or bus excursions. There are even off-road/rough road tours for motorcycle enthusiasts. You can trek in the mountainous northern regions that are home to fascinating hill tribes, or paddle your own boat through miles of slow-moving rivers and lakes. Hanoi is noisy and hectic. Everyone seems to have a motor scooter they are learning to drive as they go, with one hand on the horn. Everyone wants to sell you a ride, a tour, a postcard, or a travel book.

You can still see traces of the French architecture and culture, especially in the bakeries and museums. There are classical universities and interesting museums.

There are hole-in-the wall restaurants with pizza and CNN – quite a study in contrasts.

The trip up or down the coast is spectacular – coral islands and sampan boats fill the bays. Along the way there are many reasons to stop for awhile. One of the most interesting sights is sheets of drying "seeds" along the roadsides – this is the wonderful coffee being roasted in the sun!

You could easily spend a few days in **Hoi An** with its Chinese shop houses, sheltered harbor, and custom clothing makers. Save a few days to wander around **Hué**, the former capital, and its forbidden city. **Danang** and the **Marble Mountains** area still showcase the remnants of the Vietnam War harbors and tunnels. Vietnamese honeymooners are partial to **Dalat** with its hilly surroundings, Buddhist retreat, and curious B&B (the Mad House). And don't forget **Nha Trang** with its lovely beaches, nonstop action, diving, and resort lifestyle. **Ho Chi Minh City (Saigon)** retains far more of the French architecture and Western influence than does Hanoi, but it's not quite as frenetic. And finally there's the **Mekong Delta** area – back to an earlier, sleepier time – with quaint villages and far less Western contact than the rest of the country.

THE TOP SIGHTS & ACTIVITIES

1. The Mekong Delta
2. Bicycling – the latest tour craze
3. Sea kayaking – thousands of coves, islands, and inlets await
4. Trekking in Sapa and surrounding areas
5. The open-air university in Hanoi
6. Dalat's Mad House and monasteries
7. Hué's Forbidden City at sunrise or sunset
8. Having clothes made in Hoi An while exploring the estuary and shop houses
9. The Cu Chi tunnels, if you're not claustrophobic
10. Coffee and baguettes at a café in the former French Quarter in HCMC or Hanoi
11. Snorkeling or scuba diving in Nha Trang
12. Exploring the islands of Halong Bay
13. The bus ride along parts of the jagged coast
14. Floating lazily down the Mekong River
15. Hoa Lo Prison and Museum in Hanoi (the so-called "Hanoi Hilton")
16. Spending at least one night on the Reunification Express between Hanoi and HCMC (in soft sleeper if at all possible!). Since there isn't much to see between Hanoi and Hué, that is my preferred overnight trip.

History

The earliest traces of human presence in Vietnam have been found in caves in several areas. Little information is known about these cave dwellers, but their presence has been dated back at least 500,000 years. It wasn't until 5,000 or 6,000 years ago that wet rice cultivation began to appear. The area that now includes Vietnam was called Viet by the Chinese Zhou dynasty (1050 to 249 BC). The first Vietnamese dynasty, heavily influenced by the Chinese, appeared around 500 BC. Prior to the rise of the Ngo Dynasty in 928, the ruling influence was primarily Chinese. From that point forward, except for a few brief periods (most notably the Ming Dynasty in the early 15th century and the brief Mongol invasion in the mid-13th century), large portions of the country we now call Vietnam have been ruled by Vietnamese dynasties, albeit with significant Chinese influence.

DYNASTIES & HISTORICAL EVENTS		
Period	Dynasty Name	Country Name
500-257 BC	Hung or Lac-Vuong kings	Van Lang
207-111 BC	Trieu Dynasty	An Lac
203-544 AD	Early Chinese Han Dynasty	Giao Chi
544-603	Early Ly Dynasty	Van Xuan
603-939	Chinese Tang Dynasty	An Nam
939-967	Ngo Dynasty	Dai Viet
968-1054	Dinh and successor dynasties	Dai Co Viet
1054-1400	Later Ly and Tran Dynasties	Dai Viet
1400-1407	Ho Dynasty	Dai Ngu
1407-1428	Tran and Chinese Ming Dynasties	An Nam
1428-1802	Le and Nguyen Dynasties	Dai Viet
1802	Emperor Gia Long	Viet Nam
1832	Emperor Minh-Mang and successors	Dai Nam
1858-1945	French Colonial Administration	North – Tonkin Middle – Annam South – Cochinchina
1945-present	Tran Trong Kim and successors	Viet Nam

During the brief Ming Dynasty rule, the Vietnamese capital was, for the first time, located at Do Dong – present-day Hanoi. It was not until the founding of the Tay Su Dynasty in the late 18th century that the capital was moved to Hué. During the subsequent (and final) Nguyen Dynasty, from 1802-1945, the capital remained at Hué. It was during this period that the external borders of Vietnam aligned with what we see today. The emperors and their courtiers turned to Confucianism and away from the outside world, banning contact with foreigners. This left the country open to outside invasion and control.

The French took control of present-day Vietnam in 1858, turning it into a vassal state, keeping the Nguyen emperors as puppets. By 1861 they took Saigon, and six years later controlled the entire southern part of Vietnam. At this time the French named their holdings Cochinchina and made it a French colony. By 1883 the remnants of Vietnam in the north had been annexed by the French. The center of the country was renamed Annam, and the North was renamed Tonkin.

In 1887, Vietnam, plus Cambodia and Laos, were consolidated into a single colony called Indochina. The French exploited the area for its natural resources, and created a modernized society with working and "bourgeoisie" classes. They also changed the education system to follow the European style – infant, primary, and secondary programs.

The French created a three-tiered structure that can still be seen today – the Vietnamese were the top tier so they got a halfway-decent infrastructure, the Cambodians were in the middle so they got a bit of infrastructure, and the Laotians were at the bottom and got next to nothing.

The French used their Indochinese colonies, particularly Vietnam, as a source of soldiers and support workers in World War I. They put heavy demands on the country's infrastructure with food and financial requirements.

For a short stretch in the early 20th century, Vietnamese aristocrats and intellectuals looked to Japan for support in efforts to take back control of their country. At the same time, a group of Vietnamese who had been exiled to China saw the results of Dr. Sun Yat Sen's revolution in China (1911). They formed the Quoc Dan Dang Party to try and oust the French.

Following World War I, Ho Chi Minh began his rise to prominence. As World War II began, the Central Committee of the Indochinese Communist Party began to consolidate its goals and unify the various communist groups across the country.

On September 2, 1945, Ho Chi Minh formally announced the formation of the Democratic Republic of Vietnam, with its capital in Hanoi.

Thus began the 30-year struggle of North versus South Vietnam. The French continued to control the southern portion of the country, based on the Geneva Agreement on Vietnam in 1954. This agreement partitioned the country at the 17th parallel. The North had its capital in Hanoi, the South in Saigon. Over the next two decades, first the French and then the US governments provided military and economic support to the South Vietnamese rulers to try and prevent the communist takeover of the entire country. More information on the War, called the American War (of Aggression) by the North Vietnamese, is provided later in this section.

In 1973, after almost 20 years of fighting, with over 50,000 Americans killed and several million Vietnamese killed or permanently displaced, the US signed the Paris Agreement and withdrew from Vietnam. On April 25th, 1975, Saigon fell to the North Vietnamese, and the entire country was "reunified" under communist rule, with its capital once again in Hanoi.

Since the reunification, much of the devastation from 30 years of fighting has been repaired. At the same time South Vietnamese were trying to flee the country, refugees from other countries (particularly Pol Pot's Cambodia), were trying to enter. The strain on the damaged infrastructure of the newly consolidated country was tremendous. The first 11 years following reunification were quite difficult, but since 1986 the government has put in place very liberal foreign investment policies to help rebuild and grow the country's infrastructure. The government has also encouraged a version of free enterprise and liberalized land use policies to increase food production. As a result, the quality, quantity, and diversity of products, services, food, transport, and accommodation is surprisingly good.

The long-term goals of the Vietnamese government include self-sufficiency in food production, expansion of exports and development of new markets, and transformation into an industrial country with a modern infrastructure.

Customs & Culture

Buddhism and Confucianism have been major influences on the Vietnamese culture. In addition, there is a significant Christian population as a result of the nearly 100-year French presence. In many ways, devotion to Confucianism, to the exclusion of modernization, may have proved the downfall of the pre-communistic governments.

The people are wonderful. Most are honest, kind, and will go out of their way to help you. I have had people warn me to watch my stuff along crowded Saigon streets, moto drivers stop traffic so I could get across a busy Hanoi street, and hotel security guards help me figure out a map written entirely in Vietnamese.

Geography & Land

Vietnam is a long, narrow country hugging the far eastern side of the Indochina peninsula. It's about as long as California, but at its widest point is no more than about 300 km/200 miles wide. In many places it is only about 80 km/five miles wide. The land is quite hilly along its entire length, and in the far northwest (prime trekking territory) there are peaks approaching 3,000 meters (10,000 feet) in elevation. The entire northwestern section is high enough that altitude sickness can become a major consideration.

Much of the country is still heavily forested, outside the Mekong and Red River Delta areas. The main tree cover is referred to as double canopy jungle, with two layers of trees, virtually blocking the sunlight from reaching the forest floor. There is a wealth of hardwoods, fir trees, and various types of tropical trees such as palms, rubber, and teak.

Climate

Like the rest of Asia, Vietnam has a monsoonal climate. The arrival of the monsoon varies from north to south. Details are in the weather section, page 103. The South is very hot and humid much of the year, but does cool down and dry out in the winter months (approximately November through March). The North can get quite cool in the winter, and very hot in the summer. In the far northwest there is a true winter, with the highest peaks often seeing several snowfalls each winter.

The climate in the southern part of Vietnam is ideal for growing coffee and two rice crops a year. In the north the climate supports only one rice crop annually, but the cooler temperatures are conducive to growing many types of fruits and vegetables.

Flora & Fauna

You aren't likely to run into lions, tigers, or bears, or much other wildlife, for that matter. Nonetheless, you might encounter various wildlife, especially in the far northwestern mountains. If you take the time to go diving or boating you can view impressive

aquatic life, especially of the Nha Trang areas and in Ha Long Bay.

The most common plant life includes valuable hardwoods (especially teak) and rubber plants. Nasty critters exist, but you aren't very likely to run into them.

Government & Economy

Vietnam is a socialist/communist country, with heavy central control. However, many aspects of the economy have been liberalized, giving way to a semblance of the pre-communist/pre-war economies that thrived (at least in the

South) in the 1900s, up to the time the communists took over the entire country in 1975.

Per capita income is about $700 per year – more in the cities, less in the remoter areas. Most people still live in small villages and rural areas, but that is changing rapidly. In fact, the influx of unskilled workers from remote mountain and farming areas is causing significant problems in the larger cities – unemployment, homelessness, thievery, crimes against people and property, and begging, to name a few.

The mainstays of the economy include rice, coffee, and tourism.

Lifestyles

Vietnam is still a highly agrarian society, but increasing numbers of farmers, fishers, and hill tribe people are moving to the cities and towns. As result, the larger population centers suffer from a lack of jobs, overcrowding, and increasing poverty. Many of the people moving to the cities are doing so in search of a better life, but they do not have the skills or education to function well in big cities. As a result, there are many young men trying to make ends meet by selling postcards and travel books, while women and men may sell crafts or offer to change money on street corners.

Crimes against persons – especially foreigners – are increasing dramatically across Vietnam. At the same time, the economy is growing at a huge clip (7% or better), so things are improving for the general population. In the early 1990s the government began allowing a limited amount of free enterprise, and this has begun to dramatically improve the lot of many people, especially city dwellers who have contact with tourists. Hotels, restaurants, shops, and used bookstores are springing up like weeds, and seem to be thriving.

The idyllic days of girls in the traditional ao dai riding bicycles are long gone. Now it seems everyone has a motor scooter and no one has a license. Cars are appearing in rapidly increasing numbers, too.

Noise seems to be a unifying factor in Southeast Asia. Its absence makes the local people nervous, so expect to hear horns, shouts, bells, and other sounds almost constantly.

Traditional markets are still to be found, but retail shops and hotel arcades are making inroads.

Old women still ride around Old Hanoi with heavily laden bicycles (I call them shopping malls on wheels), and women walk home from their daily shopping expeditions balancing their purchases on their heads or carrying them in string bags.

Baguettes and strong coffee are a part of the daily routine for many Vietnamese. Bakeries and patisseries, rarely seen outside the former Indochina countries, are commonplace. Coffee shops are easy to find.

Still, much of the country has largely recovered from the effects of the War, and many people continue their rural lifestyle. That means you'll see women in conical hats planting rice by hand, standing knee-deep in water. Water buffaloes are still a mainstay for plowing the fields. Coffee beans are spread by the side of the road in late fall and early winter to "roast." The people still count on the rise and fall of the Mekong and other rivers to fertilize the fields and clean the countryside.

I find the South more to my liking – I feel less confined in the cities and towns, and find the people less rigid. However, almost every European I talked to preferred Hanoi. The feel of Hanoi is more "Old Europe," with narrow, winding streets, its shops spilling to the sidewalks and beyond. Saigon (HCMC) seems more open, with wide, tree-lined boulevards. Maybe some of the difference has to do with the minimal amount of bombing in Saigon during the War. The shorter time under communist/socialist domination has had an impact on HCMC – it seems more capitalist – freewheeling without being overbearing.

As more people have access to private transportation and the roads improve for public transportation, the boats that used to ply the rivers are becoming harder to find. It's still possible to catch a ride up or down the Mekong River, but the buses and trains are so much quicker that even the local people are turning their backs on traditional transportation. Flying is within the reach of many people now, too, so Vietnam Airlines flights are often full and the fleet is being rapidly converted from prop-planes to modern jets.

The country is becoming increasingly industrialized, but without much consideration of the consequences. As a result, the air can be very smokey and polluted, and the rivers are still the main means for disposing of waste. Still, the country-side is bucolic, if you can get deep enough into it.

Food Basics

The food is excellent, whether you buy it in a five-star hotel or from a corner pho (beef broth soup) stand. There is a wide variety of food available, from quality fruits and vegetables to meats (familiar and not-so-familiar), poultry, fish, and tofu. The food is not generally spicy. Heavy use is made of fish sauce (nam pla). The "hot pots" are not to be missed. Nothing beats the fresh fish in the Mekong Delta or in river towns across the country.

The French left some legacies that Westerners find most welcoming, namely baguettes, pastries, and real coffee. The Vietnamese have taken the coffee and made it their own, roasting it in the sun, and then serving it very strong with condensed sweetened milk. If you don't care for the taste of canned milk, ask for fresh milk.

There is an abundance of fresh vegetables and fruits available, so the menu choices are quite varied. One of my favorite dishes is tomatoes and fried tofu – simple, and very good. Another is just a plate of mixed vegetables – chef's choice.

In the large and mid-sized cities it is relatively easy to find international foods such as Italian (decent pizzas), Chinese, and Thai. There are some of the ubiquitous fast food places, but not too many yet – the average person can't afford them and most tourists avoid them.

Deep-fried foods are common, but not as prevalent as in Thailand. The most common way to cook foods is some form of stir-fry.

Clothing & Costumes

The ao dai (a long top with deep side slits worn over pants) is still seen, but not frequently. Still, if you are lucky, you might see a few young girls or women wearing the ao dai and a conical hat, riding bicycles along a canal.

The hill tribes have a wealth of unique costumes and jewelry.

Visas Requirements

Visa details are also addressed in the *Customs, Immigration, and Visas* section on page 15. Keep in mind that visa issuance rules are constantly changing. Vietnam does not currently issue visas upon arrival. Virtually all Western nationalities need a visa.

You can apply for a visa through the mail, and download the application form from a Vietnamese Embassy site (www.vietnamembassy-usa.org or www.vietnamembassy-canada.ca). Make sure to use a form of registered mail since you must send your actual passport.

My preference is to go to the Vietnamese embassy or consulate in an Asian country (generally I do this in Thailand) and get the visa there. I have also used the services of a Thai travel agent to handle the process since I hate to wait in line and would rather pay a visa handling fee!

Getting There

From Outside Asia

Several North American airlines (United and American so far) have started flights to Vietnam via Japanese and Hong Kong gateways. You can find out if your airline (or a codeshare partner) flies to Vietnam by going direct to the airline's website. Several major European airlines, including Lufthansa and Air France, serve Vietnam, as do most major Asian airlines. The long-distance cruise ships don't make calls in major Vietnamese ports, but that is likely to change in the next year or two.

From Inside Asia

 There is no viable rail service from other countries at present, so you have only a few choices. You can take a bus or mini-bus from several adjacent countries, you can fly, or you can enter via river or ferry boat. In theory you could hike or bicycle in, but the trip would be long, the terrain quite rugged, and the risks from wildlife and unexploded ordnance unacceptable to most travelers.

> **Tip:** Keep in mind that Vietnam still does not issue visas upon arrival. If you try to enter without a visa you will be refused entry.

■ Overview – Laos

The Lao People's Democratic Republic (PDR) is one of those almost-undiscovered travel destinations that is too quickly becoming a stop on the main tourist trail. It's a land of incredible contrasts – beautiful scenery, raging rivers, poor infrastructure, great food, fabulous UNESCO World Heritage Sites, and incredibly poor people. The country is slowly awakening to the possibilities of adventure and eco-tourism, but there is still a long way to go. Travel times are long – plan on a top speed of 40-50 km per hour/25-30 mph on most roads. Public transport is often primitive – rattletrap buses with people sitting on cement bags down the aisle. There are no trains. Lao Aviation flies to most places in the country, and fares are reasonable, but schedules are infrequent and inconvenient in many cases.

The recent 2004 ASEAN conference resulted in some road improvements around Vientiane, but the rest of the country is still not well off.

Still, Laos is a country not to be missed. You can see waterfalls that pass more water than Niagara Falls (in the rainy season), cycle around islands in the Mekong where life is almost unchanged from 50-100 years ago, visit hundreds of Buddhist

Laos

temples and thousands of saffron-robed monks, trek into the hill tribe areas and ride elephants, kayak in the many rivers, visit former royal palaces that are now living history museums, and so much more. There are no true beaches – Laos is a landlocked country – but there are miles of rivers that are as big as lakes after the rains fall. There's not much wildlife anymore, but the diversity of plants almost makes up for that.

The population is very diverse. Despite the wide variety of ethnic groups the undercurrent is one of cooperation and friendliness. People genuinely want you to see and enjoy their country.

Unlike several of its neighbors, the Laotian people seem incredibly honest. Even single women walking around can feel pretty safe, although caution at night is never a bad idea. Still, it pays to watch your stuff – especially your shoes!

Laos was controlled by Thailand from the late 18th century until the late 19th century, when it became part of French Indochina. The Franco-Siamese Treaty of 1907 defined the current Lao border with Thailand. In 1975, the communist Pathet Lao took control of the government, ending a six-century-old monarchy. Initial closer ties to Vietnam and socialization were replaced with a gradual return to private enterprise, a liberalization of foreign investment laws, and the admission into ASEAN in 1997.

The communist government of Laos makes the country one of the few remaining officially communist states. It began decentralizing control and encouraging private enterprise in 1986. The results, starting from an extremely low base, were striking, with growth averaging 7% in 1988-2001, except during the short-lived drop caused by the Asian financial crisis in 1997. Despite its high economic growth rate, Laos remains a country with a primitive infrastructure; it has no railroads, a rudimentary road system, and limited external and internal telecommunications. Electricity is limited outside of urban areas. Subsistence agriculture accounts for half of GDP and provides 80% of total employment.

Fast Facts

Country Name:
Lao People's Democratic Republic (conventional long form); Laos (conventional short form); Sathalanalat Paxathipatai Paxaxon Lao (local long form).

Government Type: Communist state.

Capital: Vientiane.

Location: Southeastern Asia, northeast of Thailand, west of Vietnam. Completely landlocked.

Area: Total 236,800 sq km/92,352 sq miles; land 230,800 sq km/90,012 sq miles; water 6,000 sq km/2,340 sq miles.

Comparative Area: Slightly larger than Utah.

Climate: Tropical monsoon; rainy season (May to November); dry season (December to April).

Terrain: Mostly rugged mountains; some plains and plateaus.

Elevation: Lowest point – Mekong River, 70 m/230 feet; highest point – Phou Bia, 2,817 m/9,240 feet.

Environmental Issues: Unexploded ordnance; deforestation; soil erosion; most of the population does not have access to potable water.

Natural Resources: Timber, hydropower, gypsum, tin, gold, gemstones.

Population: 6,068,117 (July 2004).

Ethnic Groups: Lao Loum (lowland) 68%, Lao Theung (upland) 22%, Lao Soung (highland) including the Hmong and the Yao 9%, ethnic Vietnamese/Chinese 1%.

Religions: Buddhist 60%, animist and other 40% (including various Christian denominations 1½%).

Languages: Lao (official), French, English, and various ethnic languages.

Currency: Kip (LAK).

Exchange Rate: 10,842 Kip = US$1.

Visa: Required of most Western nationalities. Available upon arrival at major entry points for US$20-$40, plus three passport photos.

Major Holidays

January 1 . . . . New Year's Day
January 6 . . . . Pathet Lao Day
March 8 . . . . Woman's Day
Mrch 22 . . . . People's Party Day
April 13-15 . . . . Boun Pimai, Laotian New Year
May 1 . . . . Labor Day
June 1 . . . . International Children's Day
August 13 . . . . Lao Issara, Day of the Free Laos
October 12 . . . . Day of the Liberation from French
December 2 . . . . Lao National Day

Touring

Suggested Itineraries

One Week. If you only have one week to spend in Laos, plan on seeing just one-third of the country. In the northern third it is easy to spend an entire week in Luang Prabang and nearby areas. The Luang Prabang area is by far the best developed in terms of eco-travel and adventure/active travel. It also has the greatest concentration of temples and other cultural sights. You can spend some time hiking and mountain biking, ride an elephant, raft or boat the Mekong, and visit scores of temples (wats) in this UNESCO World Heritage Site. You can take time for a massage or two, shop the night market for wonderful silks and silver jewelry, tour the former royal residence (can you say "art-deco"?) and escape the worries of the rest of the world.

Two Weeks. In two weeks you can explore Luang Prabang and add a trip to the Plain of Jars, plus take the private tourist bus to Vientiane to see the world's sleepiest international capital and fill up on baguettes and French coffee.

Three Weeks. You can do all of the above, and add a trip to Pakse and Champasak to see the fabulous ruins, then on to the Mekong's 4,000 islands and Don Khong Island for some boating, hiking, and freshwater Irrawaddy dolphin viewing.

Highlights

For some reason, Laos still seems to be off the radar screen for many travelers. It arguably offers some of the best cultural immersion possibilities with the least outside influence in all of Asia. Laos is officially landlocked, but with the **Mekong River** running virtually the entire length of the country, there's no shortage of water access. You can float, or ride a power boat from the far north to Vientiane (and beyond) if the water is high enough. The sunsets over the river are nothing short of spectacular.

Luang Prabang is a small village with enough temples to accommodate the needs of a large city, and no two are alike. The ride from Luang Prabang to Vientiane is truly beautiful – rugged, steep and thrilling. Along the way you can break up the trip by stopping at **Vang Vieng** (Van Vieng) or other sleepy towns. Vang Vieng is a backpackers' haven that has managed to keep its small town feel.

Before you leave Luang Prabang you should head north and visit the **Plain of Jars** to see where the ancestral Laotians lived and how they were buried. The Plain of Jars is a sight to behold and well worth the trip.

Vientiane is one of the smallest, slowest-paced national capitals in the world.

The **Laotian mountains** are rugged and largely pristine.

The people are warm and friendly, and the baguettes, pastries, and café au lait rival anything to be found in France. It's easy and relatively inexpensive to get around whether you choose to fly, take buses or mini-buses, hike, bike, or float down the Mekong River.

If you don't have time to get to Angkor Wat in Cambodia, visit **Champasak** and its temple complex instead.

In the southern part of the country you can travel the Mekong for days by slow boat. There are thousands of islands in a wide stretch of the river, and you can spend lazy days cycling around them, or take a boat trip to see the waterfalls and Irrawaddy freshwater dolphins. You can even cross directly from southern Laos into Cambodia if you already have your visa.

THE TOP SIGHTS & ACTIVITIES

1. The dozens of Buddhist temples in Luang Prabang.

2. Monks painting the frescos on their temple.

3. The Irrawaddy freshwater dolphins feeding.

4. The rugged hills along the road from Luang Prabang to Vientiane.

5. The waterfalls, especially in the rainy season.

6. Miles of rice paddies bursting with green, being worked by women in conical hats.

7. The pre-Angkorian temples near Champasak.

8. The sleepy international capital of Vientiane.

9. The UNESCO World Heritage Site of Luang Prabang.

10. Trekking to hill tribe villages all across Laos.

11. Kayaking or canoeing the many rivers.

12. Watching sunset over the Mekong River.

13. Watching the fishers setting their nets as the sun rises over the Mekong River.

14. Tubing near Vang Vieng.

15. Hiking in the hills and mountains that define Laos.

16. Biking along the relatively sleepy main roads and backroads.

17. Staring at the huge stone monoliths on the Plain of Jars and wondering how they got there.

18. Watching women weaving traditional silks.

19. The night market in Luang Prabang.

20. Renting a scooter and really getting around the country.

Customs & Culture

The Lao People's Democratic Republic (Lao PDR), commonly referred to as Laos, is the only land-locked country in Southeast Asia. It shares its northern border with China and Vietnam, its eastern border with Vietnam, its southern border with Cambodia, its western border with Thailand, and its northwestern border with Myanmar (formerly known as Burma). Laos encompasses almost 240,000 square km), or just under 92,000 square miles, of rugged hills, dense jungle, meandering rivers, and shifting lakes. The capital of Laos is Vientiane, a relatively small city on the Mekong River, just across the border (via the Friendship Bridge) from Thailand.

Laos offers some of the best cultural immersion possibilities with the least outside influence in all of Asia. Luang Prabang is a marvel of temples nestled along the Mekong River. Vientiane is one of the smallest, slowest-paced national capitals in the world. Vang Vieng is a backpackers' haven that has managed to keep its small town feel. The mountains are rugged and largely pristine. The Plain of Jars is a sight to behold.

The people are warm and friendly, and the baguettes and coffee rival anything to be found in France. You can even find pizza (in a restaurant owned by an expatriate Italian and his Lao family), wine, and beer when you're desperate for Western food, and enjoy them along the banks of the Mekong River at sunset.

It's easy and relatively inexpensive to get around, whether you choose to fly, take buses or mini-buses, hike, bike, or float down the Mekong River. The southern towns are hard to get to but great for relaxing and exploring.

There's so much to see and do everywhere in Laos, or you can kick back, relax, and do nothing.

HOW TO RELAX

One of my favorite ways to relax in Laos is to find a high-end massage center and spend an afternoon being pampered. For US$20 you can have several different hour-long massages, a soak in a scented bath, and a body scrub. I find the touch and technique are less aggressive than in a Thai massage.

You can visit dozens of Buddhist temples in and around Luang Prabang. Every young Buddhist boy is expected to spend at least a few months as a monk, and many of them spend several years as monks since monks get a free education. Watching the groups of young monks in their orange/saffron robes and shaved heads as they head out to beg for their meals or go to class is quite a sight to behold. Vientiane has a wonderful indoor market selling everything from cloth to exotic  spices, designer knock-offs to 22-karat gold jewelry and carved jade bracelets. The bus ride through the center of Laos between Luang Prabang and Vientiane is breathtaking and the scenery is marvelous and rugged. You can stop off in small villages, find a guide, and hike the backcountry, or rent a bike and ride around Luang Prabang. You can drift (or tube) down the Mekong and watch the spectacular sunsets. You can even collect many of your onward visas in Vientiane.

> **Note:** Women are not supposed to touch monks or have anything to them directly. Instead, put your offering of food or money into the begging bowl. Monks also get priority seating, so if you are in a public vehicle don't expect to get to keep the front seat – any monk looking for a ride is going to preempt you out of that desirable seat.

Basic History

 Evidence of human occupation in what is now called Laos goes back thousands of years, but few physical traces remain of pre-13th-century civilizations. The limited remnants of earlier civilizations have been found along the less-visited river valleys and in mountainous areas. The first inhabitants were of the

Austroasiatic group. They were hunter-gatherers and competent at navigating the many rivers that flowed through what is now called Laos. These people were traders, paddling their canoes along the Mekong River and its many tributaries, bringing valuable trade goods throughout the area. Through occasional contact with various ethnic groups and empires – most notably the Khmer (Cambodia), Cham (Vietnam by way of India), and Sukhotai (Thailand) – and ongoing migrations to and through the area, a Lao people and culture began to form.

Present-day Laos lies along the middle Mekong River Valley. Some of the earliest inhabitants were from the bronze and pottery culture of the Ban Chiang (1st century AD). They were primarily wet rice farmers. The population density of the area was sparse at best, and loosely ruled by a number of petty princes. These small fiefdoms maintained their power and spread their influence through a concept referred to as mandalas. Mandalas, loosely defined, were a kind of community and control system based on trade, arranged marriages, and warfare. These small fiefdoms fell under the influence of neighboring kingdoms, most notably the Cham in Vietnam (originating in India), the Mon (around present-day Vientiane), the Funan (in central Laos), and the Mon kingdom of Dvaravati centered in the lower Menam Valley. It was through the influence of this last kingdom that Theravada Buddhism reached Laos in the seventh and eighth centuries.

In the seventh century Lao culture and history were greatly affected by a migration of Thai tribes though the region and into parts of China. The end result was a new kingdom, the Nan-chao. This kingdom was able to greatly increase its influence and power by gaining control of the major trade routes. The most important of these routes was the southern stretch of the Silk Road. The society of the Nan-chao consisted of people from many ethnic groups in a highly organized, structured community. One of the most important contributions of the Nan-chao was the introduction and spread of Tantric Buddhism to Laos, Thailand, and other areas in Southeast Asia.

As different groups spread their culture and religions across the region, places became known by different names. When the Thai prince Khun Lo invaded the Luang Prabang area in

698 he renamed the town Muang Sua. His dynasty ruled the area for over a century. Although Muang Sua remained independent under the rule of a succession of Thai princes, the Nan-chao administrators continued to interfere in the area, actually occupying Muang Sua in 709.

In the meanwhile, there were many other outside influences vying for power and control in the area. The Khmers built an outpost at Xay Fong, near present-day Vientiane, and the Champa (Cham from Vietnam) controlled areas along the middle Mekong River in southern Laos until about 1070. During this time, Canthaphanit, the ruler of the Xay Fong, encroached on the Nan-chao administrators around Muang Sua, taking over the area without a fight.

Beginning with the rise of the Kingdom of Lan Xang in the 13th century, the country and ethnic structure seen today began to take shape. This kingdom was based in the area around present-day Luang Prabang, and was characterized by hierarchical administration. The area ruled by this kingdom was many times the size of present-day Laos, and the rulers managed to keep power for about four centuries. Quite an accomplishment in a part of the world not known for long-lasting, stable governments.

Internal power struggles caused the Lan Xang empire to fragment around 1690. Neighboring groups took advantage of this lapse of central control to attempt to absorb the people and land of Laos. The chief rivals for control of the former Lan Xang empire were Vietnam and Thailand (Siam). Until the arrival of the French in the second half of the 19th century, Laos was perilously close to dissolution and division between Vietnam and Thailand.

If any conqueror could be considered welcome, the French in Laos were certainly well-received. Amazingly, none of the Lao people were intentionally killed in the colonization process. In 1893 France took actions to ensure Laos would have an identity separate from the other countries in French Indochina (Vietnam and Cambodia). The royal family and home in Luang Prabang were preserved, and local governments were allowed to continue functioning. However, the French also encouraged immigration by the Vietnamese to provide personnel for the civil service and military.

The French did not view Laos as worthy of development – as a result the infrastructure here is the worst of the three countries. Laos never had a railroad and few roads were built under the French.

In 1945 French control over Laos and the rest of Indochina was temporarily thrown over, and the result was an abortive attempt by the Vietnamese immigrants to depose the Lao Issara or Free Lao Government. This attempt by the Vietnamese to control Laos continued with the actions of the Pathet Lao (Lao Nation) following Laos's independence. In 1975, some months after the fall of Cambodia and South Vietnam, the Pathet Lao took control of the country. The Pathet Lao fought a border war with Thailand in 1988, and it took many months to resolve the actual border location.

Visa Requirements

Visa details are given in the *Customs, Immigration, and Visas* section, page 15. If you plan to come in by any method other than by plane, you need to check with a Laotian Embassy or Consulate at least one week, but less than one month, before you plan to enter the country. Without a visa you will be turned away. Payment is almost always required in US dollars, although the Luang Prabang airport accepts Thai Baht.

There are currently at least eight land or ferry crossing points for entry to Laos, in addition to the airports at Vientiane and Luang Prabang. Entry points come and go, so you should always verify that your chosen entry point is still open. These entry points are:

From China

□ Mengla to Boten (advance visa required – land crossing)

From Thailand

□ Chiang Kong to Huay Xai (advance visa required – ferry crossing)

□ Nong Khai to Vientiane (Friendship Bridge – visa upon entry)

□ Mukdahan to Savannakhet (advance visa required – ferry crossing)

□ Chong Mek to Ban Mai Sing Amphon (advance visa required – land crossing)

From Vietnam

□ Vinh to Kaew Neua (advance visa required – land crossing

□ Danang to Lao Bao (advance visa required – land crossing)

From Burma

□ None at this time

From Cambodia

□ TBS (advance visa required – ferry crossing)

Luang Prabang Airport

□ Visa upon arrival

Vientiane Airport

□ Visa upon arrival

> **Tip:** This link has a simple map of land and ferry crossings: www.mekongexpress.com/laos/general/maps/mapsmall.htm

Getting There

From Inside Asia

There is no viable rail service at present, so you only have a few choices once you're inside Asia. You can take a bus or mini-bus from several adjacent countries, you can fly, or you can enter via river or ferry boat. In theory you could hike or bike in, but the trip would be long, the terrain quite rugged, and the risks from wildlife and unexploded ordnance unacceptable to most travelers.

By Air

Air France may fly into Vientiane by the time this book is available. **Thai Air** also flies into Vientiane from Bangkok.

Lao Aviation uses French-made ATR-72 props to fly into Laos from Chiang Mai and Bangkok in Thailand, Kunming in China, Phnom Penh in Cambodia, and Ho Chi Minh City and Hanoi in Vietnam. They are scheduled to start using Airbus 320s on the Bangkok-Vientiane-Bangkok route any day now. The service from Vietnam has been alternating with **Vietnam Airlines**, but schedules and servicing airlines change frequently. Your best bet is to consult a travel agent in Laos or an adjacent country to arrange your travel. This will also almost always be far less expensive than intra-Southeast Asian travel arranged in your home country. See *Getting There* under each country for flight route and cost information.

Since the Lao Aviation prop-driven aircraft can't fly at high altitudes (they're not pressurized), you get an up-close and personal view of the countryside. It is spectacular – so pristine and almost uninhabited – all you see are dense swathes of jungle, rivers, a few clearings, small villages, curls of smoke from cooking fires, the gilt of occasional temples, and a (very) few roads.

Lao Aviation's schedule is subject to revision without notice, so you are advised to reconfirm your flight(s) the day before and a few hours before your scheduled departure time. One way to do this is to visit http://www.mekongexpress.com/laos/schedule. This site has links to ticketing agent information for Hong Kong, the UK, Germany, Singapore, Italy, Austria, Korea, Thailand, Japan Cambodia, Laos, the USA, Taiwan, China, The Netherlands, and Vietnam. Prices also change without notice, but a reasonable planning and budgeting rule of thumb is about US$100-$150 per flight segment. The cost for a one-way flight is almost always half the cost of a round-trip, and many times you can deplane at intermediate stops for little or no extra cost, continuing your journey a few days later. That feature makes flying in Indochina an incredible bargain.

❖ **Sample Flight Costs (Lao Aviation)**

International

(all prices/schedules/routes are subject to change)

Luang Prabang to/from Chiang Mai .... $100 (daily flights)
Vientiane to/from Bangkok............ $150 (daily flights)
Luang Prabang to/from Hanoi .... $150 (daily flights)
Vientiane to/from HCMC .... $150 (weekly)
Hanoi to/from Vientiance............. $150 (almost daily)

> **Note:** Lao Aviation is continually working
> out arrangements with the national carriers
> of adjacent countries to have "code-sharing"
> type arrangements, greatly increasing the fre-
> quency of flights and convenience of connec-
> tions. The costs should be virtually identical.

Overland

Five of the seven Laotian border crossings are via
land-based transportation. With the exception of
the Nong Khai/Friendship Bridge crossing, you
must have your visa in advance. One way to see if
this rule has changed is to contact a Laotian embassy or consulate very shortly before your planned arrival in Laos.
Another way is to visit a travelers' chat room and query people who have very recently used the crossing you plan to take.

Most people enter Laos from adjacent countries by bus or
mini-bus. Be advised the trips can be very long and the roads
often leave something to be desired. For example, the trip
from Chiang Mai to Luang Prabang can easily top 24 hours.
Holes the size of Volkswagen Beetles are not unusual. Still,
you can't beat ground transportation for seeing the country
up close! The long-distance buses are reasonably comfortable,
even for tall people, and they make a reasonable number of
food and facility breaks. You may, however, find the entertainment consists of overly loud Asian videos. These long-haul
bus trips vary in price but you should plan on US$15-$35
(plus money for meals) for the 20- to 25-hour trips. The
city/town sections in this book have more detail on cost,
schedules, and bookings.

> **Tip:** Travel agents in your departure town
> should also be able to arrange your ticket and
> will often wait in lines for you and deliver tick-
> ets to your hotel.

For shorter trips across borders you may want to take a
mini-bus or share-taxi. You may or may not have to change
vehicles at the border. I would assume you will have to change
vehicles because of the border crossing formalities, and that
can add an hour or two to your planned travel time.

Tip: Chinese visas must be obtained ahead of time, and in person (by you or a travel agent). They are also quite expensive now – anywhere from $50 to $100, depending on your nationality and how fast you need the visa.

By Boat

Two of the Laotian border crossings use a ferry. You may already be on a "cruise" down the river, or you may come to the crossing by bus or other public transportation. No matter how you get there, you need a visa to cross into Laos unless you arrive from the Thai side of the Friendship Bridge. Returning to Thailand, most nationalities get a visa on the spot.

On Foot or by Bicycle

You can actually take a bus, taxi, shared taxi, or mini-bus to the Thai/Laotian border at Nong Khai and walk or bike across the "Friendship Bridge." Of course, it's a long way to Vientiane, so this walk between countries is merely a formality. However, this is one of the few places you can get a visa upon arrival, so it can be a very productive walk. Note most nationalities don't need to pay a fee to get a Thai visa going the other way.

Religion

Theravada Buddhism and Hin-duism have been major influences on the development and progression of Lao culture. Buddhism arrived in the 14th century, in some cases supplanting Hindu beliefs, but in many cases co-existing with  these beliefs. Over 60% of the Lao people are Theravada Buddhists. There is a strong Khmer influence, especially in the South, while the Thai and Burmese influences are particularly evident in the North and West. Laos, like other countries in Southeast Asia, has taken the diverse influences, symbols, and teachings from neighboring and nearby countries and synthesized them into its own symbols and stories. For example, the snake, prevalent in the designs on both religious and royal buildings, is a symbol of the benevolent spirit of the water and is considered the protector of the king.

The influences of Khmer, Thai, and Vietnamese cultures on traditional Lao culture are strong. There are still many traces of the French influence as well.

Keep in mind that in Buddhism, the head is private – it is rude to touch someone on their head, even small children. Don't touch a monk, either.

Another custom to be very conscious of – never point the soles of your feet at a Buddha image. Sit sideways so your feet point away, and use care when getting back on your feet. One must always remove shoes before entering Buddhist (and many other) temples, and always sit in the presence of Buddha.

Arts & Crafts

There are many varieties of folk art in Laos – much of it quite intricate and beautiful. Some of the more commonly seen examples include intricate woven silk and cotton cloth, bamboo and reed baskets, detailed gold and silver jewelry and other items, and carved wood and ivory goods.

Music is also important in Lao culture, and the people have developed many musical instruments, primarily reed- (bamboo) and percussion-based.

Lao theater reflects the influence of other Southeast Asian countries, especially India and Cambodia. Ballet, with orchestral accompaniment, was a major form of entertainment in the royal courts in the 16th and 17th centuries, with the dancers wearing elaborate, intricate costumes, masks, and headdresses. For the common people, Lao folk theater evolved, using dialogue, singing, and music, and taking place at the many temple fairs. Even today, dancing is a respected profession, not just a form of recreation, and professional dance troupes give outstanding performances throughout the country during religious festivals, celebrations, and holidays. All performers are males.

Museums

There are many beautiful temples, especially in Luang Prabang, but a relative scarcity of museums. The former Royal Palace in Luang Prabang houses a collection of Buddha images and many possessions of the last king. In Vientiane the Ho Phakeo museum has a collection of items depicting Lao culture from the sixth through the 20th centuries.

Lifestyles

The vast majority of the Lao people (often referred to as the Lao Lum) live in small villages with 50-60 houses. Their homes are generally made of bamboo, thatch, and timber, raised about two meters (six or seven feet) above the ground, with only the wealthiest Lao living in more substantial villas. Most villagers are subsistence farmers, and even the shop-keepers and those involved in the tourist or other trades keep chickens and kitchen gardens. The agricultural year centers around growing short-grain glutinous (wet) rice.

Most farming is still done with water buffaloes pulling the plows, and oxen-pulled carts are a common sight. Tractors or other motorized farming equipment is seldom seen.

Families live together in nuclear, rather than extended, groups. A female dowry is normally paid, and the practice of having more than one wife has been banned.

Motorized transport is becoming increasingly common, especially in the form of mini-buses and motor scooters.

Even the capital, Vientiane, is more like a village than a city. There are few fancy hotels, and a limited choice of restaurants, but things are changing.

There are increasing numbers of road, water, and other public works projects, and these are both improving and altering the lifestyle of the people. NGOs (Non-Governmental Organizations) are establishing a strong presence in Laos, and the influx of money and foreign culture and ideas is having an increasing impact on the people, expectations, and day-to-day life.

A trek to the hill tribe areas is a great way to see a fast-disappearing way of life. In many villages there is no electricity or running water, although the NGOs are working to change that. Farming is still done with water buffalo and wooden plows.

Food

Lao food revolves around rice. Meat is expensive for the average Lao and so is not a main aspect of most meals. Instead, it is more like a condiment, with vegetables as the main feature. Lime juice, coriander, and lemongrass are used to add flavor and zing and fermented fish sauce is used to give a salty taste. You will also find mint, garlic, chilis, ginger, coconut milk, tamarind juice, basil, and peanuts used for flavor, giving Lao food a strong resemblance to many Thai dishes. Food is almost always fresh since refrigeration is not common in the smaller towns and villages – don't get too friendly with the chickens pecking in the streets because they may be on the menu tomorrow!

Thanks to the years of French occupation, there is a tradition of baguettes, café au lait, fresh fruit, and other baked goods, especially at breakfast. Some of the best "French" bread in the world is found in Indochina!

Alcoholic beverages are available. The local beer is quite good. Wine is available by the bottle or glass, and is often not too bad. Whiskey is locally-brewed and very powerful. Western liquor is available but very expensive.

Bottled water and soft drinks are readily available. Fresh-squeezed juice is also common, but beware of added water or the use of ice, which may not have been from a purified source.

Clothing & Costumes

Many Lao have abandoned the traditional costumes in favor of Western-style clothes, especially in the cities and towns. It is still possible to buy the traditional ankle-length skirt in many places. The open air markets often sell the cloth (usually cotton) by lengths – the length is just right for making the skirt, and the skirt can usually be made in just an hour or two. If you are traveling with just shorts, this skirt makes a great cover-up for temples that require legs be covered.

■ Overview – Cambodia

The Democratic Republic of Kampuchea

Most Cambodians consider themselves to be Khmers. The Khmers were once a dominant force across much of Southeast Asia. The Angkor Empire extended over much of Southeast Asia between the 10th and 14th centuries. The preeminence of the Angkor Empire ended as a result of attacks by the Thai and Vietnamese.

Cambodia

In 1863, the king of Cambodia placed the country under French protection; it became part of French Indochina in 1887. Cambodia, like much of Southeast and East Asia, was occupied by the Japanese prior to and during World War II. At the end of the War, Cambodia was once again independent within the French Union and gained full independence in 1953.

After a five-year struggle, communist Khmer Rouge forces captured Phnom Penh in April 1975 and ordered the evacuation of all cities and towns. As a result of this order, over 1.5 million people died or were killed by execution, enforced hardships, or starvation. A 1978 Vietnamese invasion drove the Khmer Rouge into the countryside and began almost 13 years of civil war.

The 1991 Paris Peace Accords mandated democratic elections and a ceasefire, which was not honored by the Khmer Rouge. The UN-sponsored elections in 1993 helped restore some semblance of normalcy and the final elements of the Khmer Rouge surrendered in early 1999. Factional fighting in 1997 ended the first coalition government, but a second round of national elections in 1998 led to the formation of another coalition government and renewed political stability. The July 2003 elections were relatively peaceful, but it took a full year of negotiations between contending political parties before a coalition government was formed.

Cambodia's economy slowed dramatically in 1997-98 due to the regional economic crisis, civil violence, and political infighting. Foreign investment and tourism fell off. In 1999, the first full year of peace in 30 years, progress was made on economic reforms. Growth resumed and has remained at about 5% during 2000-2003. Tourism was Cambodia's fastest growing industry, with arrivals up 34% in 2000 and up another 40% in 2001 before the September 11, 2001 terrorist attacks in the US. Cambodia expects one million foreign tourists per year at this point. Economic growth has been largely driven by expansion in the clothing sector and tourism.

Fast Facts

Country Name: Kingdom of Cambodia (conventional long form); Cambodia (conventional short form); Preahreacheanacha Kampuchea (local long form); Kampuchea (local short form).

Former Names: Kingdom of Cambodia, Khmer Republic, Democratic Kampuchea, People's Republic of Kampuchea, State of Cambodia.

Government Type: Multiparty democracy under a constitutional monarchy established in September 1993.

Capital: Phnom Penh

Location: Southeastern Asia, bordering the Gulf of Thailand, between Thailand, Vietnam, and Laos.

Area: Total 181,040 sq km/70,605 sq miles; land 176,520 sq km/68,840 sq miles; water: 4,520 sq km/1,763 sq miles.

Comparative Area: Slightly smaller than the state of Oklahoma.

Climate: Tropical; rainy, monsoon season (May to November); dry season (December to April); little seasonal temperature variation.

Terrain: Mostly low, flat plains; mountains in southwest and north. A land of paddies and forests dominated by the Mekong River and Tonle Sap.

Elevation: Lowest point – Gulf of Thailand, 0 m/0 feet; highest point – Phnum Aoral, 1,810 m/5,937 feet.

Natural Resources: Oil and gas, timber, gemstones, some iron ore, manganese, phosphates, hydropower potential.

Environmental Issues: Illegal logging activities throughout the country and strip mining for gems in the western region along the border with Thailand have resulted in habitat loss and declining biodiversity that threatens natural fisheries; soil erosion; in rural areas, most of the population does not have access to potable water; declining fish stocks because of overfishing.

Population: 13,363,421. AIDS is having a significant impact on the overall population level and the distribution of age and gender.

Ethnic Groups: Khmer 90%, Vietnamese 5%, Chinese 1%, other 4%.

Religions: Theravada Buddhist 95%, other 5%.

Languages: Khmer (official) 95%, French, English.

Currency: Riel (KHR).

Exchange Rate: 4,262 Riel = US$1.

Visa: Required of most Western nationalities. Available upon arrival at major entry points for US$20-$40, plus three passport photos.

Major Holidays

January 7 . . . . National Day
April . . . . Chaul Chhnam (New Year, variable dates)
April 17. . . . . Independence Day
May 1 . . . . Labor Day
May 12 . . . . Khmer Republic Constitution Day
May 20 . . . . Day of Hatred
June 19/28 . . . . Memorial Day
September 22 . . . . Feast of the Ancestors

Touring

Cambodia is a rugged, beautiful country with a very poor infrastructure. Getting around is not easy, so you need to factor travel time into your plans. I recommend at least a week, and two weeks is better, to get a feel for the country.

Suggested Itineraries

Two weeks, leaving from Thailand

Day 1: Travel to starting point, from Bangkok to Poipet and on to Battambang. Note the abrupt change from relative prosperity to serious poverty as you cross the border to Cambodia. The roads also degenerate severely. Be prepared for potholes the size of VW Beetles.

Day 2: Spend the day in Battambang – a relaxing stop before hitting the temples of Angkor.

Day 3: Travel by boat to Siem Reap (Angkor Wat). Be prepared to swamp small floating villages and possibly go for an unplanned swim.

Days 4-6: Explore the "Grand Circuit" – the roads around and past the many temples at Angkor Wat. Spend part of a day in the village of Siem Reap visiting a market or two. Watch the sunrise/set at one of the temples. You can also take a boat ride to a floating village (pretty touristy but still interesting).

Days 7-8: Take the boat (beats the roads!) to Phnom Penhand spend the next day or two exploring the city.

Day 9: Take a tour to the Killing Fields.

Day 10: Travel by bus or mini-van to Sihanoukville on the coast.

Day 11: Explore Sihanoukville, then take a boat to Koh Kong (Thailand).

Day 12: Travel by bus back to Bangkok.

Two weeks, leaving from Vietnam

Day 1: Travel by train or van to Phnom Penh.

Days 2-4: Explore Phnom Penh and the Killing Fields.

Day 5: Fly or travel by bus/van to Siem Reap.

Days 6-8: Explore the Grand Circuit around Angkor Wat, visit a floating village, and explore the local markets in Siem Reap.

Day 9: Take a speedboat across the Tonle Sap to Battambang.

Day 10: Chill out in Battambang.

Day 11: Take a mini-van to Bangkok.

Possible extension: Travel by van to Sihanoukville from Battambang, then to Koh Kong and on to Bangkok.

Option: Omit trip to Battambang and fly from Siem Reap to HCMC.

If you have the time you can also take side-trips to Kompot and Takeo, and spend time in the north visiting the former hill stations.

Highlights

How do you want to travel? There are few truly international flights, but that is changing rapidly. Getting there is half the fun. You can make the road trip from Ho Chi Minh City to Phnom Penh in just a few hours if it's not the rainy season, and then on to Siem Reap (it means Thai defeated!) in about the same amount of time.

Phnom Penh has a fair amount of Colonial architecture, some interesting temples, and a few good museums. Watch your stuff and be careful of police – they have been known to accost and rob tourists, then walk away. If Phnom Penh isn't in your plans, you can fly from HCMC or Bangkok over the thick, triple canopy jungle and be in Angkor Wat (Siem Reap) in an hour or so.

Angkor Wat is a UNESCO World Heritage Site, and one of the most incredible places you could ever hope to visit. Plan on three days just exploring the main temple complex, and another day or two for the temples and sights in town and out-lying temples. You can overdose on culture and history, so a certified guide is an excellent idea. I rarely use a guide, but Angkor Wat (and Bagan in Burma) are worthwhile exceptions.

Another not-to-be-missed adventure to consider is the speed-boat ride from Siem Reap through miles of floating villages, to the former resort town of **Battambang**. There's still a lot of Colonial architecture to be seen, and much of it is in better repair than in Phnom Penh. Dinner along the river in a market restaurant is a great way to unwind after your speed boat ride.

In Cambodia there's so much to see and do, or you can kick back, relax, and do nothing.

TOP SIGHTS & ATTRACTIONS

1. **Angkor Wat** – the one must-see sight in the entire country! Plan to spend at least two full days here, and consider hiring either a car or moto (scooter) and guide. The temples are spread out and the weather is hot. You'll need a visa-type photo and US dollars to get your picture ID pass.

2. **Battambang**. Visit the last remnants of colonialism. A few traces remain, and the lake-side setting is great.

3. The **Royal Palace** and **Silver Pagoda/Emerald Buddha** in Phnom Penh.

4. The **Tonle Sap** – part lake and part river.

5. The **floating villages** in the Tonle Sap.

6. Former **hill stations** and **tea-growing areas**.

7. Other pre-Angkorian **wats** and **ruins**.

Shanty area outside Sapa

"New" Sapa town

Main city market, Sapa

Above: Vegetable sellers in Sapa market

Below: Grocery shopping Sapa-style

Above: Ancient Chinese remedies – pickled snakes
Below: Hill tribe women come to Sapa to sell woven goods and jewelry

Above: Gia Long complex, Hué tombs along the Perfume River
Below: Gia Long complex

Above: Incense drying along the road to the Hué tombs
Below: French Colonial mansion, Saigon

Above: Cathedral de Notre Dame, Saigon
Below: Former Colonial post office in Saigon

History

 Archaeological evidence indicates that parts of the region now called Cambodia were inhabited during the first and second millennia BC. By the first century AD, the inhabitants had developed relatively stable, organized societies. The most advanced groups lived along the coast and in the lower Mekong River valley and delta regions, where they cultivated wet rice and kept domesticated animals.

These early inhabitants were probably Austroasiatic in origin, related to the ancestors of the groups who now inhabit much of Southeast Asia and many of the islands of the Pacific Ocean. They worked metals, including both iron and bronze, and had good navigational skills. Mon-Khmer people, who arrived at a later date, probably intermarried with them. The Khmer who now populate Cambodia may have migrated from southeastern China to the Indochinese Peninsula before the first century AD. They are believed to have arrived before their present Vietnamese, Thai, and Lao neighbors.

The Angkorian period lasted from the early ninth century to the early 15th century. This was the golden age of Khmer civilization. The great temple cities of the Angkorian region, near the modern town of Siem Reap, are a lasting monument to the greatness of ruler Jayavarman II's successors. (Even the Khmer Rouge, who looked on most of their country's past history and traditions with hostility, adopted a stylized Angkorian temple for the flag of Democratic Kampuchea. A similar motif is found in the present-day flag of the PRK). The kingdom founded by Jayavarman II also gave modern-day Cambodia, or Kampuchea, its name. During the early ninth to mid-15th centuries, the area was known as Kambuja, originally the name of an early north Indian state.

Jayavarman II settled north of the Tonle Sap. He built several capitals before establishing one, Hariharalaya, near the site where the Angkorian complexes were built.

Indravarman I (877-89) extended Khmer control as far west as the Korat Plateau in Thailand, and he ordered the construction of a huge reservoir north of the capital to provide irrigation for wet rice cultivation. His son, Yasovarman I

(889-900), built the Eastern Baray (reservoir or tank). Its dikes, which may be seen today, are more than six km/3.6 miles long and 1.6 km/one mile wide. The elaborate system of canals and reservoirs built under Indravarman I and his successors were the key to Kambuja's prosperity for half a millennium. By freeing cultivators from dependence on unreliable seasonal monsoons, they made possible large surpluses of rice. Kambuja's decline during the 13th and 14th centuries was hastened by the deterioration of the irrigation system.

Suryavarman II (1113-50), one of the greatest Angkorian monarchs, expanded his kingdom's territory in a series of successful wars against the kingdom of Champa in central Vietnam, the kingdom of Nam Viet in northern Vietnam, and the small Mon domains, as far west as the Irrawaddy River of Burma. His greatest achievement was the construction of the temple city complex of Angkor Wat. The largest religious edifice in the world, Angkor Wat is considered the greatest single architectural work in Southeast Asia. Suryavarman II's reign was followed, however, by 30 years of dynastic upheaval and an invasion by the Cham, who destroyed the city of Angkor in 1177.

The Cham ultimately were driven out and conquered by Jayavarman VII, whose reign (1181-1218) marked the apogee of Kambuja's power. Jayavarman VII was a fervent patron of Mahayana Buddhism. He embarked on a frenzy of building activity that included the Angkor Thom complex and the Bayon, a remarkable temple whose stone towers depict 216 faces of Buddhas, gods, and kings. He also built over 200 rest houses and hospitals throughout his kingdom. He maintained a system of roads between his capital and provincial towns.

Carvings show that everyday Angkorian buildings were wooden structures not much different from those found in Cambodia today. The impressive stone buildings were not used as residences; instead, they were the focus of Hindu or Buddhist cults that celebrated the divinity of the monarch and his family. As is the case with many other ancient edifices, the monuments of the Angkorian region absorbed vast reserves of resources and human labor and their purpose remains shrouded in mystery.

Angkorian society was strictly hierarchical. The king, regarded as divine, owned both the land and his subjects. Immediately below the monarch and the royal family were the Brahman priesthood and a small class of officials, who numbered about 4,000 in the 10th century. Next were the commoners, and then a large slave class that, like the nameless multitudes of ancient Egypt, built the enduring monuments.

After Jayavarman VII's death, Kambuja entered a long period of decline that led to its eventual disintegration. The Thai were a growing menace on the empire's western borders. The spread of Theravada Buddhism, which came to Kambuja from Sri Lanka by way of the Mon kingdoms, challenged the royal Hindu and Mahayana Buddhist cults.

In 1353 a Thai army captured Angkor. It was later recaptured by the Khmer, but wars continued and the capital was looted several times. During the same period, Khmer territory north of the present Laotian border was lost to the Lao kingdom of Lan Xang. In 1431 the Thai captured Angkor Thom.

In October 1887, the French proclaimed the Union Indochinoise, or Indochina Union, comprising Cambodia and the three constituent regions of Vietnam: Tonkin, Annam, and Cochinchina. Laos was added to the Indochina Union after being separated from Thai suzerainty in 1893. The Colonial bureaucracy expanded rapidly. French nationals naturally held the highest positions, but even on the lower rungs of the bureaucracy Cambodians found few opportunities because the Colonial government preferred to hire Vietnamese.

When Norodom died in 1904, the French passed over his sons and set his brother Sisowath (1904-27) on the throne. During their generally peaceful reigns, Sisowath and his son Monivong (1927-41) were instruments of French rule. One of the few highlights of Sisowath's reign was French success in getting Thailand's King Chulalongkorn to sign a new treaty in 1907 returning the northwestern provinces of Battambang and Siem Reap to Cambodia.

The modern history of Cambodia is one of turmoil and takeovers – during World War II, by communist infiltrators from Vietnam, by Pol Pot and his cronies, and finally by a non-communist, relatively stable government.

Food

Cambodian food as a "cuisine" leaves much to be desired. There are influences from Thailand and Vietnam, and to a lesser degree China, Laos, and even India, but the food is not on a par with any of these places. You'll definitely spot the French Colonial influence in the bread, coffee, and occasional bakery. The troubles that have plagued the country for so many years have reduced eating to a matter of necessity and basic survival for most Cambodians, and the food choices and preparation reflect this. Nonetheless, there are still decent restaurants and a few specialties that are worth a try.

Overall the food is like Thai food that has been "de-spiced." You'll find curries, rice dishes, noodle bowls, and soups. There are also varieties of meat and vegetable stir-fries and a decent array of fruit. One of the few specialties you will encounter is called *an sam chruk*, sticky rice filled with bean paste, bean curd, and bits of chopped meat.

Rice (or noodles) forms the centerpiece of most meals. Usually you'll get the rice mixed with a bit of chopped, stir-fried meat and some leafy vegetables. A bit of mint, chili, or chopped fresh mystery herbs is usually the topper. Be careful of the chopped, fresh stuff or the lightly cooked leafy stuff; there is no guarantee any of it is safe to eat. Remember to stick with well-cooked or seriously pickled items, especially outside of Phnom Penh and perhaps Siem Reap (Angkor Wat). Any fish you find, away from the small stretch of coast, is likely to be of the freshwater variety out of the Tonle Sap. Fish will be either stir-fried, deep fried, or salted. You may encounter barbequed shrimp – quite nice if you can get it. There are also items most Westerners find less than appetizing – duck eggs served just before they hatch (*pong tea kon*), or fried bugs, generally cicadas (*chong roet*).

If you spend time in Phnom Penh you'll be able to sample a variety of international cuisine – decent quality and generally low prices.

The best place to find "Cambodian" specialties is to sample the wares of the street vendors. For $1-$2 you can have a decent meal, but be sure the food is fresh, hot, and served in clean conditions by clean and healthy-looking people.

Finally, if you want cheap and predictable, find the nearest backpacker's hostel or ghetto and you'll be able to get pizza, pancakes, and American breakfasts. Don't count on finding any of the ubiquitous fast food places – at least not the Western ones!

People, Culture & Customs

 Cambodian culture is defined by the influence of the Khmers, but the Khmers themselves were heavily influenced by other cultures – most notably that of India. At its peak the Khmer influence reached into present-day Malaysia, and to the borders of today's Burma (Myanmar) and Vietnam. Some of the areas where the Indian influence was strongest and still visible are in religion, astrology, some of the deities and the role of royalty, and in literature, arts, and dance.

Although Cambodia never controlled Thailand, it still influenced, and was influenced by, the Thai culture. In the 15th century many of the Cambodia intellectuals, craftsmen, and artists were forcibly taken to Thailand, and they left an imprint on Thai culture. When some of these people were able to return to Cambodia they brought back Thai ideas and cooking styles. In addition, Thailand controlled much of Cambodia for many years.

> **Did you know?** Supposedly the name "Siem Reap" comes from the defeat of the Thai – Siem is "thai" in Cambodian, and Reap means defeated.

While much of the traditional Khmer art was destroyed or stolen during the Pol Pot days and across Cambodian history, a good collection remains in the National Museum in Phnom Penh.

There were several cultures that predominated in the pre-Angkor period – chiefly the Chenla and Funan. Very little survives of the Funan period, but there is more to be found of the Chenla period, especially in the form of stepped towers embodying the Indian style, but still uniquely Chenla in form and concept. There are also some surviving statues, but most of these are in the National Museum in Phnom Penh. The primary form of art is Hindu, but there appear to be some Buddhist (Mahayana) influences as well.

> **Note:** Thanks to the efforts of the Pol Pot regime, many of the cultural relics were either destroyed or sold to collectors in other countries. Only those things that were immobile, such as the buildings in Angkor Wat and Angkor Thom, are still in situ. The few remaining artifacts of pre-colonial times are almost exclusively in the museums in Phnom Penh.

Cambodian art reached its apex during the Angkorian period, from the eighth to 14th centuries. This is the period that saw the rise of Angkor Wat and the numerous other wat complexes around the country. During this period, Javanese and Cham aspects were incorporated into the Khmer art and buildings.

There are not very many crafts choices unique to Cambodia. In general, the quality is not on par with surrounding countries, but that is slowly changing. The advent of NGOs (non-governmental organizations) and their efforts to develop sustainable, home-based industries that allow the women to work around their other chores, is slowly creating a silk-weaving industry.

Dance

Dance is an important art form in Cambodia. All the dances are highly symbolic, with a strict order and prescribed form. The Khmer Rouge killed or exiled many dancers because of their close relationship with the royal family (many dancers were well-born or actually members of the royal family). There are ongoing attempts to revive and restore this classi-

cal art form. If you have a chance to attend a performance, you really should do so, both to support the efforts to bring the art form back, and to experience a very unusual dance form.

Folk dances never really went away. The performances were used as teaching tools, so they reflect tales from Cambodia literature and a long oral tradition of story-telling.

The People

Like most of its neighbors, Cambodia is a multi-ethnic society, and this has been the source of many of its woes. There is a long history of one group trying to wipe out others – Pol Pot was just the most recent in a long line of despots. The government has historically denied the true numbers of some ethnic groups, most notably the Chinese and Vietnamese; the table that follows should give you an idea of numbers of ethnic groups, based on "official" Ministry of the Interior data (all numbers have been rounded). The dominant ethnic group is, of course, the Khmer. The total population is about 13 million, and fewer than 400,000 of those are non-Khmer.

ETHNIC MINORITIES IN CAMBODIA (2002)			
Cham 205,000	Vietnamese 96,000	Chinese 48,000	Lao 20,000
Tumpuan 16,000	Kui 15,000	Jarai 12,000	Kroeng 8,000
Phnong 5,300	Kavet 4,000	Steang 3,300	Prov 2,600
Thai 2,500	Kraol 2,000	Rabel 1,700	Other 8,000

The origin of the Khmer people is still the subject of debate. They may be from Mongol and Melanesian groups, or other groups altogether. The influence of Indian and Javanese cultures is evident in both pre-Angkor and Angkor architecture, arts, and traditions. There were also large migrations from China and Vietnam in the 18th and 19th centuries, just prior to the French Colonial era. When the Khmer Rouge took over, many of the Chinese and Vietnamese left, severely damaging both the agricultural and merchant capabilities of Cambodian society. The Khmer Rouge murdered many of the ethnic Chinese and Vietnamese who stayed, and most of those who survived left the country in 1975.

The unofficial Vietnamese population may be as high as a million, and is surely at least 200,000, since many Vietnamese returned or arrived with the Vietnamese takeover in 1979. Since the departure of the ruling Vietnamese in 1989, Cambodia has not been a good place for the remaining ethnic Vietnamese. Keep this in mind when discussing your travel plans – there is tremendous antiVietnamese sentiment, and you could feel the effects if you are perceived as too sympathetic to the plight of the local ethnic Vietnamese (or other non-Khmer groups).

> **Tip:** It is never a good idea to discuss politics, religion, or culture with the locals. There are too many ethnic issues you are not aware of. You could easily run afoul of the law. In many places, especially Cambodia, the rule of law is tenuous, and many so-called law enforcement officers are thugs in uniform who view you as an easy mark with lots of money and not much savvy. By the same token, be very careful discussing politics, culture, or ethnic issues with other travelers. You never know who will be listening, and what they might do.

Religion

 During the Angkor period, and even beyond, **Buddhism** and **Hinduism** co-existed in Cambodia. In fact, one of the reasons the Khmer empire was so powerful and lasted so long was its incorporation of the Hindu concept of the "god-king." The people believed the king's power to be divinely-inspired or granted, and no one wanted to mess with a god.

The advent of Theravada Buddhism sweeping across Southeast Asia meant the subsidence of Hinduism (although the divine aspects of the king persisted into the last century). The Hindu religion was very elitist, leaving the common people out, so the common touch of Buddhism had great appeal for the average Cambodian – they welcomed this religion, and eventually it became dominant in the country.

Language

A few elderly Cambodians still speak French, and English is spoken by people in the tourist industry and some well-educated Cambodians. For the most part, however, the language is Khmer, and the alphabet relates back to ancient Sanskrit. While there are common words with many other languages in the region, there are not enough similarities so that people from one country can understand those from another.

The Sex Trade

The Cambodians are an incredibly poor, but welcoming people. Still, they have a different set of values than most Westerners. This includes tolerating, and even encouraging, the sale of children, women, and young men into prostitution. There is a thriving sex trade and the prices are very cheap. Unfortunately, the medical care and understanding of sexually transmitted diseases, especially HIV/AIDS, is sorely lacking.

The incidence of HIV/AIDS is skyrocketing. There is no such thing as truly safe sex in a Cambodian brothel. Even if the prostitute uses contraception (and you'd better supply your own!), there is no guarantee the sheets are clean or that you won't be rolled or robbed in the brothel, or on the surrounding streets.

In addition to parents or other relatives selling children into prostitution, there are thousands of abandoned children who find the only way they can earn any money is by selling their bodies (for the lordly price of about $2-$3, if they are lucky). The police are incredibly corrupt and, if you are a Westerner, they are not on your side – unless you can outbid the other person and buy your way out of trouble.

The Adoption Racket

The Cambodians are well aware of the desire of some Westerners to adopt a baby, and they have started catering to those people. Many of the children "available" for adoption have actually been stolen by corrupt brokers or sold by their relatives. The rules have tightened considerably since 2000, so use extreme care if you are trying to adopt a Cambodian child. You may pay thousands of dollars and return empty-handed. At best, the family will get a few hundred dollars. The rest goes to baby brokers and the government.

Visa Requirements

Visa details are also addressed in the *Customs, Immigration, and Visas* section at the beginning of this book. Keep in mind visa issuance rules are constantly changing. Cambodia currently issues visas upon arrival at the major airports (Phnom Penh and Siem Reap). The cost is about US$20-$40, plus three passport photos. Virtually all Western nationalities need a visa.

Getting There

Getting there is not easy. There are some flights, but nothing on the international scene (at publication). You can fly in from Thailand, Laos, and Vietnam, or come overland on lousy roads. You can also take the slow boat route. There is no true national air carrier – the website for Royal Cambodian (Cambodge) Airlines has been hijacked and turned into a pornographic website. **Siem Reap Airlines** is, at present, the only Cambodian airline.

From Outside Asia

Currently no major North American or European airlines serve Cambodia. Since it has no true ocean ports, sailing is also not an option. You can take a ferry from Poipet in Thailand to the coast by Sihanoukville and it may be possible to take a ferry from Vietnam's Mekong Delta cities, but service is spotty at best, and downright uncomfortable in many cases. You'll need to get a visa in advance.

If you fly, you'll have to go to a major Asian gateway city, then go to either Bangkok, HCMC, or a few other cities to get a flight into Cambodia. Shop around – there are often great deals to reach an Asian gateway (Bangkok or Saigon/HCMC) if you are flexible in your routing. Check websites for the airlines you prefer, plus sites such as www.orbitz.com, www.expedia.com, and www.cheaptickets.com (my preferred non-airline site).

From Inside Asia

You can get from Vietnam to Cambodia on either **Vietnam Airlines** or **Siem Reap Airlines**. You can get from Thailand to Cambodia on **Bangkok Air** or Siem Reap Airlines. There is actually an airpass available on the Siem Reap/Bangkok Air routes, but it's hard to get information outside the associated countries. Try the websites www.bangkokair.com and www.siemreapair.com. You have to buy a minimum of three segments and a maximum of six segments, and you can't backtrack.

There is no viable rail service at present, so you have only a few choices. You can take a bus or mini-bus from several adjacent countries, you can fly, or you can enter via river or ferry boat. In theory you could hike or bicycle in, but the trip would be long, the terrain quite rugged, and the risks from wildlife and unexploded ordnance unacceptable to most travelers.

If you arrive by any means other than flying into Phnom Penh or Siem Reap, get your visa in advance.

Getting Around by Air

A good way to find flights is to check a website such as www.cheaptickets.com, then go to the direct websites for the listed carriers. The same applies for intra-Asia flights.

Siem Reap Airlines or Bangkok Air are the primary carriers for internal flights and many flights to adjacent countries. The airlines may do codeshares with Vietnam Airlines and Bangkok Air. The Siem Reap and Bangkok Air aircraft are generally up to Western standards (French ATR-72s, Boeing 737s, and/or Airbus 319s) with Western-trained pilots and maintenance staff). Always check to see which airline is actually flying your flight. The Siem Reap Airlines website is www.siemreapair.com and the Bangkok Air site is www.BangkokAir.com. The two airlines also have an airpass – a good idea to consider if your travels include Thailand. You can actually book online as well as find schedule information.

■ The Vietnam War

The Vietnam War, known throughout the region as the "American War (of Aggression)" had a major impact on the entire Indochinese region. Although officially fought only in North and South Vietnam, a flight over Laos and Cambodia makes it clear the war extended to those countries, too. Damage is still obvious – bomb craters, defoliated areas, "no-man's lands," wounded veterans, and more.

Recovery has been a long process. The lasting impact on the people of the region is still seen and felt.

The US Congress determined in the early 1970s that the incursions and battles in Laos and especially Cambodia were illegal. Nonetheless, the damage was done, and people remember.

Tip: Throughout the region the culturally aware traveler needs to treat mention of the War with care and be respectful of the feelings of the people. You shouldn't refer to it as the "Vietnam War" while you are there.

TIMELINE FOR THE WAR	
1941	Ho Chi Minh returns, secretly, to Vietnam
1945	The Japanese oust the French, famine strikes the North, World War II ends and Vietnam is divided at the 16th Parallel, Ho Chi Minh declares himself President of the "Democratic Peoples' Republic of Vietnam" (DPRV), European and US forces enter Vietnam, the first American is killed.

1946	The Chinese leave Vietnam, the French return, and Ho Chi Minh's army launches its first attack against French troops.
1947	The French fight back.
1949	The Vietnamese National Army (South Vietnam) is formed. Chiang Kai-Shek's Nationalists are defeated by Mao Ze Dong's communists.
1950	Mao's China recognizes Ho's DPRV and starts ending advisors, the US and others recognize Bao Dai's French-controlled government, fighting intensifies, "McCarthyism" and anti-communism pick up speed, the US enters the Korean conflict, the US starts sending money to aid the South Vietnamese and sends the first military advisors.
1951	Fighting intensifies, French casualties are approaching 100,000.
1952	More fighting between French and North Vietnamese troops – lots of back and forth movement, no real territorial gains on either side. The Korean conflict and McCarthyism continue and escalate.
1953	Eisenhower becomes President and continues to increase US financial and military aid to the South, Stalin dies, the Korean conflict enters a truce, the French begin building and fortifying outposts around Dien Bien Phu.
1954	General Giap (North) amasses artillery and men and beat the French around Dien Bien Phu, the first of many miles of tunnels are dug, and the US refuses to increase its role in Vietnam, despite French pleas. Over 10,000 French soldiers died at Dien Bien Phu and many went to prison camps when the French surrendered. The Geneva Convention began and divided the country at the 17th Parallel. Ho Chi Minh takes formal control of the North after spending eight years hiding in the jungle.
1955	The first direct aid shipment arrives from the US, Ho visits Moscow, PM Diem ousts Bao Dai, the Republic of South Vietnam is declared with Diem as President, and communistic purges and land grabs occur in the North.
1956	The first South Vietnamese crackdown against suspected Viet Minh (later Viet Cong) takes place, the French complete their pull-out, Diem refuses to hold reunification elections required by the Geneva Convention, and the communists put down peasant revolts in the North.
1957	The situation continues to deteriorate, with Diem spending money on the military and not the people, resulting in Viet Minh infiltrators having easy pickings.

1959	Fighting begins in earnest when Ho declares a "peoples' war." Two US advisors are killed.
1960	An attempted military coup against Diem is put down. Soldiers are conscripted for the duration of the war. These actions cause many men to flee North and later return as Viet Cong infiltrators.
1961	The Russians encourage communists everywhere to rise up, and President Kennedy promises to "fight any battle…" – the war escalates and more Americans (Green Berets) are committed to South Vietnam.
1962	Costs of the American presence in South Vietnam and support to the South are rapidly approaching several million dollars per day. The war continues to escalate. The US Military Assistance Command-Vietnam, is formed. At this point war activities are still confined to Vietnam.
1963	The Americans lose their first major battle, Buddhists demonstrate against restrictions, Diem's government is riddled with patronage and corruption and incompetency. Diem refuses to step down and is killed in a coup. Kennedy is assassinated and Johnson further escalates the US presence.
1964	Another coup takes place, Americans begin bombing the Ho Chi Minh Trail, plans are made to bomb North Vietnam, naval battles escalate, the first American POW is taken to the "Hanoi Hilton," another coup takes place. Brezhnev takes control in Russia, Johnson wins reelection in a landslide. Another coup takes place. The American presence is up to 23,000 military advisors.
1965	The war escalates yet again. Bombing begins inside North Vietnam. The Russians agree to provide unlimited assistance to the North. The first US combat troops arrive. Naval operations interdict use of the waterways causing a massive shift to the Ho Chi Minh Trail. Anti-war protests begin in earnest. Yet another power change takes place in South Vietnam. The first major US ground operations take place. Bombing of the North is halted twice to try to pressure the North to accept a negotiated peace. Troop strength approaches 200,000.
1966	The war escalates as bombing of the North resumes. Anti-war protests increase. Captured US pilots are paraded through the streets of Hanoi on the way to Hoa Loa prison. The Ho Chi Minh Trail in Laos is bombed. The DMZ area is bombed for the first time. Defoliating chemicals (Agent Orange) are being used, as is napalm. President Johnson makes his first visit to Vietnam. Troop levels are approaching 400,000, and over 5,000 combat deaths have occurred.

1967	Further escalation, including a dogfight where eight to 10 MiG-21s were shot down over the South. A truce is declared during Tet. Pro- and anti-war activists march across the country. CA Governor Reagan says the US should get out of Vietnam. Battles are now occurring along the Laotian and Cambodian borders, and planes that crossed Chinese airspace were shot down. Defense Secretary McNamara resigns. President Johnson makes his final visit to Vietnam. Troop levels are approaching 500,000, and over 16,000 combat deaths have occurred.
1968	The Tet Offensive takes place, despite a declared truce. Hué and Saigon are strenuously attacked and defended. The My Lai Massacre takes place. Johnson announces he will not seek reelection. Reverend Martin Luther King is assassinated. Peace talks begin in Paris but end quickly with no progress. Robert Kennedy is assassinated. Nixon is chosen as the Republican Presidential candidate. Almost 1,000 US aircraft have been shot down so far. Bombing of North Vietnam is once again halted. Nixon wins the Presidency.
1969	There is no Tet truce. The My Lai Massacre investigation begins. Bombing is halted in the North, but begins in Cambodia. Troop levels reach their peak of almost 550,000, with over 33,000 killed in action. The North refuses to meet the US for peace talks. The first US troop withdrawals begin. Nixon makes his only visit to Vietnam. The draft lottery is held for the first time since World War II. About 115,000 troops have been withdrawn and over 40,000 killed.
1970	Peace talks are ongoing, but deadlocked, in Paris. A Cambodian coup ousts Prince Sihanouk in favor of General Lon Nol. The ousted Prince and the communist Khmer Rouge, led by Pol Pot, begin to try to retake the country. More troops are scheduled to be withdrawn. The US and South Vietnamese continue to fight in Cambodia. Four student protestors are killed by National Guard soldiers at Kent State. The use of Agent Orange is ended. US troops leave Cambodia. Troop levels are under 350,000. US ground troops are no longer allowed in Laos or Cambodia. By the end of the year troop levels are down to 280,000 and drug use is considered to be a major problem. ■
1971	The war is slowly de-escalating. Lieutenant William Caley is found guilty in the My Lai Massacre. Deaths are over 45,000, and the last Marine combat units have left Vietnam. The "Pentagon Papers" are published. Troop withdrawals continue to accelerate. Soldiers begin refusing to perform assigned missions. Saigon releases some of the POWs it holds. Australia and New Zealand withdraw their troops. Troop levels are under 160,000. Bombing of the North is resumed.

1972	Hanoi rejects Nixon's peace plan again. Nixon visits China. Further troop withdrawals take place. General Giap stages a massive attack against the reduced forces to try and capture the South. Nixon orders massive B-52 bomb strikes against the North. US troop levels drop below 70,000. Nixon visits Russia. The Watergate break-in occurs. Paris peace talks resume and collapse again. The last US combat troops leave on August 23rd, 1972. Nixon wins reelection in a landslide.
1973	Peace talks resume in Paris. January 27, 1973, the Paris Accords are signed by the US and the North Vietnamese. The draft ends and the last US death in Vietnam occurs. 591 POWs are released from Hanoi. The final troops (advisors) are withdrawn on March 29th. Vice President Agnew resigns.
1974	Impeachment proceedings begin against Nixon. Nixon resigns. President Ford announces a clemency program for many draft evaders. The North's Politburo decides to invade the South in 1975.
1975	April 30th, 1975, the last Marines leave the US Embassy in Saigon and the city falls to the North Vietnamese Army.

Vietnam

■ Introduction

The Country at a Glance

Vietnam is divided into several main areas:

- ☐ The Northwest mountains
- ☐ Hanoi and nearby sights (Halong Bay, Perfume River)
- ☐ The Middle (Marble Mountains, Danang, Hoi An, Hué, Nha Trang)
- ☐ The Hill country (Dalat)
- ☐ Saigon
- ☐ The Delta

In this Chapter	
■ Introduction	87
■ Hanoi	108
■ Hué	131
■ Danang	139
■ Hoi An	145
■ Nha Trang	152
■ Dalat & the Southern Highlands	158
■ Ho Chi Minh City	164
■ The Mekong Delta	177
■ Adventure Travel	182

The Northwest Mountains. This is where most people choose to go trekking. The hill tribes (Montagnards) are interesting and diverse, the scenery is beautiful, with a 3,000-m (10,000-foot) peak as its centerpiece, and the trekking can be as easy or strenuous as you wish. The town of Sapa (Sa Pa) has Colonial French remnants and lots of decent hotels in new and restored villas. The Chinese border is very close – if you come in on the night train from Hanoi you'll arrive at a town less than two km from the Chinese border. If you come overland from China the Sapa area is probably your first major stop in Vietnam. Don't plan to get your Chinese visa here, though.

Hanoi and the nearby areas. It seems most travelers define Vietnam in terms of the first major city they come to – either Hanoi or Saigon, now called Ho Chi Minh City. Hanoi is a city of crowded, narrow, winding streets and has a more frenetic pace than Saigon. There are far more sites of historical interest in Hanoi than in its southern sibling. Prosperity is obvious, but so is grinding poverty and the presence of huge numbers of refugees from the mountainous northwestern areas. Hanoi is a great place to make onward plans for the rest of the country, or plans for your next country. It's also a long way from any of the other places people normally want to visit – at least a full night on the Reunification Express to either Sapa or the sights in the middle, and much longer (by train) to the hill country, HCMC, or the Delta. If you can't get a first-class (soft) sleeper, I highly recommend flying to your next destination. The roads aren't good enough to make the bus trip very pleasant for more than a few hours.

Halong Bay is high on most travelers' lists once they have made it to Hanoi. It's an easy day trip to go out, around the bay, and back, but it's far more pleasant to spend a night (or two) in a local guesthouse. You can take a boat tour of the bay and the limestone (karst) caves, scuba, kayak, and just chill for a day or two. If your plan is to spend some quiet time, use a travel agency for transportation, then book your own hotel and leave the tour group until it's time to return to Hanoi.

> **Note:** There is a great handicraft shop on the outbound trip to Halong Bay. The products are made by disabled people, are of excellent quality, and reasonably priced. Most tour buses stop there, and it's one of the few such stops I found worthwhile. The embroidery is fabulous, and you are helping some of the most downtrodden people in the country get and keep gainful employment.

The Middle. This area is quite diverse, but the main attractions are within a half-day bus trip from one another. This is the area where the old demilitarized zone, or **DMZ**, divided the country into North and South for much of the 20th century. The barbed wire is gone now, but your guide can show you where the line used to be. Most buses traversing the area stop at the Marble Mountains if you're in the mood for a souvenir. **Hué** has the old Forbidden (Imperial) City and the emperors' tombs, so it's an absolute must. **Hoi An** is filled with Chinese shophouses and is a paradise if you want to get

Vietnam

Vietnam

tailor-made clothes that are ready in as little as 24 hours. **Danang** isn't much, but it's the place to get trains and bus connections north and south. **Nha Trang** is the old US Army rest and relaxation station, and has some excellent diving and sailing facilities, as well as the laid-back beachfront atmosphere.

The Hill Country. Dalat and environs are set in rolling hills amid pine trees and monasteries. The town itself is pleasant and relaxing, especially if your idea of relaxing involves places that are not along a beach.

Saigon. Now called HCMC, it has more large-scale French Colonial period leftovers than Hanoi, and I find the city more open, tourist-friendly, and relaxed. But the capitalistic influences that are more prevalent here than anywhere else in the country have their downsides, too – more crime and more persistent touts.

The Mekong Delta. Going here is like stepping back in time. There aren't many roads and the cities depend on the river and its tributaries for commerce and transportation. That makes travel inherently slow, and you get used to shopping on the river, eating on the river, and even sleeping on the river in some cases. This is Vietnam's bread (or rice) basket; several crops can be grown each year due to the warm weather and rich soil.

Currency: US$1 = 14,891 Vietnam Dong (VND).

Getting There & Around

By Air

 In the last few years there has been a veritable explosion of airlines flying to Vietnam. Even the major international airlines have started flying Boeings and Airbuses into Hanoi and HCMC (Saigon) again. Since the list is ever-growing, a good way to find flights is to check a website such as www.cheaptickets.com, then go to the airline websites for specific flight information. The same applies for intra-Asia flights.

Vietnam Airlines is the primary carrier for internal flights and many flights to adjacent countries. The airline does code shares with Siem Reap Airlines, Lao Aviation and Air France. Keep in mind that many Lao Aviation aircraft are not up to Western standards. Always check to see which airline is actually flying your flight. The Vietnam Airlines website is www.vietnamairlines.com; you can book online.

Vietnam Airlines covers much of the country, and the flights are reliable and safe. The trip from Hué to HCMC takes about an hour by plane and costs $70-$100, as compared to $10-$15 or so for the bus, which takes 14-16 hours. There are airports in or near Sa Pa, Hanoi, Da Nang, Hoi An, Hué, Da Lat, Nha Trang, HCMC, and other major travelers' destinations. The Hanoi-to-HCMC flight costs about $200, but may be less through some travel agents. Most other flights are about $100 or less.

INTERNAL FLIGHTS – ONE-WAY		
City	**City**	**Cost/Time**
Hanoi	HCMC	$125-$200/3 hours
Hanoi	Dalat, Danang, Nha Trang, Hué	$100-$150/1½-2 hours
Dalat	Nha Trang	$75/1 hour
HCMC	Dalat, Danang, Nha Trang, Hué	$100-$150/1½-2 hours

FLIGHTS TO OTHER COUNTRIES IN SOUTHEAST ASIA		
City	**City**	**Cost/Time**
Hanoi	Bangkok	$150-$200/3 hours/Air France, Vietnam
HCMC	Bangkok	$150-$200/3 hours/Air France, Vietnam
HCMC	Siem Reap/Angkor Wat	$100/1 hour/Lao, Vietnam, Bangkok Air
Hanoi	Luang Prabang	$100/1 hour/Lao Aviation, Vietnam Air

Vietnam

By Road

 Roads in Vietnam are generally OK, but not great. There are few "super-highways," and those are around the major cities. Since these and all other roads are choked with scooters, motos, cyclists, cars, animals, and many other things not seen on Western highways, travel is risky at best. I have been in several fender-benders and one more serious accident on Vietnamese roads, and the delays were not welcome. Once the bus I was in hit a cow and was rear-ended by a dump truck. It took hours to bring another bus to get us to Da Lat. Another time a van clipped a young woman weaving on her bicycle in the middle of a super-highway near Hanoi. Vietnam is well-equipped with vans, mini-buses, tourist buses, and regular buses, as well as cars for hire, so it is easy to get around by road. As a general rule, tourist buses leave and arrive on time, and are relatively cheap and quick. There are a number of "tourist cafés," such as Sinh Café, that run all kinds of bus services to almost any place you may want to visit. For short trips, or trips to the interior (to Da Lat, for example), buses or mini-vans, or private cars are the way to go unless you want to fly.

The tourist café buses are notorious for taking you where you want to go, then driving into the courtyard of a favored hotel, and locking the gates behind you, forcing you to stay in their hotel for the night. About all you can do is refuse to hand over your passport. Without your passport they can't register you with the police and hotel owners are rarely willing to take the risk of an unregistered "guest" so they will probably open the gates and let you out. If you've been to Thailand you've probably encountered similar tricks with the Khao San Road tour companies.

By Rail

 Vietnam has a decent railroad system – a legacy of the French. Indochina was a three-tiered Colonial empire, with Vietnam at the top, Cambodia in the middle, and Laos at the bottom. As a result, the French provided lots of training in Colonial administration to the Vietnamese, and needed rail infrastructure to move these trainees and employees around the country.

During and following the Vietnam-American War, the rail infrastructure deteriorated significantly, but the post-war government has restored the lines along the coast and inland to the northern hill country (towards Sa Pa) so it is now possible to travel from the far northwest corner (to within two km of the Chinese border) to Hanoi, down the coast, and into HCMC by train. You can even connect to the Trans-China Express and onto to the Trans-Siberian Express trains and hence to Europe – if you're so inclined and have the time and visas! To travel by train the entire length of Vietnam, without stopping, is going to take about three days and two nights.

Tip: If you travel by first-class soft sleeper (the only way I recommend), you do get "meals" of a sort, but I strongly encourage you to bring your own food, drinks, and snacks. When the train stops, your window will be deluged by local women selling lots of stuff –

corn-on-the-cob, bananas, baguettes, and more. My favorite of their many offerings is what I call "road-kill chicken." I call it that because the poor thing is simply plucked, smashed flat, and grilled, head and all.

If you plan to travel by train – and I highly recommend doing at least a part of your trip that way – book at least a few days ahead (more on weekends) to get a soft-sleeper berth.

> **Tip:** Many times it is best to go through a travel agent since they have pre-booked large blocks of soft-sleeper tickets and may be your best only source. Going to the train station will save a few dollars but the wait and hassle are not worth the small savings, especially since the ticket offices keep irregular hours and may not even have tickets.

For short hauls, buses, private mini-vans, or private (hired) cars make the most sense.

By Boat

 One of the most interesting and relaxing trips is a boat trip along the Perfume, Red, or Mekong Rivers. It is possible to spend weeks on motorized and "poled" boats seeing the backwaters of Vietnam. At a minimum a two- or three-day boat trip through the Mekong Delta is an experience not to be missed – a trip back in time. There are passenger and cargo boats going both directions on the Mekong River, tourist boats that take you to caves, tombs, and temples along the Perfume River, and many more choices. It is possible to arrive in the Mekong Delta by boat from Cambodia, but the options are not very comfortable and the schedules are "catch-as-catch-can." You can also kayak the coast or Ha Long Bay.

Weather & When to Visit

 Vietnam is a long (1,600 km/990 miles), narrow, climatically diverse country so the weather is correspondingly changeable and varied. The technical term is "tropical monsoon climate." There is no one good time to go if you want to sample much of the country. However, with a bit of planning you can travel in a direction that minimizes the most likely hot, steamy, or rainy times. While the worst of the seasonal monsoons hit different parts of the country at different times of the year, you will often encounter hot, humid weather, except in the far north and the highlands of the central areas. Even in the coolest of times, humidity rarely goes below 75-80% during the day and usually hovers in the 80-90% range. Of course, when it rains the humidity is close to 100%.

Since most people seem to prefer easing their way into the country from the south, here are some guidelines on what to take and when to go.

The South

Weather patterns in the South (and the Central Highlands) are controlled by the south/southwesterly monsoon.

As with most of the country, when it rains, it rarely pours all day, but it can be misty and overcast for several days at a time. The seasons are:

□ Monsoon – May to September. Hot and steamy. The rains actually ease a bit but continue through November. This is when temperatures are often at their lowest, but "low" is a relative term!

□ Dry season – December to late April/early May. Temperatures rise steadily during this time. This is when it is likely to be really hot. Temperatures in the day are in the 30-40°C/86-105°F range, dropping to the 20s°C/70s°F at night. March, April, and May are the hottest months – expect 40°C/100°F+ temperatures on an occasional basis.

The humidity can present a real problem, making temperatures feel much warmer than the thermometer indicates. Heat stroke and dehydration can be serious problems. If either or both conditions persist they can even be life-threatening.

Ho Chi Minh City is located at 10.82°N 106.60°E.

						HO CHI MINH CITY						
					Average Temperature							
	Jan	Feb	Mar	Apr	May	Jun	Jul	Aug	Sep	Oct	Nov	Dec
°C	25.8	26.6	27.7	28.7	28.2	27.4	27.1	27.3	26.9	26.6	26.2	25.7
°F	78.4	79.9	81.9	83.7	82.8	81.3	80.8	81.1	80.4	79.9	79.2	78.3
					Average Rainfall							
mm	14	3.8	9.4	51.4	212.9	308.7	294.9	27.3	271.2	341.8	260.5	118.8
inches	.6	.1	.4	2	8.5	12.2	11.8	1.1	10.8	13.7	10.4	4.7
					Humidity							
%	61	56	58	60	71	78	80	78	80	80	75	68

The Mekong Delta has similar monsoonal and dry season patterns as in HCMC, but overall temperatures are usually warmer. Flooding can be a problem at any time of the year, but is worst in the monsoon season. Floods can cut off entire towns, and wash out roads and bridges, making road travel difficult. Of course, the Delta is well covered by rivers and boats!

The Central Highlands

The climate is similar to that of the South in terms of the monsoonal and dry seasons, but higher elevations help moderate temperatures. Keep in mind the sun is far more intense at higher elevations, and Dalat is about 1,500 meters/4,900 feet high.

The Central Coast

Continuing north the weather patterns follow the northeast monsoon, essentially reversing the pattern found in the South.

The seasons are:

□ Monsoon – late fall into winter. Misty and overcast, with very heavy rains at times.

□ Dry season – March-August. It still rains quite a bit at this time of year.

The rainy season in Nha Trang and nearby areas begins fairly abruptly in November and runs through December. As you head north to Hué, Danang, and Hoi An, it lasts longer – from September into February.

Spring (March to May) or before the fall monsoon (early September) or near the end of the rains (late November to December) are the bet times for these cities.

Summer brings the highest temperatures, generally with highs in the 30s°C/high 80s°F. Dalat can be very appealing at this time of year. At 1,500 meters (about a mile high) the day-time temperatures are much cooler – into the 20s and low 30s°C/60s-70s°F.

As you head farther north the climate becomes more extreme. The rainy season shortens, with the worst part coming in September and October. Winter follows the rains, bringing cooler, drier, pleasant weather. The northern stretches of the central coast experience a weather phenomenon familiar to people from the coastal regions of North America and other parts of the world – hurricanes, known as typhoons in this part of the world. Typhoon season generally runs from August to November. Summers along the north central coast are very hot and dry.

Hanoi & The North

The sunniest time of year is the last three months, although rains can come at any time, and December can be cool (even cold), drizzly, and misty. January into March is the cool or even cold season, and the mist and drizzle can last for days. From the later part of March the weather begins to improve and temperatures start rising. By summer, day time highs can approach 40°/105°F.

Hanoi is not as consistently warm as the South, but it can get quite warm in July and August. The weather is driven by the northeast monsoon, bringing the rainy weather in the summer, but the likelihood of mist and overcast conditions lasts much of the year, until spring. While summer temperatures tend to be in the 30s°C/high 80s°F, it is not unusual to hit 40°C/100°F+ for several days running. When you combine these temperatures with the summer monsoon, it can get pretty steamy and uncomfortable.

It is cool enough from November to March that a jacket is a good idea, and a sweater is useful in the coldest months – December to February.

❑ Monsoon – May to September. Hot, humid, sticky, and generally nasty.

❑ Dry season – October to December. Even then it can be misty and overcast, with rain more often than not as winter approaches.

The Red River Delta has the added dimension of floods when the summer rains hit.

The weather patterns are very similar to those of Hanoi. However, increasing elevation has a moderating effect on temperatures. It has been known to be frosty and even to snow in the winter months around Sapa. A jacket and sweater can be welcome almost any time of year in the mountains.

Vietnam

	Jan	Feb	Mar	Apr	May	Jun	Jul	Aug	Sep	Oct	Nov	Dec
HANOI												
Average Temperature												
°C	17	18	20	24	28	30	30	29	28	26	22	19
°F	62	64	68	75	83	86	86	84	83	79	72	66
Average Rainfall												
mm	18	28	38	81	196	239	323	342	254	99	43	20
inches	.7	1.1	1.5	3.2	7.8	9.5	12.9	13.7	10.1	4	1.7	.8
Humidity												
%	68	70	76	75	69	71	72	75	73	69	69	6

If you want to stay in the North and perhaps the central coastal areas, October to December is probably the best time. If you stay in the central highlands and south, December to early May is probably your best bet.

If you want to combine both monsoonal areas, November to January might work, but September, October, March, and April also offer decent chances of good weather. If you go in the winter, you might want to avoid the far north in November and December.

What to Take

While detailed packing lists are included in the *What to Bring* section, the information you just read makes a few necessities pretty obvious:

☐ A waterproof jacket such as a windbreaker with a light or removable lining.

☐ A poncho.

☐ An umbrella.

□ Waterproof, anti-slip walking shoes.

□ A sweater if you'll be in the North, especially in winter.

□ Long pants, preferably waterproof and breathable.

Before you go to Vietnam it's a great idea to track the weather for your intended destinations for a few weeks and note the long-term (10-day) forecast for the time just before, during, and after your intended visit. Monsoonal climates are unpredictable at best. The most familiar source for weather forecasts online is www.weather.com.

Hotel Basics

The budget hotels ($$ and $$$) are fairly standard across the country. Generally, you can expect en suite facilities, although the bathrooms are not up to Western standards. For example, the shower often does not have a curtain, so the entire bathroom gets wet. There may or may not be a tub. The hot water is often "on-demand" using a hot water "geyser" – a system that heats the water as it passes through a box on the wall. That means you may have to flip a switch to get power to the geyser. It also means the hot water doesn't run out if everyone in the building takes a shower at the same time. Breakfast is often included and combines the best of French continental with Asian, plus lots of fresh fruits.

■ Hanoi

History

 Hanoi is not all that old as international capitals go. It was first settled in the seventh century by Chinese invaders of the T'ang dynasty. They liked the climate, and growing conditions in the Red River Valley and Delta. Prior to this time there was just a small fort in the area. The Chinese held what they called Amman – the Pacified South – for about three centuries. For a century the site was abandoned, until King Le Thai To – the erstwhile founder of Hanoi – located his capital there. For most of the next 800 years (until the capital was moved to Hué), Hanoi was the Imperial City.

During this time the Chinese periodically invaded and retook the city, but their control never lasted very long. As a result, Hanoi saw a flowering of culture, with the founding of the country's first university – the outdoor Temple of Literature.

From about the early 16th century, following the death of the last strong emperor, King Le Thanh Thong, the city underwent a gradual decline, and finally Emperor Gia Long moved his entire court to Hué in 1802.

As a provincial backwater, the remnants of the former Imperial city were easy picking for the French invaders, and in 1882, they took over, named the area Tonkin, and made Hanoi the seat of government for the entire region in 1887. So it remained until the French were pushed out of the North in 1954. That's when the city once again became the capital of Vietnam.

Arrival

 If you come in by bus you are going to end up at one of the three long-distance bus centers, none of which are centrally located. Plan on taking a taxi to your hotel, at a cost of about $10. If you come in by mini-bus you may be able to negotiate a drop-off at your hotel for a small additional fee.

The train station is only about a kilometer from the center of town, and a bit farther from the old French Quarter. A taxi should cost a few dollars to get to hotels in those areas.

 I recommend not taking a taxi alone – you may need a witness in case the driver decides to raise the agreed price and refuse to give you your luggage until you pay up. Two Westerners are usually enough to preclude this behavior. Rental cars are not usually a problem – the hotel or car service collects the money from you and handles the transaction on your behalf.

If you arrive by air you will come into the relatively new, rather stark **Noi Bai Airport**. It has money-changing facili-

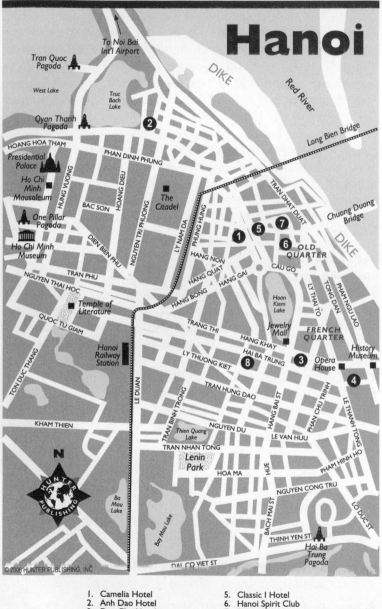

Hanoi

To Noi Bai Int'l Airport

Tran Quoc Pagoda

West Lake

Truc Bach Lake

Qyan Thanh Pagoda

2

DIKE

Red River

Long Bien Bridge

HOANG HOA THAM

PHAN DINH PHUONG

Presidential Palace

Ho Chi Minh Mausoleum

HUNG VUONG

HOANG DIEU

BAC SON

The Citadel

TRAN NHAT DUAT

Chuong Duong Bridge

DIKE

One Pillar Pagoda

DIEN BIEN PHU

NGUYEN TRI PHUONG

PHUNG HUNG

LY NAM DA

1 **5** **7**

6 OLD QUARTER

Ho Chi Minh Museum

HANG NON

CAU GO

TRAN PHU

HANG QUAT

HANG GAI

LY THAI TO

TONG DAN

PHAM NGU LAO

NGUYEN THAI HOC

HANG BONG

Hoan Kiem Lake

Temple of Literature

QUOC TU GIAM

TRANG THI

HANG KHAY

Jewelry Mall

FRENCH QUARTER

TON DUC THANG

LY THUONG KIET

HAI BA TRUNG

8

History Museum

Hanoi Railway Station

LE DUAN

TRAN BINH TRONG

HANG BAI ST

3 Opera House

4

LE THANH TONG

TRAN HUNG DAO

PHAN CHU TRINH

KHAM THIEN

NGUYEN DU

Thien Quang Lake

TRAN NHAN TONG

LE VAN HUU

HUE

PHAM HINH HO

Lenin Park

HOA MA

N

HUNTER PUBLISHING

Ba Mau Lake

Bay Mau Lake

NGUYEN CONG TRU

BACH MAI ST

LO DUC ST

THINH YEN ST

Hai Ba Trung Pagoda

DAI CO VIET ST

© 2006 HUNTER PUBLISHING, INC

1. Camelia Hotel
2. Anh Dao Hotel
3. Dan Chu Hotel
4. Hilton Hanoi Opera Hotel

5. Classic I Hotel
6. Hanoi Spirit Club
7. Prince I Hotel
8. Lotus Hotel

ties but they've never been open when I went by. You should be able to take the Vietnam Airlines mini-bus to their office in town (several km from the center). You may even be able to persuade the driver to take you to the center and drop you at a hotel. If you have already booked a hotel, they will send a car and you pay the driver $10 for the ride. This price is per car, not per person.

Where to Stay

 There are two main areas to stay in Hanoi – the French Quarter and the Old Quarter. The budget hotels are in both areas, but the higher-end hotels are largely in the French Quarter. The Old Quarter is at the north end of Hoan Kiem Lake and the French Quarter is to the east. Some people also like to stay around West Lake, but that's a bit far from many of the more popular sights.

Hanoi is a great base for traveling to the northeast and northwest, as well as to Halong Bay. It's easy to catch a flight out of Vietnam or to other places inside the country. The travelers' cafés that seem to be everywhere can arrange flights, and are your best source for overnight soft sleeper train accommodations.

My personal favorites are the members of the Camellia Hotels, particularly Anh Dao Hotel. The staff is accessible and responsive – they even helped settle a dispute with a cab driver at 5 am. The Anh Dao Hotel offers free high-speed Internet access for all hotel guests. The cheapest rooms don't have "real" windows, though – just fake windows that open into the stairwell. Breakfast is included, and is substantial – a complete buffet with a half-dozen kinds of fruit, baguettes, cheese, meat, hard-boiled eggs, and local food too. Fresh flowers on the tables, clean, comfortable rooms, with CNN, lots of hot water... what more do you need? All this for about $15-20 double or single.

Hotels come and go; new ones are appearing faster than any travel guide can

HOTEL PRICE CHART	
Rates are per room based on double occupancy.	
$	Under $12
$$	$12-$25
$$$	$26-$40
$$$$	$40-$80
$$$$$	Over $80

keep up with. There is no reason to choose a place without satellite TV, breakfast, and private bath unless your budget is below $15 a day (total for one or two people). Any of the travelers' cafés can help you find a room if you haven't reserved one.

> **Tip:** Always look at the room before you sign on the line. Some rooms have windows opening into noisy stairwells, which means there's no natural light. It also allows easy access to your room. Some rooms set above an unventilated kitchen or next to the sewer pipes can smell very bad.

 Your hotel must register you with the police. To do this they need your passport. Most budget hotels (and many high-end ones, too) will not give your passport back, unless you insist, until you have paid and checked out. This is not always a bad thing since thievery is an increasing problem, and passports are a target. Consider taking a photocopy of your passport with you and letting the hotel keep the original. The only times you may need the original are to cash traveler's checks (a waste since commissions are so high), if you run afoul of the law, or if you are applying for onward visas.

Old Quarter

$$ **Anh Dao Hotel** at 37 Ma Ma, Old Quarter, www.camellia-hotels.com, ☎ 04/8267151. All rooms have private facilities. There's an ODC tour desk in the lobby – not the low-end travelers' café, but a good mid-range agent for small or private groups and quality services. We used them to visit Halong Bay and Sapa, and were very pleased. They can arrange adventure and active trips, including trekking in Sapa or other hill tribes areas, kayaking on Halong Bay, and much more.

$$ Camellia Hotel II at 13 Luong Ngoc Quyen Street, Old Quarter, www.camellia-hotels.com, ☎ 04/8283583. fax 8244277. Newly refurbished in January 2004. Very similar in features and services to the Anh Dao. Part of the same hotel group.

$$ Classic I at 22a Ta Hien, Old Quarter, ☎ 04/8266224. This new, fairly large (40-room) hotel is not far from the original Little Hanoi Restaurant (see below). Like most hotels it has an on-site tour arranger and Internet access.

$ Hanoi Spirit Club at 50 Hang Be, Old Quarter, www.az-queencafe.com, ☎ 04/8267356. This is one of the many cheap backpackers' hostels, with space in dorm rooms for just a few dollars per person. It has a bar and restaurant, Internet access, and is co-located with Queen Travel, one of the many budget travelers' cafés in Hanoi. There are also rooms with/without private bath. Many rooms are not air-conditioned.

$$ Prince I Hotel at 51 Luong Ngoc Quyen, Old Quarter, www.hanoiprincehotel.com, ☎ 04/8280155. This is a nice hotel with full facilities and decent-sized rooms.

> **Tip:** Hotels have secure places to leave your luggage. If you don't want to do that, many hotels will let you pay for a half-day and keep the use of your room – a great deal if you are on the night train.

French Quarter

$$$$$ Hilton Hanoi Opera at 1 Le Thanh Tong, French Quarter, www.hilton.com, ☎ 04/9330500. This is one of the top hotels in Hanoi. It has over 250 Western-standard rooms, three restaurants (one is a great coffee shop for an afternoon break), and outdoor swimming pool.

$ Lotus at 42v, Luong Kiet, French Quarter, www.lotus-guesthouse.com, ☎ 04/8268642. An old standby, with dorm spaces and very basic private rooms. The location is great, but the amenities are lacking.

$$$ Dan Chu at 29 Trang Tien, French Quarter, www.danchuhotel.com, ☎ 04/8254937. Located in an older, French-era building, this hotel is reminiscent of French Colonial days, with courtyards and roomy hallways. The rooms have satellite TV and A/C.

This is only a sampling of the broad range of hotels in Hanoi. It's always advisable to book ahead since the city can be crowded at any time of year. Many of these hotels will pick you up at the airport or train station for a small charge – generally about $10 for airport pick-up/drop-off and $3 for the train station. I have found this service far preferable to taking a chance with a taxi. Unfortunately, there are too many taxi drivers who will quote a price (few will use their meters) and then raise it at the end of your trip, or take you somewhere you didn't ask to go.

Where to Eat

Hanoi is over-stuffed with restaurants. You can get almost any type of food, from local and regional specialties or pizza to Indian, vegetarian or afternoon tea and cakes. You can eat on street corners, in the many markets, or in top-of-the-line restaurants in the Hilton. Restaurants do have two shortcomings – they are often small, so they fill up quickly, and they don't stay open very late.

As with hotels, new restaurants are sprouting up like mushrooms after the monsoon. Be adventurous. The menus are almost always in English, even in the smallest places. Sometimes the translations leave much to be desired, though, so flexibility is key. An example – one restaurant indicated the translation of something as "fried bull's thing." I just assumed it was part of a "don't ask, don't tell" program and let it go at that.

If the staff, tables, floor, or food look dirty or unappealing, go somewhere else. Every restaurant has its good and bad days. Remember the advisories at the beginning of this book, too. Don't drink the water. Don't eat food that isn't cooked or peeled, at least until you've been in-country several weeks. Yes, this applies even at the Hilton. Be careful eating food that is creamy and/or has been out in the hot sun.

Old Quarter

$-$$ **Little Hanoi**, 25 Ta Hien (the original) and 14 Ta Hien (the annex), ☎ 04/926-0168. This is my favorite restaurant in Hanoi. The food is authentic, inexpensive, and good. The service is great. The original is on two levels in an older house. Try to

RESTAURANT PRICES	
$	Under $2
$$	$2-$5
$$$	$6-$10
$$$$	$11-$20
$$$$$	Over $20

avoid the upstairs, which has low ceilings and is hot and cramped. The seafood and chicken dishes are excellent. The portion sizes are more than adequate. Open all day from about 7 am to 11 pm. The Dalat wine is pretty good if you want a change from beer, tea, and soft drinks.

$-$$ **Ily Café**, 97 Ma Ma, no phone. I was underwhelmed by this restaurant. It is more of a brew pub with mediocre food and lousy service. Stay away until the staff and food improve. Ask around before you try this place – maybe it's improved.

$$ **Tamarind Café**, 80 Ma May, no phone The food is well presented and a bit quirky. Lots of vegetarian selections in an eclectic setting. My second favorite after Little Hanoi. Open all day from about 6 am to 11 pm.

$-$$ **Tandoor**, 24 Hang Be, no phone. Decent Indian food and good service. The owner actually had the cook come out and discuss my meal choices. The food can be quite spicy, so take care if that's not your style. At lunch you can get a thali for about $4. Lunch from 11 am to 2 pm and dinner from 6 pm to 10 pm.

Along the west side of Hoan Kiem Lake there are numerous cafés and ice cream parlors. Perfect for a break after a few hours of shopping or walking around the Temple of Literature.

French Quarter

$$$ **Al Fresco's**, 23 Hang Ba Trung, ☎ 04/8267782. Get your Italian food/pizza fix here. There are two sister restaurants with balconies, Pepperoni's (I and II) in the Old Quarter near the Cathedral. They serve large portions, including Ameri-

Vietnam

can, Australian and Italian dishes. Open from about 9 am until 10 pm.

$$ **Asean Food**, 53 Ba Trieu, no phone. Malaysian. Curries, sambals, vegetarian delight. There is also Western and Indian food. I have heard this one is good, but haven't tried it yet. Open from about 11 am to 9 pm.

$ **Hoa Sua**, 28a Xom Ha Hoi, ☎ 04/9424448. If you want excellent food while helping disadvantaged children (who are trained here), this is the place to go. A wide variety of food with a French influence, served on the garden-like patio or in the rooms of a French Colonial villa. This place is a bit hard to find, but worth the effort. The smoked duck salad was my favorite. There is often live music Saturday evenings and Sunday at lunch. Open from about 7 am to 10 pm.

$ **Hanoi Hilton** coffee shop, 1 Le Thanh Tong. A luxurious bargain for afternoon tea. I enjoy ducking in for afternoon coffee/tea and cakes. They have an afternoon special and the pastries are as good as many in France. There's a small courtyard away from the crowds. Another of my favorite places.

Markets & Supermarkets

There are a number of supermarkets and local markets where you can buy quality, low-cost food and build a picnic.

Cho Dong Xuan, Dong Xuan Street. This is the largest covered market in Hanoi, at the far north end of the Hoan Kiem Lake area. The shopping is wondrous, and the food stalls, at the rear of the main floor, are well-stocked with vegetables, fruits, and other delectables.

Cho 19-12, between Hai ba Trung and Ly Thuong Kiet, is a street where they sell fresh foods – open during the daylight hours.

Need a yogurt fix, some milk, packaged cheese, or canned fruit? Try one of these grocery stores:

Citimart, Hanoi Towers, 49 Ha Bang. This small grocery is well stocked with the stuff expats like. If you've been on the road awhile, this place is worth a visit.

Intimex, 22-23 Le Thai To (the southwest end of Hoan Kiem Lake). This is a fair-sized store with a good range of Western-style food and household goods.

The Trade Center, 7 Dinh Tien Haong. Close to the Old Quarter. Dried and canned foods and toiletries.

The Deli, 59a Ly Thai To, on the ground floor of the Press Club. Good wine selection, as well as breads, quiches, and other baked goods. Both eat-in and carryout.

Au Délice, 19 Han Thuyen. A wide variety of pâtés, deli meats and cheeses, and wine.

Nightlife

Water Puppets, Kim Dong Theater, 57 Dinh Tien Hoang (right at the northeast edge of Hoan Kiem Lake). This is a traditional form of entertainment, and goes on every evening, with multiple shows. It is OK for an hour or so, but that's about enough. The shows cost between $1.50 and $3, depending on where you sit.

Folk Music, Temple of Literature, Nguyen Thai Hoc Avenue, across from the National Fine Arts Museum – #66). Times and places vary. Ask at the museum or the entrance to the Temple.

The Opera House, 1 Trang Tien, ☎ 4/825 4312. Classical (Western) concerts and ballets.

Bars & Clubs

New Century, 10 Trang Thi. Something for everyone, with bands, laser shows, dancing, and drinks. The cover charge (about $3) includes one drink. Open from 8 pm to 2 am, and sometimes much later.

Press Club, 59a Ly Thai To. This is a high-end bar for Western businesspeople. Not cheap, but very elegant and comfy.

Summit Lounge, 20f Sofitel Plaza, 2 Yen Phu. Great views and happy hour from 4:30 to 8 pm. Open until midnight, with live music after happy hour ends.

The Wave. Part of the Summit Lounge, this is a nightclub with DJ and occasionally live, local musicians. Football on TV, happy hours, and no cover charge.

Shopping

Hanoi is a shopper's paradise. The array of crafts and consumer goods is overwhelming. The streets closest to Hoan Kiem Lake on the west and north sides, as well as the entire street around the Lake, are filled with specialty shops selling embroidered pillows and wall hangings, scarves, clothes, carved furniture, raw silk, lacquerware, painted fans, artwork, CDs, and much more, at prices that are (almost) too good to be true. And to make a good thing better, you are expected to bargain.

> **Tip:** Don't start to bargain if you have no intention of buying. It's OK to start bargaining for one item (to get a feel for prices and flexibility) and change to another item. To simply waste the shop-owner's time is rude and gives Westerners a bad name.

I find the Thai and Laotian **silks** to be better quality than the Vietnamese versions, but the Vietnamese material is decent and lower in cost. There are **tailors** all over the city and the country who can make quality clothes in no time. If you see some silk in Hanoi, you could buy it and take it to a tailor in Hoi An or elsewhere.

The detail work in the **embroidered wall hangings** and **screens** has to be seen to be believed. If you want to contribute to a worthy cause, consider buying your embroidered goods at the Disabled Center on the bus trip to Halong Bay.

There are stores offering ethnic **crafts** from minority and hill tribes, but you are usually better off buying direct if you are going to go trekking. T-shirts are cheap, but not of the quality found in the Night Market in Chiang Mai (Thailand).

Artwork, such as pencil or charcoal sketches, is a good bargain. I bought five small cat drawings – charcoal outlines – for $2.

> **Tip:** If you like something enough to buy more than one (or maybe you're with someone who wants the same item), ask the price of one item. Start to bargain. When you have the price down by about 30-35%, ask the price for two of the same item. Bargain some more. If you want a third, repeat the process. Each additional items should reduce the average price per item by another 5-10%. Don't start out asking "How much for two." That overplays your hand at the outset. Happy shopping!

Ipa-Nema, 59b Hai Ba Trung, carries avant-garde clothes.

Co, 18 Nha To, is the place for handmade silk clothes (at a price).

Kana, 41 Hang Trong, sells traditional Vietnamese silk clothing.

Song, 5 Nha Tho offers clothes that show a French influence.

Tan My, 66 Hang Gai, has three levels of embroidery, silks, and clothes.

Lan Handicrafts, 38 Nha Chung, is a non-profit outlet. The merchandise is made by disabled and disadvantaged young people.

The Restored House at 87 Ma May. In the museum shop you can examine a wide variety of handicrafts – chopstick rests, porcelain, hangings, jewelry, pottery, and more. Prices are on the high side, but at least you'll know where to start the bargaining at other stores.

Any shops along the north side of Hoan Kiem Lake or the streets just west of the Lake are worth a look. Or browse the myriad shops in the Old Quarter.

Tours & Travels

There are hundreds of travel agencies in Hanoi. Your hotel will have its own agency or an arrangement with several agencies nearby. These are far better options than using Vietnamtourism (30a Ly Thuong Kiet, www.vn-tourism.com) or Vinatour (54 Nguyen Du, www.vinatour.com.vn). The government agencies are generally expensive, inflexible, and will want to organize your entire stay in the country down to the second. They also can't (or won't) get you rail or air tickets unless you sign on for one of their tours.

Here are some agencies to try:

☐ **Handspan Adventure Tours**, www.handspan.com. These are tailored, small group tours. Many hotels contract with this group. I have used them.

☐ **Queen Travel**, www.queencafe.com.vn. This is another middle market, reasonably priced tour organizer and operator that I have used.

□ **Explore Indochina**, www.exploreindochina.com. This group sets up very personalized, higher-end adventure tours. An excellent reputation in the bicycle touring market.

Sinh Café. This a low-end tour group and I don't recommend it. They have a tendency to hijack you into "their" hotel in a town and lock the gates behind you, forcing you to stay at least one night. It happened to me in Dalat, and the hotel was smelly (sewage) and dirty. You can contact them through the Hanoi Toscerco at www.tosercohanoi.com.

Getting Around & Away

Short Haul

Walking is the easiest way to see Hanoi, although the myriad scooters, cars, and other means of conveyance don't make it the safest means. You can cycle in Hanoi, but you are taking a big risk. Still, many hotels and street-side kiosks will rent bikes for $5-$10 per day. You can also take the cheap city buses, pedi-cabs (also known as cyclos), catch a ride on the back of a scooter, or take a taxi to get around the city.

You can rent cars for about $25-$30 per day. Ask at your hotel. Vehicles are not well-maintained and your fellow drivers are nuts.

Scooter drivers are glad to offer you a lift for a few dollars.

Car hire to the airport is about $10. Metered taxis cost about the same but you'll only find them outside the big hotels.

Buses are cheap, but make sure you get on the right one. Ask at your hotel to get the bus number and tell the driver where you need to go. Since the buses cost a flat amount (about 25¢) regardless of distance, you could travel a long way and no one would wonder what you are doing until you reached the end of the line.

Taxis don't want to use meters and are known for altering (upping) the agreed rate when you reach your destination.

Be very aware how poor the drivers are. They drive wherever it suits them, don't always stop for red lights, drive on sidewalks, and rarely give way to pedestrians. Watch for all types of transport coming down the wrong side of the road.

Long Haul

Unless you have lots of time and flexible bones, take the first class (soft) sleeper or fly to get out of Hanoi. Fares are very reasonable.

The long distance train fare to Sapa or Hué will run $30-$40; the airfare is about twice that, but costs are always changing. You can book your own flights at any Vietnam Air office or agent, or get a travel agency to handle everything. Don't even bother to go to the train station for sleeper tickets – let the travel agent do it. It will cost more, but they have a lock on the soft sleepers. They buy the tickets ahead of time and resell them to you through their offices and those of their buddies.

You could ride a bicycle, and the route from north to south (or the other way) is very popular with hardcore cyclists.

What to See & Do

Here are the top sights, in no particular order. Plan to get around to most of them via cyclo (bike-propelled cart) and you'll have a very enjoyable trip and be able to see the highlights in two days or the entire city in less than a week.

Central Hanoi

In Central Hanoi you will find most of the sights, shopping, accommodations, restaurants, and resources of interest to travelers.

Take time to immerse yourself in the vibrant street scenes and life of the central core – the women hauling mini-malls on bicycles, the men playing cards on street corners, the laborers toting huge loads in two baskets at the ends of a bamboo rod across their shoulders... another world.

❖ Ho An Kiem Lake

The central area lies around Hoan (Ho An) Kiem Lake. The lake itself is peaceful, with the three-tiered pagoda in the middle and the small footbridge at the north end near the Water Puppet Theater. Walking around the lake is great for exercise, and you can watch the local people doing their T'ai Chi exercises in the morning. There are numerous ice cream parlors and over-priced restaurants on the west side of the lake.

❖ The French Quarter

This is the area where the Opera, Governor's house, and villas of the wealthy were located. The southeast corner of Ho An Kiem Lake is very pleasant. This is also where many of the international standard hotels and auberges (such as the Hanoi Hilton) can be found. Spend some time wandering the leafy streets and picturing the way the area must have looked, all pastels and elegant colonials, in its heyday.

The **Hanoi Hilton Hotel**, overlooking the Opera, makes a pleasant stop for tea and pastries, especially if you are staying in one of the two- or three-star tourist hotels at the north end of the lake. 1 Le Thanh Tong Street; ☎ 4/9330500.

The **Opera** is a sight in and of itself. It stands in August Revolution Square; ☎ 4/825 4312. You'll find yourself transported back to the luxurious lifestyle of French colonialism when the residents tried to recreate the life they left behind in La

Belle France. There are no tours – too bad since the interior is fully restored to its marble, gilt, and crystal glory. You might luck into a performance; that's the only way to get inside nowadays. But the outside is quite splendid and worth a walk around.

The **History Museum** is one block east of the Opera House. I found the contents to be fascinating, but the outside is even better – a mix of Vietnamese and French Colonial.

A block north of this museum is the **Museum of Vietnamese Revolution**, in another French Colonial building. Of particular note is the exhibit covering the American War.

Walk back to the Opera House and head two blocks north on Ly Thai To to see the **Residence of the Governor of Tonkin** and the **Metropole Hotel**. These are two of the most attractive Colonial-era buildings in all of Vietnam.

Walk along Trang Tien if you want to to do some shopping, especially for books and jewelry. If you head west you'll end up at the lake.

If you continue south (from the eastern end of the lake) you will see two tall towers, and in the shadow of these buildings is the pre-Colonial, much dreaded, **Hoa Lo Prison**. This is the infamous site called the "Hanoi Hilton" by American prisoners of war during the Vietnam-ese-American War. It has a much longer history though, dating back to the early 20th century, and most of the displays focus on the time the prison was used by the French to hold Vietnamese prisoners prior to 1945.

❖ **The Old Quarter**

This is where I prefer to stay. There are lots of basic hotels with free Internet, quiet rooms, decent food, and CNN/satellite TV. You're close to Hoan Kiem Lake, several markets, lots of good restaurants, and plenty of travel specialists to arrange your onward travel, confirm flights, and set up tours.

Ma May is one of the main streets in the Old Quarter. As you walk along it you will come to another main road – **Hang Buom** – passing a large collection of variegated architecture – pre-Colonial shophouses, Colonial villas, and Soviet-inspired concrete slab buildings. On Hang Buom you will see one of the oldest remaining temples – the **Bach Ma Temple** (founded in the ninth century), dating from the 18th century.

Dong Xuan, the largest covered market in Hanoi, is on the eastern edge of the Old Quarter – not too far from the Water Puppet Theater. It's three levels of anything and everything you can imagine (and a few things you might not want to think about). I love walking through the food stalls and shops. Some of the items used in food preparation are amazing; others make me never want to eat again unless I know all the ingredients and watch the preparation!

 With the increasing incidence of bird flu showing up in humans in Vietnam, stay away from any markets that include food stalls. Live chickens go with food stalls, so discretion is the better part of valor for the time being.

If you proceed to the south (toward the lake) you'll come to the **Museum of Independence** at 48 Hang Ngang. This site is noteworthy because it is where Ho Chi Minh drafted his Declaration of Independence for the "Democratic" Republic of Vietnam in 1945. There is no cost to enter, and the two upper levels are certainly worth a look to see how he lived.

From here walk south to the lake – you'll be entering a shopper's paradise.

❖ The West Side

Immediately to the west of Hoan Lake is a pair of shopping streets – they parallel the lake from one end to the other (running north-south). You can find drawings, paintings, fabric, silk, clothes, lacquerware, gold and silver, and

Temple of Literature

much more. Continuing to the west you will find the most important monuments and historical sites in the city.

The **Temple of Literature**, Quoc Tu Giam St, Dong Da District, was founded in the 11th century as Vietnam's first university and includes an open-air temple complex. It is a fascinating place to walk through, with its arched open rooms, steles carved with historical information, and peaceful garden-like atmosphere. Other sites in the area worth a visit (hire a cyclo driver for $10 for the day) are: the **One Pillar Pagoda, Presidential Palace, Ho Chi Minh's Mausoleum, Cot Co Flag Tower,** and the **Museum of Military History**. All of these places are close together and can be easily visited in a single day.

Another of my favorite places is the **National Fine Arts Museum**, located south of the Temple of Literature at 66 Nguyen Thai Hoc. The eclectic mix of styles, periods, and themes is fascinating. The museum is open during business hours Tuesday-Sunday.

Outside the Central Area

Another area worth a visit is the smaller West Lake. It is primarily a fashionable residential area, but there are a few sights such as the **Museum of Ethnology** and the **Yen Phu Temple** that you should see.

Useful Information

Hanoi is reasonably well equipped for the traveler, and the situation and services are improving constantly.

Airlines

Vietnam Airlines has several locations, including at the main airport and south of Hoan Kiem Lake. All travel companies should be able to handle flight confirmations and reservations for you.

The main airline addresses and telephone numbers are:

Air France, 1 Ba Trieu, ☎ 04/823-3484

Cathay Pacific, 49 Hai Ba Trung, ☎ 04/826-7298

China Southern Airlines, 360 Kim Ma, ☎ 04/771-6611

Japan Airlines, 63 Ly Thai To, ☎ 04/826-6693

Lao Aviation, 269 Kim Ma, ☎ 04/846-4583

Singapore Airlines, 17 Ngo Quyen, ☎ 04/826-8888

Thai International Airlines, 44b Ly Thuong Kiet, ☎ 04/826-6893

Vietnam Airlines, 1 Quang Trung, ☎ 04/825-0888

Embassies & Consulates

Australia, 8 Dao Tan, Va Phuc, ☎ 04/831-7755

Cambodia, 71 Tran Hung Dao, ☎ 04/942-4788

Canada, 31 Hung Vuong, ☎ 04/823-5500

China, 46 Hoang Dieu, ☎ 04/845-3736

Thailand, 63-65 Hoang Dieu, ☎ 04/823-5092

United Kingdom, 41/31 Hai Ba Trung, ☎ 04/936-0500

United States, 7 Lang Ha, ☎ 04/772-1500

Internet/Communications

Most post offices offer international calls at a steep price. Better is to buy a calling card and use it at one of the many calling centers popping up all over.

Many hotels let guests use high-speed Internet for free. There are also dozens of Internet cafés now, and the cost for high-speed is about $3 per hour.

Medical Facilities

There are decent hospitals in Hanoi, but it is best to try to get to Thailand if you need serious care. Pharmacies will dispense almost anything (such as antibiotics) without a prescription. Make sure you know what you are taking and that it is not expired.

If you need serious treatment, try the **Hanoi French Hospital** at 1 Phuong Mai.

Day-Trips from Hanoi
Halong Bay

Most visitors plan this as an overnight or two-night excursion from Hanoi. Any of the many travel companies can arrange this trip for you. I recommend going with a company that keeps the group size under 10.

The typical trip is a morning departure from your hotel in Hanoi, a three- to four-hour bus ride to the bay, and then a cruise across the bay to **Cat Ba Island**, which has a number of mid-range hotels. Your trip will probably include all meals.

> **Tip:** There is usually a lower-cost option to stay on your boat. The accommodations are cramped but the food is better than on the island.

The outbound trip usually includes a stop at one or more craft shops. If you get to stop at the large complex run by the agency to provide jobs for the disabled, that's the place to spend your money.

The first or second day of your trip includes a cruise around the bay, with several stops to see floating villages and karst caves. You can extend the trip and spend a few days sea-kayaking to other caves – a very interesting experience.

Expect to pay about $10-15 per day for your trip, accommodations and food.

You can also go by train to the harbor area and hire a boat or take the ferry or hydrofoil to Cat Ba Island, but the trips arranged out of Hanoi are really quite good.

Sapa & the Mountains (then off to China)

It is possible to fly to Sapa, but I find the night train (soft sleeper, of course) to be a pleasant trip. The train ride is eight or nine hours to the town of **Lao Cai** (right at the Chinese border) and then a 90-minute bus ride up a steep road to Sapa.

Travel companies in Hanoi will arrange three- and four-day trekking excursions to Sapa for $50-100 per person. The cost varies depending on the level of accommodation in Sapa and the size of your group. I went with a friend in 2004 and we paid $80 each for a group of two, and stayed in a new hotel

(Bamboo Sapa) with all meals included, guide included, two days of trekking, the night train each way, and two nights in the hotel.

Sapa is a trekking heaven. You can go it alone if you wish – the paths are well marked and not too strenuous. With a guide you get to go into tribal homes, see sights you might otherwise miss, and learn the local history of the various ethnic groups. You can also stay overnight at various villages, and this requires a guide.

The town of Sapa is interesting. There are Colonial remnants such as restored villas and a church, as well as some adequate restaurants with patios and views of the hills.

The highest point in Vietnam is **Fan Si Pan Mountain** (10,000 feet or 3,000 meters). It can be trekked in a single day if you're in good shape, or you can overnight in the warmer seasons. Don't even think about going without a guide, though. Mountain weather is treacherous and can change so fast. You can go from sunny and warm to snowing in less than an hour, and then all paths disappear.

If you want to explore the many ethnic villages on your own, consider renting a four-wheel-drive vehicle. You can self-drive, but you may want to hire a driver. Figure $30-$50 per day for the vehicle, and another $20-$25 for the driver. If you're a heavy-duty mountain biker and brought your own gear you might try biking, but you'll have a hard time finding a guide or accommodations.

❖ Where to Stay

$$ **Bamboo Sa Pa**, Cau May, ☎ 020/871075. A great hotel, newly remodeled and expanded. The rooms have views over the hills (on the back side of the hotel). The facilities are clean and modern and the food in the attached restaurant is good. There is a good tour desk in the lobby. Our room had a balcony, a fake fireplace and tile floors, plus a tub-shower combo.

Other choices, all along or near the main streets, $$$ **Baguettes & Chocolat**, $$ **Chau Long**, $$$$ **Prince**, $$$ **Royal**.

Above: Floating market in the Mekong Delta
Below: Floating village, Mekong Delta

Above: Riverside homes in Can Tho town (Mekong Delta)
Below: Typical Mekong Delta home and vegetable garden

Above: River scene, Don Khong island, Laos
Below: Home in the 4,000 Islands area, Laos

Above: Village on the Mekong, Southern Laos

Below: School along a path in the 4,000 Islands area, Southern Laos

❖ Where to Eat

Any of the places along the main roads in town are good. The menus are posted so you can decide before you go inside. Keep in mind that many tours from Hanoi include all your meals (at your hotel). There is a place just across from the Bamboo Sa Pa that serves decent pizza if you get a hankering.

❖ What to Do & See

Trek. Climb Mount Fan Si Pan. Hang out on a nice patio and drink Chinese beer. Get your laundry done. Trek some more. Go to the weekly market at various nearby towns. Fight off the tribal women wanting to sell you things you don't want or need.

Vietnam

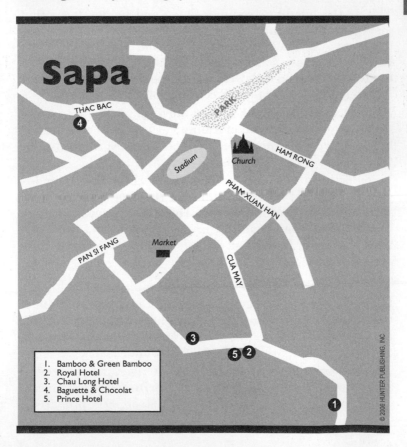

Sapa

THAC BAC
4

PARK

Stadium

Church

HAM RONG

PHAM XUAN HAN

PAN SI FANG

Market

CUA MAY

3

5 2

1. Bamboo & Green Bamboo
2. Royal Hotel
3. Chau Long Hotel
4. Baguette & Chocolat
5. Prince Hotel

1

© 2006 HUNTER PUBLISHING, INC

If you make your own way to Sapa your hotel can set you up on a small group (four or fewer people) tour and trekking excursion. If you want to climb the mountain, the guide selection is better in Sapa and you can check out the gear before you sign on.

Take a trip to one of the surrounding villages. That's what most of the treks do, visiting Cat Cat, Sin Chai, Ta Van, Lao Chai, Su Pan and other nearby villages.

Go to **Bac Ha**, a town about 40 km/24 miles northeast of Sapa. Make sure you visit on Sunday when the people from several hill tribes come to the market in all their tribal costumes.

Lao Cai

This is the bustling trading village and border town that marks the end of the Reunification Express. From here you can cross to China if you have a visa. You can continue on to Kunming by train (twice a week) or walk or take a taxi to the border and cross on foot. On the Chinese side you can get more frequent trains or a bus and continue onward.

Keep in mind the border is open only from 7:30 am to 5 pm; China is one hour ahead of Vietnam, so you actually need to cross earlier – by 4 pm – or you'll be stuck overnight in Lao Cai.

If you do have to spend the night here, check out the many guesthouses and hotels on the road running from the train station to the border (Nguyen Hué). The prices are high because of all the Chinese who come on two- and three-day trips. Weekends fill up fast. The restaurants around the train station offer decent, cheap food.

The Red River Estuary & Delta

If you are not going to get the Mekong Delta this is the next best thing. There are no particular sights – rather one goes for the experience. Life is slow and you are in the heart of the second broadbasket, prime rice-growing country.

The most popular trip here is along the river, in boats rowed almost exclusively by women, to the **Perfume Pagoda** (actually a cave). The trek up is slippery and steep, so be prepared.

It's easy to arrange this day trip from Hanoi. The cost should be about $8-$10, including lunch and all other costs, plus the boat trip.

 The tribal people who row the boats will become quite insistent on a large "tip" at the end of the trip. This is not the norm in Vietnam, but be prepared for a nasty confrontation with the boys and men at the end of your trip if you don't hand over a few dollars.

Leaving Hanoi

The route from Hanoi south the former DMZ is not very interesting to most travelers. If you are cycling, you may want to take the train for the long leg to the central coastal area. The night train is a great way to make this trip. Trains are not cheap, but you do save the cost of a night in a hotel. Plan on about $35-$40 for the train to Hué, Danang, or Hoi An. The flights to Danang are $90-$100 and take about an hour.

You can also take the buses run by various travelers' cafés such as Sinh Café. You can arrange intermediate stops and hotels in non-tourist places at the same time you buy your ticket.

■ Hué

History

 In 1802 Emperor Gia Long, left, moved his court and capital from Hanoi to Hué. Prior to that time the town had belonged to the Kingdom of Champa (until 1306) and then was ceded to Vietnam. The town itself remained a relative backwater under the Nguyen emperors for several hundred years. The citadel was built in the 16th or early 17th century, and moved to its present location in the late 17th century. The arrival of Emperor Gia Long in 1802

began the flowering of Hué, with the building of a Chinese-style Forbidden City and the construction of royal tombs along the Perfume River.

When Emperor Bao Dai abdicated in 1945, Hué ceased to be the capital of Vietnam, and Hanoi was reinstated. Two years later the wooden buildings were largely destroyed in a fire. During the 1968 Tet Offensive Hué was a center of the fighting and was mostly reduced to rubble.

Hué was declared a UNESCO World Heritage Site in 1993, and massive reconstruction has been going on since then.

Hué is a wonderful city to stroll around, and the tombs along the Perfume River are a peaceful oasis not to be missed.

Getting There & Away

If you arrive via the night train from north or south you are going to be a few km outside the main town. A taxi should cost $2-$3 for a ride to a hotel in the center. If you come by boat (hydrofoil) from Danang, you'll be at the wharf right in the center.

The airport is called **Phu Bai** and is 15 km/nine miles southeast of Hué. There is a bus (about $2) to the central hotel area. Taxis cost $7-$8 and should use their meters.

If you come in on a Sinh Café Open Tour bus you'll be right in the thick of the center and the hotel district.

Getting Around

Hué is one of the few cities in Vietnam where the tri-shaw (a bicycle rickshaw) is still a common sight. This is the easiest way, other than on foot, to get around. You can hire one for the day for $10 or so, and be pedaled to the various tombs outside town.

Bicycles are plentiful and cost $5-$8 per day to rent. They are a wonderful way to get around the area.

Taxis are persistent – bargain hard if you plan to use one.

Where to Stay

 There are new hotels popping up frequently in Hué so reasonably priced accommodations are easy to come by. You may want to pre-book (www.asia-hotels.com) but it is rarely necessary. Most of the hotels are within a block or two of the Perfume River on the south side, but a few places are opening inside the Citadel on the north side.

Pre-Booked/Pre-Paid Hotel Options

You can always book the hotels below using their websites, but I have found the rates through a site such as www.asia-hotels.com to be very competitive, especially for the higher-end choices.

Huong Giang Hotel, 51 Le Loi Street, Hué. The hotel has 135 rooms, gracefully situated on the south bank of the Perfume River in the heart of the city. Reached by a 30-minute drive from the Phu Bai airport (12 km/seven miles away) and only a five-minute drive from the railway station. Popular landmarks such as the Imperial Citadel, Royal Tombs, Mausoleum, art galleries and museums are all within easy reach. All rooms and suites are decorated in traditional Vietnamese style and equipped with modern conveniences such as satellite TV with CNN, mini-bar, hairdryer and Internet connection. Room rates vary from $48 to $79, depending on size and view. Rates include taxes and breakfast.

General Hotel Options

$$$$ **Saigon Morin Hotel**, 30 Le Loi, ☎ 054/823526, www.morinhotel.com.vn. This is a far better choice than the Century Riverside. It's a restored pink villa hotel with nearly international standard rooms.

$$$-$$$$ **Century Riverside Hotel**, 49 Le Loi, ☎ 054/823390, www.centuryhotels.com. This is an international-style hotel that is not up to international standards. The riverside location is nice though.

$$ **Binh Minh I**, 36 Nguyen Tri Phuong, ☎ 054/825526, binhmunhhue@dng.vnn.vn. I usually stay here or at the Binh Minh II (45 Ben Nghe). The rooms are spacious, clean and

bright. Most have their own bathrooms, but you can save a few dollars with shared facilities. Breakfast is included.

There are many other choices in all price ranges so it pays to look around and see what's available.

Hotels are the best source of tourist information and tour arrangements.

HOTEL PRICE CHART	
Rates are per room based on double occupancy.	
$	Under $12
$$	$12-$25
$$$	$26-$40
$$$$	$40-$80
$$$$$	Over $80

Where to Eat

Hué has some of the best food in the country. It's a wonderful mix of French and Vietnamese, with a number of international options thrown in to liven the mix.

$$$ Club Garden, 8 Vo Thi Sau, ☎ 054/826327. Serves traditional food in a pleasant setting with garden seating available. There are set menus that allow you to sample a variety of dishes at a reasonable prices.

$ Dong Tam, 48/7 Le Loi. A vegetarian restaurant with a courtyard.

$$ La Carambole, 19 Pham Ngu Lao, ☎ 054/810491. Serves a blended French-Vietnamese cuisine and international dishes.

Most of the restaurants are located near the hotels, and almost all are good value and quality.

RESTAURANT PRICES	
$	Under $2
$$	$2-$5
$$$	$6-$10
$$$$	$11-$20
$$$$$	Over $20

Nightlife

There are several bars for evening entertainment, including the **DMZ Bar** near the Saigon Morin Hotel and the **Café on Thu Wheels**.

Shopping

There are craft shops and stalls, but Hué is not a shoppers' destination.

Tours & Travels

Ask at your hotel or any other hotel for information. Try the **Mandarin Café** at 12 Hung Vuong, ☎ 054/534485, mandarin@dng.vnn.vn.

What to See & Do

The Citadel and the Forbidden City are the highlights in Hué itself, and the Emperors' Tombs along the Perfume River are also not to be missed. You can also get to Bach Ma National Park (see page 143) easily if you have your own transport or arrange a tour.

The Citadel

The present Citadel was laid out by Emperor Gia Long in the early 19th century. It consists of three layered enclosures, and used to have a moat (where the young boys now play soccer) You enter the Citadel  through the Flag Tower, and then you will see spread before you the restored Imperial City and the purple/mauve Forbidden City.

You can walk around the entire Citadel on the in- or outside. But beware – it's huge – 10 km/six miles in circumference.

The Flag Tower

The Flag Tower is actually three towers flanked by nine sacred cannons. You can climb to the top. The view at sunrise or sunset is spectacular.

The Imperial City

The second moat and interior wall form the protective fortifications for the Imperial (administrative) City. The layout is

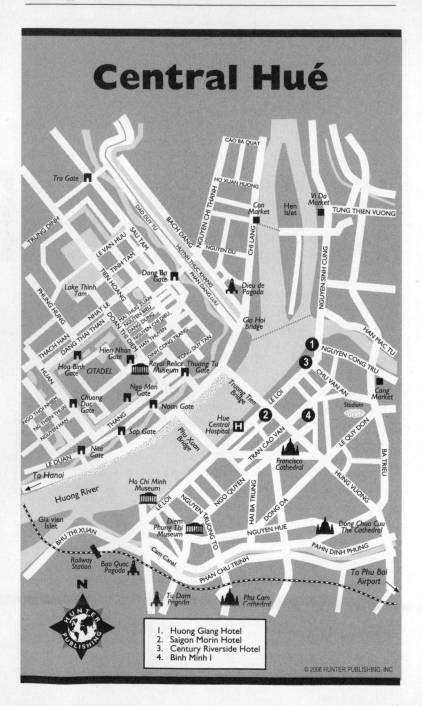

Central Hué

1. Huong Giang Hotel
2. Saigon Morin Hotel
3. Century Riverside Hotel
4. Binh Minh I

similar to Beijing's Forbidden City. There are four gates, one at each compass point, with the most impressive being the southern one. The southern gate (Ngo Mon) is the main entrance to the Imperial City. Most of the buildings were already in poor condition before the Tet Offensive in 1968, and subsequent fighting and neglect have taken their toll. Massive restorations are ongoing, however.

The main buildings are:

The **Ngo Mon (Southern) Gate**, with the pavilion on top called the Five Phoenix Watchtower.

The **Thai Hoa Palace**, the most impressive of the palaces in the town. It is lacquered with gold and red, and seems to glow in the morning and evening light. This was the palace that held the throne and was the site of many important ceremonies.

The Forbidden City is approached from the Great Golden Gate. It is contained inside the third enclosure. Most striking is the purple color of the buildings. The remaining buildings (many were destroyed in a fire in 1948) are:

The **Left and Right Houses** where mandarins would prepare for audiences with the emperor,

The **Thai Binh Reading Pavilion**, a two-story building surrounded by bonsai.

The **Ancestral Altars** at the southwest corner.

Museums

The **Museum of Fine Arts**, 3 Le Truc, with its displays of royal memorabilia. The museum is inside the Long An Palace. This palace was built in 1845 and was located in the Imperial City. It was moved to this location in 1909.

The **Provincial Museum**, across from the Museum of Fine Arts, is probably still closed. If it's open, you can see materials related to the Tet Offensive and the rest of the War.

Phu Cat

This is the area alongside the Citadel where the merchants and other civilians lived. There are a number of Chinese Assembly Halls (as in Hoi An), and pagodas.

The European part retains much of the French Colonial influence and buildings.

Nearby Sights

The main attraction close to Hué is the collection of Emperors' Tombs along the Perfume River. You can visit these on a boat tour, or rent a bicycle or hire a tri-shaw and explore them from the land.

Heading south from town, here are the tombs and related buildings you will come to:

Nam Gao, the altar of heaven. This was a key element in the religious life of Hué.

Van Mieu, the temple dedicated by Emperor Dia Long to Confucius.

The **Royal Arena**, on the other side of the Perfume River, where elephant fights were held.

Thien Mu Pagoda and **Hon Chen Temple**, noted for their beautiful settings.

The Royal Tombs or Mausoleums

Tu Duc's Tomb is the most harmonious tomb. There are pavilions, trees, a lake, and more. Emperors built their tombs while they were alive and used them as retreats from the Forbidden City.

Khai Dinh' Tomb looks as if it escaped from somewhere in Europe and landed near Hué. It is a mish-mash of styles – European Baroque, Vietnamese, and even Cham.

Minh Mang's Tomb is a series of pavilions and mounds set in a lake.

Gia Long's Tomb was badly damaged during the War so there isn't much to see any more.

Dong Khanh's Tomb wasn't built since he died at a young age. Instead, he is buried near a temple dedicated to his father.

Thieu Tri's Tomb is very similar to his father's (Minh Mang), with a determined avoidance of any Western influences.

Duc Duc's Tomb is rarely visited.

Useful Information

Airlines

All travel companies should be able to handle flight confirmations and reservations for you.

The main airline is: **Vietnam Airlines**, in the Thuan Hoa Hotel at 7 Nguyen Tri Phuong, ☎ 054/824709.

Internet/Communications

Most post offices offer international calls at a steep price. Better is to buy a calling card and go to one of the many calling centers popping up all over.

Many hotels let guests use high-speed Internet for free. There are also dozens of Internet cafés now, and the cost for high-speed is about $3 per hour.

Medical Facilities

Try to get to Hanoi, HCMC, or Thailand if you need serious care. Pharmacies will dispense almost anything (such as antibiotics) without a prescription. Make sure you know what you are taking and that it is not expired.

■ Danang

History

Danang is the third-largest city in Vietnam. It sits on a large, sheltered bay, making it an excellent harbor and shipping port. The War resulted in the creation of a large air base here, but few signs remain.

Marines coming ashore at Danang, March 9, 1965

When Hoi An's harbor began silting in the 18th century, shipping traffic moved to Danang. The French had a concession here from the late 19th century. When Vietnam was partitioned after World War II, Danang ended up on the

South Vietnamese side, but was only 200 km/120 miles away from the DMZ.

During the Vietnamese-American War, the nearby China Beach became well-known as a rest and relaxation site for American military personnel. The city also became a destination for refugees fleeing the communist North.

The city was "liberated" on March 29, 1975.

Getting There & Away

 Danang is a transportation hub in the area. If you want to go to Hoi An you will likely go through Danang.

The airport is really close to the city. You can take a taxi for $2 to town. It should cost $10-$15 to go on to Hoi An.

The train station is also close to town and costs about $2 by taxi. It should cost $10-$15 to go on to Hoi An.

The long-distance bus station is just past the train station.

Open tour buses drop you at the Cham Museum or their in-town offices.

Getting Around

 Danang is too spread-out for much walking. Your best bet is to rent a bicycle ($2 per day) or a motorbike ($6-$10 per day) at your hotel or a tour agency.

Car rentals will run about $25 per day, but driving is risky and chaotic.

Where to Stay

 Most people don't spend a lot of time in Danang. It is convenient to the Marble Mountains, China Beach, and the former DMZ. The airport has more flights than some nearby cities can offer.

Pre-Booked/Pre-Pay Options

You can always book the general hotels that follow using their websites, but I have found the rates through a site such as www.asia-hotels.com to be very competitive, especially for the higher-end choices.

$$$$$ **Furama Resort**, 68 Ho Xuan Huong Street, Bac My An, Da Nang. Furama Resort Danang is an award-winning beach resort offering 200 luxuriously furnished rooms and suites, each having a spacious and private terrace, overlooking the lush tropical gardens of the resort. The architecture displays a luxurious contem-

HOTEL PRICE CHART	
Rates are per room based on double occupancy.	
$	Under $12
$$	$12-$25
$$$	$26-$40
$$$$	$40-$80
$$$$$	Over $80

porary resort in a very natural setting. The resort is within two hours drive of some Vietnam's most stunning cultural heritage sights, including the ancient sea port of Hoi An, the former Imperial capital Hué and the Holy Valley. Both the interior and public areas are inspired by the French Colonial period, rooms and suites feature polished timber floors and fittings with plantation-style shutters, ceiling fans and comfortable cane furniture.

Pre-paid online rates start at about $140 and go up depending on the season and view. Rates include breakfast and taxes.

$$ **Saigon Tourane Hotel**, 5 Dong Da Street, Hai Chau District, Da Nang. Saigon Tourane Hotel is a modern, five-story establishment that overlooks the Han River and Tien Sa Bay. It has about 80 rooms. One of its best features is its location, less than five minutes from both the airport and the railway station. The rooms are well furnished and equipped with individually controlled air-conditioners, IDD telephone, satellite TV, mini-bar, hairdryer, table lamp, tea-making facilities, bathrobe, toilet kit, and slippers.

Pre-book pay at hotel rates at press time: $30-$45, including breakfast and taxes.

General Hotel Options

$$$-$$$$ **Bamboo Green Resort**, 158 Phan Chu Trinh, ☎ 0511/822996, bamboogreen1@dng.vnn.vn. Decent hotel with a good range of amenities. Tour groups often stay here. One of the better choices in Danang.

$-$$ **Da Nang**, 1-3 Dong Da, ☎ 0511/821986, dananghotel@ dng.vnn.vn. This was the US military's officers' quarters during the War. Rooms have great features for the price – satellite TV, A/C, and often en suite facilities. Stay in the western block; avoid the eastern block.

Where to Eat

There are plenty of decent restaurants in the area. Here are some choices to start.

$ **Bamboo Bar**, 11 Bach Dang, On the river, with decent food, cheap beer, and music some evenings. They

RESTAURANT PRICES	
$	Under $2
$$	$2-$5
$$$	$6-$10
$$$$	$11-$20
$$$$$	Over $20

can also help with bike hires and tour arrangements.

$$ **Hana Kim Dinh**, 15 Bach Dang. This is a floating restaurant, just north of the Han Bridge. It serves a good mix of Asian and Western food, and is not as expensive as it looks.

Nightlife

There's not much to choose from, the **Bamboo Bar** (see *Restaurants*) is probably your best choice.

Shopping

Not much except the usual local market.

Tours & Travels

An Phu Tourist Agency is considered the best in the area. They are at 147 Le Loi, ☎ 0511/818366, anphucndn@yahoo.com.

What to See & Do

Few people (except some American military who served in the area) come to Danang for the sights. They come to visit surrounding areas (China Beach, Marble Mountains), or they stop here en route to or from the DMZ. Or they use Danang as the entry point to Hué or Hoi An. Still, there are a few sights worth a day of your time.

The Cham Museum

The Cham Museum, located at 1 Duong 2 Thang 9, is small, but well worth seeing. Visiting here before you go to the Cham ruins at My Son provides historical and cultural perspective. The museum is open every day and

charges a small admission fee. There are terracotta figures displayed in a courtyard garden, and numerous other artifacts throughout the museaum.

The Coa Dai Temple

The temple, located at 63 Hai Phong, was built in 1956. It is the second-most important temple (after Tay Ninh).

Day-Trips from Danang

The Beaches

China Beach, and many other beaches (**Red Beach**, **Non Nuoc**, all the way south to **Hoi An**), is the main reason many people give Danang more than a passing glance. The beaches are usually clean, with fine white sand. The riptides and undertows make swimming very risky. Lifeguards are non-existent.

Marble Mountains

This is the site of marble quarries and sacred caves. Most tour buses will stop here for a few hours to give you time to hike up to a cave (admission fee). You can also wander the many carving shops – some of the work is quite good.

Bach Ma National Park

This park (www.bachma.vnn.vn) is about 70 km/42 miles north of Danang, or 40 km/24 miles south of Hué. You can arrange a tour form either place. The area is well suited to hiking and biking. There are plans to develop it as an eco-resort, but the location so far off the main tourist track is slowing things down for now.

Note: There are over 1,400 species of flora and 230 species of birds in the park. You may also see the Asian black bear, leopards, and other interesting mammals.

If you don't arrive with a tour, you can go to the Visitors' Center and arrange transportation, tickets, and accommodation. You can also get several useful guidebooks and find out about the six nature trails in the area. You'll need a motorbike, car, or strong legs and a good bike to come on your own.

Useful Information

Airlines

 All travel companies should be able to handle flight confirmations and reservations for you.

The main airline addresses and telephone numbers are:

Pacific Airlines, 35 Nguyen Van Linh, ☎ 0511/583538

Siem Reap Airways, 84 Nguyen Van Linh, ☎ 0511/582361

Vietnam Airlines, 35 Tran Phu, ☎ 0511/821130

Embassies & Consulates

None – the closest are in Hanoi or HCMC.

Internet/Communications

You can go to most post offices and make international calls at a steep price. Better is to buy a calling card and go to one of the many calling centers popping up all over.

Many hotels let guests use high-speed Internet for free. There are also dozens of Internet cafés now, and the cost for high-speed is about $3 per hour.

Medical Facilities

Try to get to Hanoi, HCMC, or Thailand if you need serious care. Pharmacies will dispense almost anything (such as antibiotics) without a prescription. Make sure you know what you are taking and that it is not expired.

■ Hoi An
History

The maritime importance of Hoi An stretches as far back as the second century BC. Hoi An has been occupied by Japanese and Chinese, as well as Europeans, leaving an interesting legacy and culture. As far back as the 16th century the river and seaport of Hoi An bustled with activity, as evidenced by the large numbers of Chinese shophouses and 18th- and 19th-century homes of Chinese merchants still present in the town today. The harbor began to silt up in the late 18th century, and that spelled the demise of Hoi An as an international trading center.

Today you can still see the homes, shophouses, temples and Cham monuments in and around Hoi An and My Son. You can wander the narrow, winding streets, hear the babble of languages and see the myriad goods being carted up and down steps and streets – if you let your imagination run.

Hoi An was listed as a UNESCO World Heritage Site in 1999. It could easily be one of the highlights of your trip, especially if you add the attraction of made-to-order clothes.

Getting There & Away

The nearest airport is 30 km/18 miles away in Danang. The easiest way into Hoi An is by taxi, at a cost of about $10-$15.

If you arrive or leave by train you will also arrive in Danang, and take a taxi or Honda Om to town.

The open tour buses will drop you at their respective offices in town.

Getting Around

Bicycle rentals are very inexpensive – a few dollars a day – and easy to arrange at almost any hotel. Motorbike rentals are also cheap – less than $5 a day through your hotel.

To see the central part of Hoi An plan on walking. Traffic is restricted, and that includes bicycles.

Vietnam

Where to Stay

 Hoi An is filled with budget hotels of varying standards, but there are no truly international standard facilities.

HOTEL PRICE CHART	
Rates are per room based on double occupancy.	
$	Under $12
$$	$12-$25
$$$	$26-$40
$$$$	$40-$80
$$$$$	Over $80

Pre-Book/Pre-Pay Options

$$$$$ Hoi An Beach Resort, Cua Dai Beach, Hoi An, Quang Nam. Hoi An Beach Resort consists of 110 rooms equipped with modern comforts and other services housed in traditional Vietnamese village-inspired villas. Deluxe rooms are 60 sq m/666 sq feet and complete with modern appointments like air conditioning, mini-bar, safety deposit box, IDD phone, satellite TV, writing desk, complete bathroom supplies, tub and shower and extra outdoor Vietnamese bathroom, plus a private balcony for outdoor viewing. Rooms look either over the garden or the De Vong River.

Pre-pay/pre-book Internet rates at press time are $59-$70 with breakfast and taxes included.

$$$-$$$$ Hoi An Hotel, 06-Tran Hung Dao Street, Hoi An, Quang Nam. A 160-room, three-wing, quiet French-Oriental business hotel surrounded by a huge garden. All rooms are equipped with air conditioner, IDD phone, satellite TV, mini-bar and en suite bath/shower.

Pre-book/pre-pay Internet rates for 2005-2006 are $36-$52 with breakfast and taxes included.

General Hotel Options

$$$ Hai Yen 22a Cua Dai, ☎ 0510/862445. This is a slightly better than basic hotel that is fairly close to the beaches. It has en suite facilities, bike rentals, Internet access, and tour services.

$$$ Hong Phat, 41 Nguyen Thai Hoc, ☎ 0510/910100, quanghuy.ha@dng.vnn.vn. This is a 350-year-old building and quite a deal if you can get one of the four rooms and don't mind not having an exterior window.

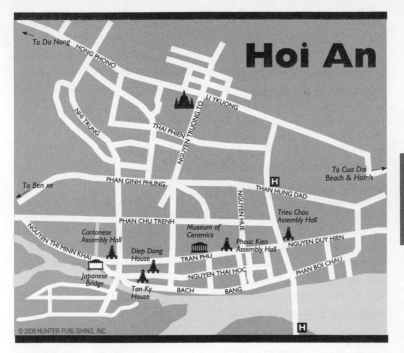

Where to Eat

Restaurants are plentiful and good.

$$ Faifoo, 104 Tran Phu (beach). Try the five-course sampler of Hoi An dishes.

$$ $$$ Hoi An Hai Sen, 64 Bach Dang. The main specialty is seafood, but the sources – Vietnamese, Turkish, and Scandinavia – are curious. Still, the food is good but a bit pricey.

$ Quan An, 18 Hoang Van Thu. Simple, cheap, local food.

Nightlife

Not much goes on here at night.

Shopping

The area is becoming a clothesmaking and crafts center for the entire region. Silk custom-tailored clothes can be made in 24 hours (but more time is better) and prices are much lower than in the rest of the country. For the best deals check out the market with its tailors' stalls.

If you head out of town there are numerous villages, each with a crafts specialty. This is where the bicycle comes in handy.

Tours & Travels

Your hotel is a good source of information, especially if you want to go to My Son or the nearby craft villages. Try **An Phu Tourist** at 29 Phan Dinh Phung, anphutourist@ hotmail.com, for help and services.

What to See & Do

 Too many travelers come to Hoi An for one reason – to get custom silk, wool, and cotton clothes made in a hurry. They miss the charms of this truly lovely, interesting city and nearby My Son. Hoi An was, and still is, an important part of Vietnamese culture, and has the buildings, temples, and monuments to prove it.

The Old City

Start by wandering the narrow streets of the old town. As soon as you leave the main street, with its art galleries, tailor shops, and souvenir vendors, you enter a different world. Take note of the tiled roofs, pas-

The Japanese Covered Bridge

tel-colored two-story residences and shophouses, and then go into the bustling market. There are only three short streets that comprise old Hoi An so it's a brief, pleasant stroll.

> **Tip:** You can buy a single ticket that allows entry to many of the monuments and museums in Hoi An. Ask at your hotel.

You'll come to the **Japanese Covered Bridge** at the western end of Tran Phu. It's a red-painted arched wooden bridge first built in the 16th century and reconstructed several times since then. This is the bridge used as the symbol of Hoi An.

❖ **Assembly Halls**

The entire old city is filled with Chinese assembly halls – meeting places for Chinese of different regional origins. If you came from Fujian, or Guangzhou, and so forth, you had a dedicated assembly or meeting place. The assembly halls are:

Phouc Kien (46 Tran Phu). This is the Fujian assembly hall, built in the late 17th century and added to several times. It has an ornate, gaudy entrance and a number of interesting statues and carvings.

Trieu Chau (157 Nguyen Duy Hien). This assembly hall belongs to the Chaozhou group, and is on the eastern edge of town. It is heavily carved and ornate, and dates from the late 18th century.

Hai Nam (10 Tran Phu) was founded by the Hainanese group in the late 18th century. It has an ornately carved, gilded altar.

Cantonese (just east of the Japanese bridge). This assembly hall was built in the 18th century by immigrants from Guangzhou (Canton). It is impressively ornate and gaudy with a pleasant courtyard.

Chinese Assembly Hall (center of town). Built in 1740 as a facility for all the Chinese groups in Hoi An – a general meeting place.

❖ **Merchants' Houses (Shophouses)**

Walking along Tran Phu and towards the river you will see a number of two-story merchants' houses. The best known is the **Tan Ky House** at 101 Nguyen Thai Hoc, a carved, wooden, two-story building in excellent condition. Note the amalgamation of styles: Chinese, Japanese, and Vietnamese. Take particular note of the rich woods and beautiful inlaid areas inside.

Other merchants' houses worth a look include the **Diep Dong Nguyen House** at 80 Nguyen Thai Hoc (across from the Tan Ky House), which was converted to a pharmacy and still has the old cases, and the **Phung Hung House** at 4 Nguyen Thai Hoc, still lived in eight generations later by the descendants of the original builders.

❖ Museums

There are several museums that are worth a peek. Probably the most interesting is the **Museum of Trade Ceramics** at 80 Tran Phu. The building itself is intriguing since it typifies the building style of warehouse and residence combined. The ceramics trade in Hoi An was in its heyday in the 15th and 16th centuries and there are a number of ceramic samples from those days.

The **Museum of Sa Huynh Culture** features artifacts from the culture that occupied Hoi An from the second century BC to about the second century AD.

❖ The Market

You can buy almost any goods or services in the market. This is the place to order those custom clothes, get a pedicure, or even a haircut. Just avoid the areas that sell chickens or other birds.

Day-Trips from Hoi An

The other big destination in the vicinity of Hoi An centers on the Cham culture (the culture that spread to Cambodia and points beyond in the sixth-eighth centuries).

My Son

This is the biggest concentration of Cham towers and buildings in the area. The site is 40 km/24 miles from Hoi An. The road has been improved so now it can be a day trip from Hoi An. Get your hotel to arrange a guided tour. It only costs $2-$3 plus entrance fees. Some tours arrange part of the return trip by boat. If you are feeling really ambitious you might be able to get your hotel to help arrange a bicycle or motorbike trip to My Son.

My Son was named a UNESCO World Heritage Site recently. It is nothing close to the marvels of Angkor Wat or Bagan, but still impressive.

Until recently, My Son was almost totally surrounded by dense jungle. The immediate area has been cleared, but you still will get the feeling of the original forests that covered much of this part of Vietnam.

The majority of the excavated buildings and towers date from the seventh-13th centuries, although there is evidence the site was used as early as the fourth century. This was the burial place of Cham kings.

Be careful – this area was heavily mined in the 1970s and '80s, and there may also be unexploded ordnance in the vicinity. STAY ON THE PATHS! It is really best to go with a guide.

Useful Information

Airlines

All travel companies should be able to handle flight confirmations and reservations for you.

See the *Danang* listings, page 139-40, for airline information.

Embassies & Consulates

None – Plan to go to Hanoi or HCMC.

Internet/Communications

You can go to most post offices and make international calls at a steep price. Better is to buy a calling card and go to one of the many calling centers popping up all over.

Many hotels let guests use the Internet for free. There are also dozens of Internet cafés now, and the cost for high-speed is about $3 per hour. Many connections here are still very slow, though, so forget about sending your photos home from here.

■ Nha Trang

History

There is a little bit of history in the form of the Cham Towers, but Nha Trang has never been a big stopping place for tribes, kings, or marauding armies. It was a big (R&R) site for the US military during the War, however.

Getting There & Away

Nha Trang is well served by flights from all over Vietnam. It is a short trip from the airport to the town, costing a few dollars by taxi or Honda Om.

The train station is also close to town, as is the bus station.

Where to Stay

Nha Trang has a huge variety of hotels, almost all within a few blocks of the Pacific beaches.

Pre-Book/Pre-Pay Options

$$$$ **Ana Mandara Resort**, Beachside Tran Phu Blvd, Nha Trang, Khanh Hoa. Reminiscent of an old Vietnamese village, furnished with native wood and rattan, the resort reflects the real image of Vietnam, with its warm hospitality, rich culture and unique tastes. Located directly on the beach of Nha Trang, the resort rests comfortably on extensive private tropical gardens overlooking the sea. Blending graceful architecture and gracious service, peaceful atmosphere and captivating scenery, Ana Mandara offers its guests a unique experience in simplicity, serenity and refinement. The resort has 16 villas containing 68 well-appointed guest rooms and suites scattered along the beach. All rooms come with a private covered terrace, open timbered roofs, bathrooms with vanity counter, bathtub and shower, plus all the conveniences of a five-star resort.

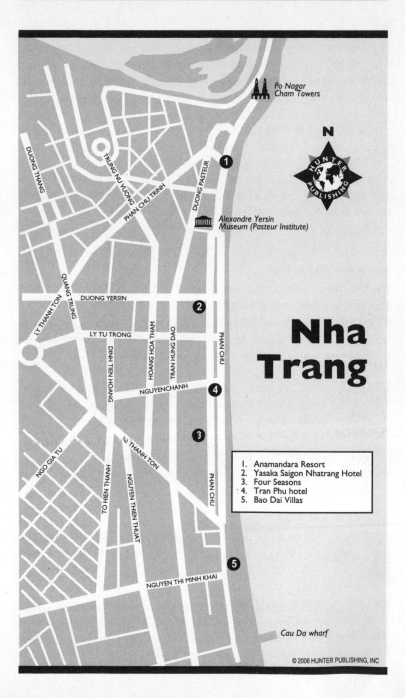

Po Nagar
Cham Towers

N

HUNTER
PUBLISHING

Alexandre Yersin
Museum (Pasteur Institute)

Nha
Trang

1. Anamandara Resort
2. Yasaka Saigon Nhatrang Hotel
3. Four Seasons
4. Tran Phu hotel
5. Bao Dai Villas

DUONG THANG

TRUNG NU VUONG

PHAN CHU TRINH

DUONG PASTEUR

QUANG TRUNG

LY THANH TON

DUONG YERSIN

LY TU TRONG

DINH TIEN HOANG

HOANG HOA THAM

TRAN HUNG DAO

PHAN CHU

NGUYENCHANH

NGO GIA TU

TO HIEN THANH

THANH TON

NGUYEN THIEN THUAT

PHAN CHU

NGUYEN THI MINH KHAI

Cau Da wharf

© 2006 HUNTER PUBLISHING, INC

Pre-booked/pre-paid Internet rates at press time start at $150 per night and escalate rapidly depending on time of year and type of room. All rooms include breakfast and taxes.

$$$$ **Yasaka Saigon Nhatrang Hotel**, 18 Tran Phu Boulevard, Khanh Hoa, Nha Trang, Khanh Hoa. This is an 11-story, 174-room beach resort hotel, offering sea views from rooms and suites. It is within a few minutes of the beaches, airport, and railways stations. Room facilities comprise satellite TV, IDD telephone, mini-bar, hairdryer, bathtub, shower, toiletries. Superior, Deluxe and Senior Deluxe rooms are all 35 sq meters/389 sq feet in size and enjoy daily servicing, free daily mineral water and buffet breakfast.

Pre-nook/pre-pay Internet rates at press time: $46-$48 for standard rooms, including breakfast and taxes.

General Options

$$-$$$ **Tran Phu**, 52 Tran Phu, ☎ 058/524228. This is a newer, beach-front hotel with standard amentities.

$$$-$$$$ **Bao Dia's Villas**, Tran Phu. These beach-front villas were once used by the emperor of Vietnam. Now they provide rooms and suites set in gardens by the sea. The hotel is pretty far out of town.

There are many other options along Tran Phu by the beaches.

HOTEL PRICE CHART	
Rates are per room based on double occupancy.	
$	Under $12
$$	$12-$25
$$$	$26-$40
$$$$	$40-$80
$$$$$	Over $80

Where to Eat

 Most of the hotels have gardens with restaurants, and all offer decent Asian and Western food. Some to try:

$$ **Four Seasons**, Tran Phu. Seafood specials.

RESTAURANT PRICES	
$	Under $2
$$	$2-$5
$$$	$6-$10
$$$$	$11-$20
$$$$$	Over $20

$-$$ **La Bella Napoli**, Tran Phu. As the name suggests, you can get pizza here, along with other pasta dishes and seafood.

Nightlife

There are lots of ocean-front bars and some discos open until all hours. Try:

Crazy Kim's Bar, 19 Biet Thu, with its late-night happy hour and two-foot-tall drink specialties.

Nha Trang Sailing Club, 72074 Tran Phu. Great views and a beach-front bar.

Shopping

There are a few souvenir shops in the area. Try **Cua Hang Luu Niem Git Shop** at 8 Phan Boi Chau or **Bambou** at 15 Biet Thu.

Adventures on Water

People come to Nha Trang for three reasons: To eat seafood, to chill out, and to try the various watersports.

The **Nha Trang Sailing Club** rents Jet Skis and windsurfers.

For scuba diving, plan on coming in January to May. There are more than a dozen dive sites in the area. Try **Rainbow Divers**, ☎ 058/829946, www.divevietnam.com, based at the Nha Trang Sailing Club, or **Octopus Dive Club**, ☎ 058/810629, at 62 Tran Phu. You can rent equipment, get your PADI certificate, and dive all day.

Tours & Travels

Any of the agencies and your hotel should be able to assist with tours, tickets, and reservations. A few options:

Khanh Hoa Tourism, 1 Tran Hung Dao, ☎ 058/823709, is the place for visa issues and extensions.

Mama Linh, 2a Hung Vuong, ☎ 058/826693.

Hanh Café, 26 Tran Hung Dao, ☎ 058/814227.

Getting Around

The town of Nha Trang stretches for several km along the Pacific, but doesn't go more than a few blocks inland. Walking is easy and pleasant, especially along the ocean-front boardwalk.

Bicycling is another excellent way to get around, and most hotels rent bikes for a few dollars a day.

To venture farther afield consider renting a car or a motorbike. The bigger hotels and any travel agency can help with this. Prices are comparable to the rest of Vietnam.

What to See & Do

You are in a scuba, sailing, snorkeling, beach paradise, and the activities reflect that.

There are miles of pristine beaches, or you can learn to scuba-dive on any of 20 different dive sites. You can hire a boat to take you island-hopping. You can explore ancient Cham monuments, or venture farther out to hot springs.

Inside the city limits you'll find the **Alexandre Yersin Museum** at the Pasteur Institute (north end of Tran Phu). Yersin was a bacteriologist celebrated for his discovery of the bacillus responsible for the bubonic plague. His house has been turned into a museum. As you head back to the south you can visit the **Nha Trang Cathedral** and the **Long Son Pagoda**, neither of which is of great interest.

Outside of the northern end of town are the **Po Nagar Cham Towers**, 10 towers constructed between the seventh and 12th centuries. Rent a motorbike to take you out there – definitely worth a look.

Near the Cham Towers, off to the northwest, you'll come to the **Thap Ba Hot Springs**. Your hotel can arrange transport for you. Call ahead to price and reserve treatments (☎ 058/835335).

❖ Islands

There are several islands of note in the area. Boats leave from Cau Da Wharf – expect to pay about $50 per day for a boat. **Hon Mieu** is the closest island and can actually be reached by a ferry from the wharf. There is an aquarium that is worth a quick look, then off to the next island, **Hon Tam**.

Hon Tam has a decent beach and you can do some snorkeling.

Hon Tre is the next island, and it is much different in appearance from the others – rocky with cliffs.

Useful Information

Airlines

All travel companies should be able to handle flight confirmations and reservations for you.

Vietnam Airlines, 91 Nguyen Thien Thuat.

> **Note** that in small towns there are few English speakers in such offices. You will usually have to visit them in person or have a local do so for you.

Embassies & Consulates

None. The closest are in HCMC or Hanoi.

Internet/Communications

You can go to most post offices and make international calls at a steep price. Better is to buy a calling card and go to one of the many calling centers popping up all over.

Many hotels let guests use high-speed Internet for free. There are also dozens of Internet cafés now, and the cost for high-speed is about $3 per hour.

Medical Facilities

It is best to try to get to Hanoi, HCMC, or Thailand if you need serious care. Pharmacies will dispense almost anything (such as antibiotics) without a prescription. Make sure you know what you are taking and that it is not expired.

Vietnam

■ Dalat & the Southern Highlands

History

 This is one of the most beautiful, laid-back parts of Vietnam, but it wasn't always that way. During the War this was one of the most heavily contested areas in the southern half of the country.

This is the coffee, tea, and mulberry (silkworm food) growing area of Vietnam. Farms and cattle abound, amid villages of thatched and tile-roofed houses, lakes with floating villages, and fishermen who row their boats with their foot so they have both hands free for the nets.

Dalat is on the Cam Ly River at an elevation of 1,500 meters (a bit less than 5,000 feet). Surrounded by rolling hills and forests, the area is quite beautiful, and well suited to trekking, hiking, biking, or just walking. It is also home to two very interesting sights – the oldest golf course in Vietnam, and the strangest hotel in Southeast Asia. If you need to retreat from the heat in the South, this is the place.

In order to go trekking to the minority villages it is best to arrange a guide and let him handle the permissions and arrangements for you. See *Tours & Travels*, page 155, for resources.

Getting There & Away

 Dalat has an airport with connections to HCMC, Hanoi, and the Danang area. There are also a few international connections, but few people enter Vietnam through Dalat. Flights on Vietnam Airlines cost about $100 each leg.

From the airport you can take the Vietnam Airlines bus to their office in town for about $3. It's 30 km/18 miles (allow 45 minutes) to town. A taxi will cost about $10 and a ride on the back of a motorbike about the same as the airline bus.

If you arrive by bus you will come to the bus station at the west end of Xuan Huong Lake. Buses come from all over Vietnam, but most travelers arrive from Nha Trang to the north or HCMC. If you come in on the Sinh Café open tour bus you will arrive at the Trung Cang Hotel.

Getting Around

Unless you are in outstanding condition you will find biking around the city of Dalat a challenge. Better to get your cycling legs on a trip outside the urban area. That also means there won't be any tri-wheeled vehicles or cyclos (bike-propelled carts). Your options really come down to three: your feet, taxis, or Honda Oms.

If you want to do a day-long tour of the area, visiting waterfalls, monasteries, silk farms, and ethnic villages, look for the group called the "**Easy Riders**." Their bikes are larger and they speak decent English. You can also call them at ☎ 063/822194, or seek them out at the Phu Hoa Hotel (if they don't find you first). A day trip in a taxi is about $20-$25.

You can rent bikes at the Sofitel, Novotel, Hoa Binh, and Duy Tan hotels (and through the travel agencies) for about $5-$10 per day. Check the equipment carefully and bring your own helmet.

Where to Stay

Dalat has a good variety of hotels. The quality is rather uneven, though. The Sinh Café hotel (Trung Cang) is a smelly dump.

Dalat is one of the few places in former Indochina with a golf course. The course is at the former Royal Palace, so there are no on-site hotels – yet. In the meanwhile there are lots of reasonably priced hotels. The first two are available through www.asia-hotels.com at very favorable rates.

> **Tip:** If you arrive on the open tour bus they are going to try to lock you into their place, so watch out. When the bus pulls in, grab your bags and walk out to the street. Right across the street is a plain, but much better basic hotel, or head down the hill into the main part of town.

Pre-Book/Pre-Pay Options

$$$ **Golf 3 Hotel**, 04 Nguyen Chi Minh Khai, Dalat City, ☎ 063/826042/49. This is in the heart of Dalat City only steps from the market. It is well located for many of the attractions in the surrounding area. Rooms feature IDD phones, en suite showers, mini-bars, satellite TV. Rooms with hairdryers, tea/coffee facilities and video/CD players are also available.

Internet rate at press time: $38 per night with breakfast and taxes.

$$$$ **Novotel Dalat**, 7 Tran Phu Street, Dalat, ☎ 063/825777. The original Du Parc Hotel has been transformed into the four-star Novotel Dalat, retaining its former French Colonial style in 1997. Guests can choose to explore the surrounding waterfalls on a mountain bike, take a paddle boat on the serene Xuan Huong Lake, make use of the superb golf and tennis facilities or simply relax at one of the excellent bars or restaurants within the resort. Located 30 minutes from Dalat Airport and only five minutes from the shops, market and Dalat Palace Golf Club. Rooms are all equipped with satellite TV, in-house movies, IDD telephone, mini-bar and fridge, safe, and hairdryer.

Pre-book/pay at hotel rate at press time: $65. Does not include 15% tax or breakfast.

HOTEL PRICE CHART	
Rates are per room based on double occupancy.	
$	Under $12
$$	$12-$25
$$$	$26-$40
$$$$	$40-$80
$$$$$	Over $80

General Hotel Options

$-$$ **Chau au Europa**, 76 Nguyen Chi Thanh, ☎ 063/822870, europa@hcm.vnn.vn. This is a fairly basic, small hotel, but the rooms are clean and you can get breakfast for a few dollars extra.

$$-$$$$ **Hang Nga's Crazy House**, 2 Huynh Thuc Khang, ☎ 063/822070. This is the most bizarre hotel in Southeast Asia. The building looks like it is made from tree trunks, the rooms are filled with huge animals and have an Alice-Through-The-Looking-Glass quality. There are tours of

Dalat that include this place as a stop. If you stay here you have to vacate the premises during the day and take your valuables since there will be tour groups coming through.

$-$$ **Hoa Binh II**, 67 Truong Cong Dinh, ☎ 063/822787. This is the alternative to Hao Binh I (the backpacker haven). The hotel is styled like a French country inn. There is plenty of hot water and private facilities.

Where to Eat

There are small restaurants up most of the streets running out from the main market and square. The main square also has a number of somewhat overpriced but decent restaurants.

RESTAURANT PRICES	
$	Under $2
$$	$2-$5
$$$	$6-$10
$$$$	$11-$20
$$$$$	Over $20

$ **Art Café**, 70 Truong Cong Dinh (near the Hoa Binh I and II hotels), popular and cheap, with decent local food and Western-style basics. Most dishes cost about $2. Open late.

$-$$ **Long Hoa**, 3 Thang 2. Styled to be a French café with Vietnamese food. One of the few places to offer fresh yogurt – a food many Asians avoid since they often suffer from lactose intolerance.

$$ **Trung Dong**, 220 Phan Dinh Phung. Lots of seafood and great ambience.

Nightlife

For the view over Dalat and its environs, especially at night, try the **Skyview Café** at the Golf 3 Hotel. There is also a disco in the basement of the Golf 3.

Other than that there isn't much in the way of nightlife. This is a city in the middle of a farming area, after all.

Shopping

Dalat is at the center of the Vietnamese silk-worm-growing industry. It is also the center of a revived embroidery tradition that produces amazing works. Most of the Dalat tours include at least one embroidery center on the itinerary.

Tours & Travels

In order to go trekking you need official permission and the red tape can get messy. Better to go with one of the two specialist agencies (located almost across the street from one another):

Phat Tire Ventures, 73 Truong Cong Dinh, ☎ 063/829422, www.phattireventures.com.

Hardy Da Lat, 66 Phan Dinh Phung, ☎ 063/836840, hardydl@hcm.vnn.vn.

Figure $15-20 per person per day for trekking – that includes all activities, food, accommodations, and your guide. Bring your own sleeping bag if you plan to trek, or at least your own sleeping sheet if you plan to rent equipment. In addition to trekking these agencies arrange mountain biking, sailing, canoeing, rock climbing, and canyoning trips. Bring your own helmet if you plan to climb or bike.

Da Lat Travel Service, 3 Thang 2, ☎ 063/822125, can help with air and other arrangements.

What to See & Do

The city curves around the western side of man-made Lake Xuan Huong. A walk around the lake is a pleasant excursion, and takes you to a botanical and rose garden that is beautiful when the flowers are in bloom.

> **Note:** Dalat is a university town so expect to be approached by students wanting to practice their English or ask you to help them with a survey. Please try and help them out. Dalat is also a major honeymoon destination for Vietnamese couples.

Although the hill country was bombed with some regularity, Dalat itself was not hit. You can still see largely unscathed (but not well maintained) French Colonial buildings snuggled up to by ugly communist-built concrete block buildings.

Make sure you go to the **Cho Da Lat market**. It's centrally located in a concrete multi-level building. You'll get a real appreciation for the variety of food that is grown in the area. There are a few craft shops in the area.

The train station, **Ga Da Lat (Gare Dalat)**, was built in the late 1930s and is typical of the period. Trains run on-demand to the nearby village of Trai Mat where you can see the **Linh Phuoc Pagoda**, right, and enjoy the pastoral scenes on the short trip.

There are several nearby pagodas that are worth a visit, and this is where your guided taxi or Honda Om trip really pays off. You can visit the **Linh Phong Pagoda** and the **Thien Vuong Pagoda** (with its wooden pillars and huge Buddha statue).

Another stop on your tour could be one or two of **Emperor Bao Dai's palaces**. Dinh I and III are the most interesting, giving glimpses into the royal Vietnamese lifestyle in the first half of the 20th century. **Dinh I** was the more day-to-day palace, and **Dinh III** was the summer palace. The gardens at Dinh III are lovely. Another palace to visit on your tour is **Dinh II**.

To the west of Dinh II are two enduring monuments to the French Colonial era – the **Palace Hotel** (at the Sofitel) and the **Cathedral**. Both are worth a look around.

Many tours stop at **Hang Nga's Crazy House** – it is certainly worth a quick tour. See page 160.

Day-Trips from Dalat

The waterfalls are south of Dalat and are certainly worth a trip. The two main ones are **Datanla Falls** and **Prenn Waterfall**. The $10-$20 Honda Om/Taxi tours will include these sights. The Prenn Waterfall is by far the more impressive, but the steep hike up to the Datanla Falls is exhilarating and the surrounding forest is impressive.

Useful Information

Airlines

All travel companies should be able to handle flight confirmations and reservations for you.

The main airline contact is: **Vietnam Airlines**, 40 Ho Tung Mau, ☎ 063/822895.

Embassies & Consulates

The closest facilities are in HCMC, a four- or five-hour bus trip or a one-hour flight away.

Golf/Tennis

There is an 18-hole golf course at the **Da Lat Palace Golf Club,** ☎ 063/821201. Bring your own clubs. As for tennis, you may be able to pay a fee to use the courts if you aren't a guest. Bring your own racket and tennis balls.

Internet/Communications

You can go to most post offices and make international calls at a steep price. Better is to buy a calling card and go to one of the many calling centers popping up all over.

Many hotels let guests use high-speed Internet for free. There are also dozens of Internet cafés now, and the cost for high-speed is about $3 per hour.

Medical Facilities

It is best to try to get to Hanoi, HCMC, or Thailand if you need serious care. Pharmacies will dispense almost anything (such as antibiotics) without a prescription. Make sure you know what you are taking and that it is not expired.

■ Ho Chi Minh City (HCMC/Saigon)

History

 I find HCMC more to my liking than Hanoi. The people are more focused and less aggressive – remnants of a less distant non-socialist past perhaps. There are more trees and wider streets. At the same time there is probably more to see in Hanoi than HCMC.

Located at the top of the Mekong Delta, HCMC is still a capitalistic paradise, despite 30 years of communist rule. When the govenment relaxed its restrictions on small business a few years ago, the economy took off. HCMC was the biggest beneficiary, having never fully given up on capitalism after the fall of Saigon in 1975.

The city is much more modernized and glittery than Hanoi. There are high rises, international standard hotels, quality restaurants, and elegant shopping.

Little is known about the early history of HCMC. In the first to fifth centuries the area of present day HCMC was under Funan Empire control (like Angkor in Cambodia). The main population of this sleepy backwater was Khmer fisherman. As Angkor rose, this area benefited as the starting point for shipping and receiving goods into the Angkorian Empire.

During the 17th and 18th centuries the northern Viets entered the area, followed by the Nguyen dynasty in Hué in the early 19th century. This is when the city was first known as Saigon.

During a period of rebellion (Tay Son brothers) in 1772, members of the Nguyen dynasty fled south from Hanoi, building the Gia Dinh Citadel. The leader, Nguyen Anh, returned north, this time to Hué, and renamed himself Emperor Gia Long.

The Tay Son brothers' rebellion provided the French their first chance to enter Vietnam; they did so by assisting Gia Long in putting down the rebellion. It took seven decades, but the French finally gained control over the southern part of Vietnam and established a trading post in Saigon. In 1861 they seized control of Saigon and in 1862 named Saigon the capital of French Cochinchina.

The French set about busily remaking the city in the image of Paris – wide avenues, villas, a cathedral, tree-lined boulevards, an opera house, and much more. They also started creating an infrastructure of railroads and roads.

The French rule, often quite harsh, extended to the entire country. Interrupted by World War II, the French lost control of the north but retained control in the south. They gradually eased out of the country and the Americans eased in. The end of colonialism came with the fall of Saigon in April 1975.

Since the fall of Saigon, the renamed city has been treated with less than highest favor by the powers in Hanoi. Nonetheless, the effects of capitalism are far more evident here, and the benefits of economic liberalization (almost 20 years ago) are more far-reaching than in the north.

Getting There & Away

By Air

Flying in to HCMC is easy, although not that cheap. If you arrive in Hanoi and want to fly the entire way (or vice versa) the trip on Vietnam Airlines is going to cost over $200 each way, unless you catch a special deal. You can also fly in from Dalat, Nha Trang, Hoi An/Danang, Hué, and other parts of the country. The airport, **Tan Son Nhat**, is about seven km/four miles from the center of HCMC. It takes 20-30 minutes in a taxi or hired car, and both cost about $10. There are also buses and motorbikes (about $2 for the trip).

The airport is quite well equipped. You can find "left luggage" services, plenty of ATMs and money changing facilities, a decent array of duty-free shops, and a Saigon tourist desk. Make sure to buy a city map at the tourist desk or in SASCO books nearby. If you want to reserve a hotel, the tourist desk can help with that, too

By Train

Many people either start or end their journey in Vietnam with a trip by train. The train station is about three km/two miles northwest of town (for northern arrivals and departures). The best way to get soft sleeper or soft seat tickets is to go through your hotel or a tour operator. You will rarely get one by going to the train station yourself.

Since it's a bit of a trip to town and the traffic is awful, take a taxi ($4), even if you have to call for one (☎ 08/842-4242 or 811-1111).

By Bus

There are several terminals for bus arrivals, depending on the bus company and the city you are coming from or going to. Plan to take a motorbike, cyclo ride or taxi to your hotel ($3-$5).

By Boat

It is possible to come in by boat from points along the Mekong. Only the hydrofoil from Vung Tau arrives in the city proper – other arrivals are a few km north or south of the center. Again, call for a taxi (☎ 8111-1111) or hop a motorbike or cyclo (bike-propelled cart) for a few dollars.

Where to Stay

There are three main areas for hotels in HCMC. The Dong Khoi area is a bit more upmarket than the other two – Pham Ngu Lao and the region to the west of Pham Ngu Lao. The backpackers tend to flock to the latter areas; as a result, there are many use-

HOTEL PRICE CHART	
Rates are per room based on double occupancy.	
$	Under $12
$$	$12-$25
$$$	$26-$40
$$$$	$40-$80
$$$$$	Over $80

ful facilities such as used bookstores there. I usually stay in the Pham Ngu Lao area, in the Le Le Hotel. The staff are friendly, there is 24-hour security, and the rooms run the gamut from tiny to huge, with private facilities and satellite TV. If you come to town without a reservation, the Pham Ngu Lao area is probably your best bet for "walk-in" accommodations. Between the huge New World Hotel and the multitude of guesthouses down the Pham Ngu Lao alleys, you should be able to find a decent room any time of the year (except Chinese New Year).

Pre-Booked/Pre-Paid Hotel Options

You can always book the general hotels that follow using their websites, but I have found the rates through a site such as www.asia-hotels.com to be very competitive, especially for the higher-end choices.

$$$$ Amara Hotel Saigon, 323 Le Van Sy Street, Ho Chi Minh City. This is a four-star business-class hotel with 305 rooms, including suites and Executive accommodation on the Amara Royal Club floors. Rooms all have en suite bathrooms with bath and shower stalls, mini-bar, 24-hour room service, safes in the room, Internet, hairdryers, color TV with in-house movies and satellite.

Online booking rates are $59 per room.

$$$ Asian Hotel, 146-150 Dong Khoi Street, Ho Chi Minh City. The hotel is small and basic with a good location. It's less than five-minute walk to the Notre Dame Cathedral and Reunification Palace.

Pre-book/prepay Internet rate at press time: $35 with taxes and breakfast.

Vietnam

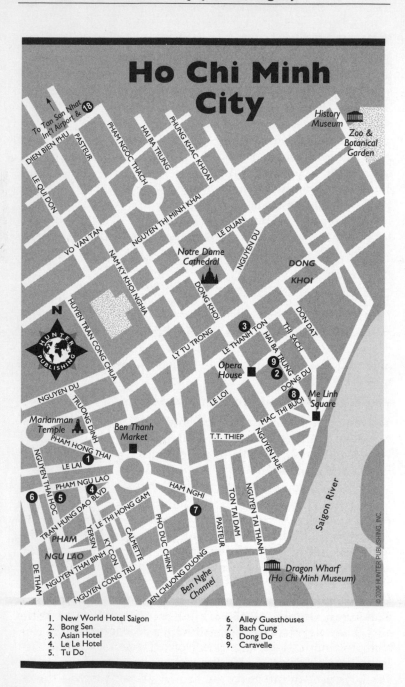

Ho Chi Minh City

To Tan Son Nhat Int'l Airport & 18

History Museum

Zoo & Botanical Garden

DIEN BIEN PHU
PASTEUR
PHAM NGOC THACH
HAI BA TRUNG
PHUNG KHAC KHOAN
LE QUI DON
VO VAN TAN
NGUYEN THI MINH KHAI
LE DUAN
NGUYEN DU
DONG KHOI
Notre Dame Cathedral
DONG KHOI
NAM KY KHOI NGHIA
HUYEN TRAN CONG CHUA
LY TU TRONG
LE THANH TON
TH SACH
DON DAT
Opera House
HAI BA TRUNG
DONG DU
Me Linh Square
NGUYEN DU
TRUONG DINH
LE LOI
MAC THI BUOI
Marianman Temple
PHAM HONG THAI
Ben Thanh Market
T.T. THIEP
NGUYEN HUE
LE LAI
NGUYEN THAI HOC
PHAM NGU LAO
TRAN HUNG DAO BLVD
LE THI HONG GAM
HAM NGHI
TON TAT DAM
NGUYEN TAI THANH
PASTEUR
Saigon River
PHAM NGU LAO
YERSIN
KY CON
CALMETTE
PHO DUC CHINH
BEN CHUONG DUONG
Ben Nghe Channel
Dragon Wharf (Ho Chi Minh Museum)
DE THAM
NGUYEN THAI BINH
NGUYEN CONG TRU

N

1. New World Hotel Saigon
2. Bong Sen
3. Asian Hotel
4. Le Le Hotel
5. Tu Do
6. Alley Guesthouses
7. Bach Cung
8. Dong Do
9. Caravelle

© 2006 HUNTER PUBLISHING, INC.

$$$$ **First Hotel**, 18 Hoang Viet Street, Ho Chi Minh City. The hotel has 108 well-equipped modern rooms and suites plus extensive sports, health/fitness and business facilities, all set against a traditional Vietnamese backdrop. Strategically located only 1.5 km/one mile from Tan Son Nhat International and domestic airports, six km/3.6 miles from the city centre, four km/2.4 miles from the Saigon Railway Station and on the way to Cu Chi Tunnels and the Mekong Delta. Ho Chi Minh City Exhibition and Convention Center are within walking distance. Rooms are furnished in traditional Vietnamese rattan style, with a full range of modern amenities including individually-controlled air conditioning, cable TV, IDD phones, en suite bath and mini-bar.

Pre-book/pre-pay Internet rates at press time: $46-$52, including breakfast and taxes.

General Hotel Options
❖ Pham Ngu Lao Area

$$ **Le Le Hotel**, 171 Pham Ngu Lao, lelehotel@hcm.fpt.vn, ☎ 08/8368686. This hotel is my favorite for price, service, and convenience. It is a "mini-hotel" with 24 rooms. The rooms range from miniscule (about $10) to palatial (with a balcony and sitting area). There is a security guard on duty at all times, as well as desk staff. The staff is unfailingly pleasant and English-speaking. They can help arrange tours to the Mekong Delta and around Vietnam. Rooms include breakfast. All rooms have private facilities and satellite TV.

$$$$ **New World**, 76 Le Lai, www.newworldvietnam.com, ☎ 08/8228888. This is a huge hotel, with over 500 very nicely appointed rooms, and facilities that include a swimming pool and fitness club.

$$$ **Tu Do**, 267-269 Pham Ngu Lao, ☎ 08/8367345. This is another mini-hotel with 45 rooms. A bit larger and more luxurious than the Le Le Hotel just down the street. Also includes breakfast and satellite TV, and some rooms have bathtubs – a feature not often found in Vietnam.

$ **Alley Guesthouses**. There are several alleys running perpendicular to Pham Ngu Lao. These are the sites for numerous small, very inexpensive guesthouses. Double rooms can be had for well under $10 per night, and dorm accommodations are available for a few dollars per person.

Vietnam

❖ Dong Khoi Area

The hotels here are definitely pricier than in Pham Ngu Lao, but there are still decent places for under $20 double. It's in this area that you'll find converted French houses and luxury hotels (Sofitel, Caravelle, Continental, Grand, Sheraton, and Renaissance Riverside), with lots of mid-range hotels, too. It's definitely not a backpacker enclave. The restaurant selection is varied and excellent.

$$ **Bach Cung**, 170-172 Nguyen Thai Binh, ☎ 08/8212777. The façade looks like a mixture of a wedding cake and a castle, but the rooms are excellent value for this part of HCMC. All rooms have full facilities and satellite TV.

$$$ **Dong Do**, 35 Mac Thi Buoi, donghotel@hcm.vnn.vn, ☎ 08/8273637. A mini-hotel with full facilities and a restaurant.

$$$$ **Bong Sen**, 117-123 Dong Khoi, bongsen@hcm.vnn.vn, ☎ 08/8291516. Right in the heart of Dong Khoi. Great location, excellent facilities. There is a second hotel (**Bong Sen II**) around the corner if this one is full.

$$$$$ **Caravelle**, 19 Lam Son Square, ☎ 08/8234999. The place to stay if money is not a concern! A luxury hotel with suites and rooms, too many amenities to list, and fabulous views.

Where to Eat

HCMC is a food-lover's paradise. There are restaurants of every imaginable style and price range. The backpackers' area is the best place for inexpensive Asian and Western food, especially if your taste runs to burgers and pizza. Most of the international-caliber hotels have buffets and lunch and dinner and these are quite reasonably priced.

Dong Khoi Area

$$-$$$ **Chu**, 158 Dong Khoi, serves American-style food and Asian dishes.

$$-$$$ **Manhattan's**, 94 Hai Ba Trung (Saigon Square), serves the best burgers in HCMC, as well as chicken and pizza dishes.

$$$ **Amigo**, 55 Nguyen Hué, a place for grilled steaks and seafood.

$$-$$$ **Gardenstadt**, 34 Dong Khoi, a German restaurant with imported food and beer.

$$ **Vietnam House**, 93-95 Dong Khoi, with very traditional Vietnamese food in a Colonial building.

RESTAURANT PRICES	
$	Under $2
$$	$2-$5
$$$	$6-$10
$$$$	$11-$20
$$$$$	Over $20

Vietnam

Pham Ngu Lao (the backpacker area)

$-$$ **Asian Kitchen**, 185/22 Pham Ngu Lao, with Vietnamese, Japanese, and vegetarian choices at good prices.

$$ **Bodhi Tree**, 175/4 Pham Ngu Lao (a personal favorite), is a vegetarian restaurant with a pleasant atmosphere.

> **Café culture:** Cafés abound and are occupied from early morning to late at night with coffee-sipping, pastry-eating locals and tourists. You will think you're in Paris.

Nightlife

If its nightlife you're after, you've finally come to the right part of Vietnam!

In addition to hanging out at the numerous cafés, check out the larger hotels. Many have rooftop bars, basement discos, and live entertainment of surprisingly good quality.

Check out some of the bia hoi bars for a taste of local draft beer served over ice.

Shopping

There are bookstores by the dozen, and several high-end shopping centers. There are only a few craft shops, and you are better off buying your souvenirs in Hanoi.

There are several public markets worth a walk-through. Check out **Be Thanh Market** (junction of Tran Hung Dao, Le Loi, And Ham Nghi), or **Thai Binh Market** on the west end of Pham Ngu Lao.

Tours & Travels

There are hundreds of tour and travel specialists in Saigon/HCMC. The state-run operations are OK, but pricey. They are:

Saigontourist, 49 Le Thanh Ton, ☎ 829-8914, and **Vietnamtourism**, Room 101, Mondial Centre, 203 Dong Khoi, ☎ 824-2000.

The backpacker havens along Pham Ngu Lao are good choices for less partisan information. Any hotel should also be able to help you.

Other choices include:

Ann Tours, 58 Ton That Tung ☎ 833-2564, anntours@yahoo.com.

Diethelm Travel, International Business Centre, 1a Me Linh Square, ☎ 829-4932, dtvlsgn@hcm.vnn.vn.

Getting Around

The best way to see HCMC is to walk, but the best way to get from one place to another is by cyclo or Honda Om.

There are cyclo thieves all over HCMC. They ride in pairs. One drives, the other snatches your jewelry, purse, wallet, daypack, or luggage. Watch your stuff.

Riding a bicycle is possible, but not really practical. You can rent a scooter or motorbike for $10-$15 per day. Just remember there are few rules of the road and even those are rarely followed.

Tip: When you start to cross the street, keep moving steadily and slowly, no matter what the traffic does. Don't freeze, dart or dash.

The omnipresent cyclos (bike-propelled carts) and Honda Oms (left) are the main transports in this crowded, maddening city. Figure on about $1-$2 per hour for a cyclo ride; point-to-point fares need to be negotiated. Honda Oms cost a bit more per ride. Taxis are pretty common and can be found with metered services.

Buses are not very reliable or prevalent.

Cars, Scooters & Cyclos

You can rent a car or scooter and self-drive, but I don't recommend it. If you are determined to do so, try your hotel, and expect to pay $10-$15 per day for a motorbike and $30 or more per day for a car.

What to See & Do

Sights tend to be clustered in a few places, and you'll need motorized transport to travel between these clusters. Many of the French Colonial era sights and museums are along Dong Khoi and Le Duan. The old French Quarter is in District One, along the river.

The Dong Khoi Area

Dong Khoi starts at Notre Dame Cathedral and runs essentially southeast to the Mekong River. Along this road you'll find souvenir shops and designer boutiques, restaurants and hotels, and Colonial French buildings.

❧ The Cathedral

Notre Dame Cathedral is a red-brick building with twin spires. The inside is not much to look at. Right next door is Diamond Plaza for upscale shopping.

❖ The Old General Post Office

Now called the Reunification Palace, this is a yellow-stucco building that makes a pleasant picture against a blue sky. The building is southwest of the Cathedral, in Cong Van Hoa Park. Take a look inside to see the nave-styled interior and map-murals.

❖ Lam Son Square

As you continue toward the river on Dong Khoi you will come to Lam Son Square and the Hotel Continental. This is the heart of the former French Quarter and still a desirable area to live in today. The **Municipal Theatre** is on the east side of the square, looking much as it did 100 years ago.

Continuing on to the riverbank you'll pass souvenir shops and restored villas, and a few good places to eat.

The Nguyen Hué Area

At one time this elegant tree-lined avenue was known as the Champs Elysée of the East. At the northern end of the street is the impressive **Hotel de Ville** with its yellow and white striped façade and Greek columns.

❖ The Ho Chi Minh City Museum

This museum is housed in the former Gia Long Palace. It lies a block to the west of the Hotel de Ville at 65 Ly Tu Trong, and is almost 120 years old. It was the residence of the Governor of Cochinchina. The museum is open daily from 8 to 4, and there is a small admission fee. Many of the exhibits focus on the Vietnam-American War and the Vietnamese struggle against the French overlords.

Along the River

At the end of Dong Khoi is the Ben Nghe Canal where the Colonials used to promenade in the evenings. This is also the location of the **Ho Chi Minh Museum** (not the City Museum), at 1 Nguyen Tat Thanh. It's not one of the better museums – I'd give it a miss. The quay here is where Uncle Ho left in 1911 to go to Europe.

Ben Thanh Market Area

This is the busiest, if not the largest, market in HCMC. You can see bizarre sights and pick up interesting souvenirs.

If you walk down Pho Duc Chinh you will find HCMC's **Fine Art Museum** in a Colonial mansion. This is the place to see many pieces from the first millennium. You can also buy more recent artworks if you wish. Across the street **Le Cong Kieu** is the antique shopper's dream.

Le Duan Boulevard to the Botanical Gardens

On the other side of Notre Dame Cathedral is Le Duan Boulevard. This street crosses the top of Dong Khoi and runs between the Presidential Palace and the Gardens. It is also the site of the former American Embassy, best remembered with helicopters hovering overhead and people fighting to get off the roof and flee the approaching North Vietnamese army on April 30, 1975.

❖ The Botanical Gardens & Zoo

This area is almost certainly closed due to bird flu. If not, don't go there unless the bird flu cases have ended.

❖ The History Museum

This museum is adjacent to the zoo and gardens, and may not be accessible if the zoo and gardens are still shut down. If you can get in, the museum is open every day and there is a small admission fee. It is worthwhile since it has a comprehensive collection of artifacts spanning two millennia.

The Reunification Palace & Surrounding Area

Heading northwest from the Cathedral, walk about five minutes to the **Palace** next to Cong Vien Van Hoa Park. It is open every day and costs about $2 to enter. As you enter the Palace you may think you've entered a 1960s and '70s time capsule. The last President of South Vietnam actually lived here – this is his stuff.

The **War Remnants Museum** is just north of the park. It is a very popular attraction with its exhibits showing the horrors of modern warfare. It is open every day and there is a small admission charge.

North of Dien Bien Phu Area

This area has a variety of temples and pagodas that are worth a visit. The best choice is to hire a Honda Om for a few hours to make the trip. You can include a trip to Cholon, the Chinese Quarter, while you're there.

Vietnam

Cholon is a shopper's dream, with stalls and markets selling junk, kitsch, souvenirs, and some good quality items. There are also dozens of temples and pagodas.

Day-Trips from Ho Chi Minh City

The biggest nearby attraction is the **Cu Chi Tunnels**. These tunnels were used by the Viet Cong as safe havens in the South. They are fully equipped for long-term living and incredibly claustrophobic, so beware. The best way to go is on a tour; make sure the price includes the $5 admission charge.

Useful Information

Airlines

 Any local tour and travel agent can help with flight arrangements and confirmations. You can reach the main airlines serving HCMC as follows:

Air France, 130 Dong Khoi, ☎ 829-0981.

Japan Airlines, 17th floor, SunWah Tower, 115 Nguyen Hué, ☎ 821-9098.

Lao Aviation, 181 Hai Ba Trung, ☎ 822-6990.

Siem Reap Airways, 132-134 Dong Khoi, ☎ 823-9288.

Thai Airways, 65 Nguyen Du, ☎ 829-2809.

United Airlines, 7th floor, Jardine House, 58 Dong Khoi, ☎ 823-4755.

Vietnam Airlines, 116 Nguyen Hué, ☎ 829-2118.

Embassies/Consulates

Embassies are in Hanoi; consulates are in HCMC, as follows.

Australia, Lamdmark Building, 5b Ton Duc Thanh, ☎ 829-6035.

Cambodia, 41 Phung Khac Khoan, ☎ 829-2751.

Canada, 235 Dong Khoi, ☎ 824-5025.

Laos, 93 Pasteur, ☎ 829-7667.

United Kingdom, 25 Le Duan, ☎ 823-2604

United States, 4 Le Duan, ☎ 822-9433.

Above: Home, sweet home along the Mekong, southern Laos
Below: Mekong gas station for boats and scooters

Above: Temple in Southern Laos
Below: Falls on Don Det in the 4,000 Islands

Above: Privy in Southern Laos
Below: Homes on Don Khong Island, Laos

Above: Streets newly paved by the French, Luang Prabang, Laos

Below: Typical old-style dirt roads and open gutter, Luang Prabang

Above: Monks at a Don Khong wat or temple, Laos
Below: Luang Prabang night market along the Mekong River

Above: Typical Don Khong Island guesthouse (great prices!)

Below: The only border crossing from southern Laos to Cambodia

Above: Steps to the beach at the Laos-Cambodia border

Below: Water's edge, Laos-Cambodia border

Above: Typical wooden temple, Don Khong Island

Internet/Communications

Internet cafés are everywhere, and your hotel probably has free Internet service for guests. Costs are very low – perhaps $1-$2 per hour for high-speed access.

Telephone calls can be made from the main post offices. Ask at your hotel for better deals.

Medical Facilities

There are reasonably good quality medical services available. If all you need is an antibiotic for a sinus infection, go to a pharmacy and order what you need. Just make sure the medication is not damaged or expired, and look online for information about doses and side-effects.

Check out the **International SOS Clinic**, 65 Nguyuen Du, ☎ 829-8484, if you need assistance.

Vietnam

■ The Mekong Delta

History

 This is Vietnam's breadbasket. It is possible to grow two or even three crops of wet rice each year. The fertile soils support orchards, vegetable farms, coconut groves, and sugar cane. The Delta rises from the nine tributaries of the Mekong River that form it. This area grows over one-third of Vietnam's food on less than one-tenth of its land.

The highlights of the Delta are the timeless scenes of river life – markets, villages, farms, and fishing.

Getting There & Away

 The quickest way to get to or from the Delta is by bus or hydrofoil from HCMC. The most pleasant is by slow boat from HCMC with a switch to a power-boat to navigate the narrow canals and tributaries, or ride by bus to the north end of the Delta and then switch to the powerboat.

There is no airport in the area, but that may be changing.

HCMC tour agencies are the easiest way to arrange a trip through the Delta, lasting one day to one week or longer.

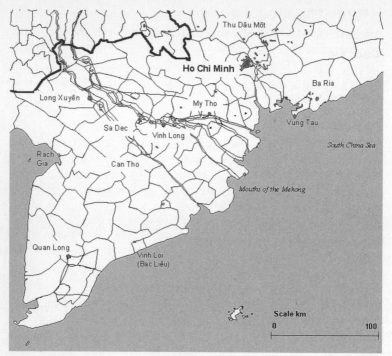

The Mekong Delta

If you go by bicycle you are in for a wonderful trip once you are clear of HCMC and its environs. You can even put your bicycle on some of the local boats – you'll have to to get across a few of the tributaries.

Where to Stay

 If you come on a tour from HCMC your hotels will be included, as will your meals in most cases. If you are on your own, here are a few options:

My Tho

$-$$ **Rang Dong**, Thang 4, ☎ 073/874400.

$$-$$$ **Chuong Duong**, by the Post Office on Thang 4, ☎ 073/870875.

Ben Tre

$$$ **Hung Vuong Hotel**, on the river, ☎ 075/822408.

Vinh Long

$$$ **Cuu Long "B"**, Along 1 Thang 5, ☎ 070/823656.

Can Tho

$$ **Can Tho Guesthouse**, 41 Chau Van Liem, ☎ 071/811772.

$$$$ **Golf**, 2 Hai Ba Trung, ☎ 071/8122210, golfcanthohtl@ hcm.vnn.vn.

$$$-$$$$ **Quoc Te**, 12 Hai Ba Trung, ☎ 071/822080.

There are also some pricier pre-book options at www.asia-hotels.com.

Where to Eat

My Tho

The majority of the restaurants are at the north end of Tet Mau Than. None stands out from the others.

Ben Tre

Try the hotel restaurants at **Hung Vuong** or **Dong Khoi**.

Vinh Long

Most of the restaurants are along the river. You might want to avoid the Phuong Thuy – it sits out over the river but the food and service are only so-so.

Can Tho

There are many more choices in this, the largest of the Delta's cities.

$$ **Hoang Cung Restaurant**, 55 Phan Dinh Phung. Reasonably priced Vietnamese and Western food.

$ **Mekong Restaurant**, 38 Hai Ba Trung. Cheap Vietnamese and Chinese food. Open 24 hours.

$$$ **Spices**, Victoria Can Tho Hotel. A bit out of the way, but the elegant atmosphere and food can be worth the trip.

Nightlife

There are a few 24-hour restaurants and some bars, but generally speaking they roll up the sidewalks and tributaries at about 10 pm.

Shopping

The main highlight in the Delta is the floating markets. The stationary markets, especially in Can Tho, are good for souvenirs, but the floating markets are much more interesting and fun. There are three floating markets in the Can Tho area. They are best reached by boat, but some can be reached from the road.

One of the crafts that permeates the Delta is basket weaving, so most tours will stop at least once.

Tours & Travels

The **Can Tho Tourist Travel Centre** at 20 Hai Ba Trung is your best bet for arrangements and assistance. They can be reached at ☎ 71/821852 or canthotourist@hcm.vnn.vn.

Getting Around

The best, if not the only, ways to get around are boat and bicycle. You will miss a lot in a bus, and the area is much too large to cover on foot.

Most of your travel will be by motorboat. You'll likely dock across from your hotel and re-board the boat to continue your journey.

There are local buses if you leave the boat and want to travel by other means.

Hiking, Cycling & Walking

The Delta is a bicycler's haven. It's flat and not too heavily traveled. Many hotels and street-side kiosks will rent bikes for $5-$10 per day.

Cars, Scooters & Cyclos

You can rent cars for about $25-$30 per day. Ask at your hotel. Vehicles are not well-maintained and your fellow drivers are nuts.

Scooter drivers are glad to offer you a lift for a few dollars.

What to See & Do

The two places I suggest spending time (other than actually on your bike or in a boat) are Ben Tre and Can Tho.

Ben Tre

The town is completely surrounded by water. It is an island known for its coconut groves and fruit orchards, and also as the site of one of the worst bombings in the War during the Tet offensive of 1968. This is the town a US military spokesman said we would "have to destroy in order to save it" since it was infiltrated by the Viet Cong.

There is a town market on the north bank, and hundreds of boats on the south bank. This is one of the best areas to explore on a bicycle or even on foot. You can also try the local rice wine at the factory just west of the bridge.

Can Tho

Can Tho is a large city with about 500,000 people. It has canals, floating markets, land-based markets, good restaurants, and rice paddies everywhere you look.

The main reason people come here is to take boat trips into the surrounding Delta and explore towns and markets.
Still, there are a few things in Can Tho to occupy a day or so. Check out the **Ho Chi Minh Museum** and the **Can Tho Museum**; each has its own charms.

The market along the waterfront is also interesting in its variety and for its people-watching. You can stop by the **Ong Pagoda** (late 19th century) and take a walk around its somewhat gaudy interior.

Useful Information

The majority of the resources are in Can Tho.

Airlines
All travel companies should be able to handle flight confirmations and reservations for you.

Vietnam Airlines, through Can Tho Tourist, 20 Hai Ba Trung.

Note that in small towns there are few English speakers in the regional offices. Rather than call, you will usually have to visit them in person or have a local do so for you.

Embassies & Consulates

None – you have to go to HCMC.

Internet/Communications

You can go to most post offices and make international calls at a steep price. Better is to buy a calling card and go to one of the many calling centers popping up all over.

Many hotels let guests use high-speed Internet for free. There are also dozens of Internet cafés now, and the cost for high-speed is about $3 per hour.

Medical Facilities

It is best to try to get to Hanoi, HCMC, or Thailand if you need serious care. Pharmacies will dispense almost anything (such as antibiotics) without a prescription. Make sure you know what you are taking and that it is not expired.

■ Vietnam Adventure Travel

Mekong Delta

The rice belt in the south is easily accessed from HCMC. From Vinh Long, travel by boat, sampan, foot around the Delta, through floating markets and dry land markets. Experience a peasant lifestyle that's laid back and way off the beaten path. Include the city of Can Tho, and excursion to a Khmer village.

Mekong Delta by Bike

 This is an easy seven-day bike trip including the bus trip to and from HCMC. Make sure the company that provides the bikes is reputable and the bikes are in good condition. Bring your own helmet if your plans include biking, and don't forget a few tools and basic patch kit and spares!

Most tours start with a bus/mini-van trip to My Tho. From here you will use a combination of bike riding and ferries/boats to get around. Most accommodations will be basic, but should include a single bed rather than mats on the floor. A possible itinerary is:

Day 1: My Tho to Ben Tre. Ferry to cross the Mekong, then a 12-km/7.5-mile ride to Ben Tre.

Day 2: Ben Tre to Cai Mon to Binh Hoa Phuoc. Cross the Mekong by ferry. A 20-km/12.5-mile bike ride to Cai Mon. Boat ride to Binh Hoa Phuoc Island. Most people stay in a local villager's home.

Day 3: Ride around Binh Hoa Phuoc – 20-30 km/12.5-20 miles. Most people stay in a local villager's home.

Day 4: Binh Hoa Phuoc to Vinh Long to Can Tho. Travel by boat to Vinh Long. Ride around the town through the local markets and then to Ba Cang. From here you can take a boat to a local Khmer village, and then ride to Can Tho.

Day 5: Can Tho. Take a boat to the local floating markets. Many of these people almost never set foot on land! Ride back to Can Tho (about 18-20 km/11-12.5 miles).

Red River Delta

The rice belt in the north – easy access from Hanoi. Hanoi to Ninh Binh by bus, bike ride (12 km or 7.5 miles) to boat landing, boat to Tam Coc, then bus to Hanoi.

Sa Pa (Sapa) Trekking

Always book the small (four-eight people max) tours! Otherwise you'll be in a group of 12-16 or more and spend lots of time fending off hawkers and visiting so-called "factories and craft shops."

Take a bus (or go with a group) from Hanoi to Lao Cai. Catch the night train to Sa Pa. Make sure you book a first-class/soft sleeper. A small group tour is really useful here. The next stop could be **Can Cau**, but you'll need 4WD to get there. If you can get there on a Saturday, so much the better – there's a weekly market you should visit. You can trek about six km/3.6 miles through the villages of **Phu La** and the **Flower Hmong** in Ta Chai, and then take a 4WD to **Lan Den Thang** village. Be prepared – the roads are rough to nearly non-existent, and the overnights are either in tents (on cots) or villagers' huts (with your sleeping bag and a woven mat on the floor). The opportunity to see a fast-disappearing way of rural life is more than worth the short periods of discomfort. If you come back in five years you may be too late.

There is another weekly fair – this one is on Sundays in **Bac Ha**. It's about an eight-km/five-mile trek through mountains, paddies and vegetable fields. Then you can return by either mini-bus or 4WD to Sa Pa to catch the night train back to Hanoi.

Another option is to base yourself in Sa Pa, and either have a guide arranged by an agent in Hanoi or arrange one in Sa Pa, and spend several days trekking out and back to various hill tribe villages (Black Hmong, etc.) in the area, returning to your Sa Pa hotel each night. That's what we did – we trekked 10-15 km/six-10 miles each day, and our guide arranged to carry lunch or took us to a local villager's house for lunch, then back to our hotel and dinner in local restaurants. Pizza after a day of up and down hills was rather nice!

Other towns you can trek to or from (accessing them by mini-bus): **Hang Kia** (Red Hmong), **Xa Linh** (Black Hmong), **Cun Pheo**, **Mai Chau**, **Son La**, **Lai Chau**.

Mount Sapa

 You can climb Mount Sapa, usually done as a two-day, one-night trek. You need to be in excellent condition – you are hiking to an elevation of about 3,000 m (10,000 feet) from a starting elevation of about 1,700 m (one mile). If you have not pre-arranged this, most hotels in Sa Pa can handle the tour for you. Going solo is not a good idea.

The trip is strenuous but worth every grueling step! The scenery is beyond spectacular – almost as good as the Alps or Rockies.

ALTITUDE SICKNESS

About one in 10 people experience serious altitude sickness at 3,000 m, and many people experience mild symptoms (headache, trouble sleeping, loss of appetite) at that elevation. The local people really don't know the symptoms or the treatment. For your information, the serious symptoms of altitude sickness include shortness of breath, dizziness, disorientation, a wet cough, pulmonary edema and heart problems. Be careful. The only treatments are to return immediately to an altitude where the symptoms ease, or take oxygen. Your guides live at altitude, so they rarely have problems. Even if you live at altitude, you have probably been elsewhere in Asia and in Hanoi (and other low-elevation locations) for several days to several weeks or longer. Altitude is something you can usually acclimatize to, but it takes a few days (figure a day or two in Sa Pa before you head higher).

Here are some ideas for tours that emphasize walking and biking, with ground or air transportation between the main destinations. Of course, you can always reverse the order. And this may be a good idea depending on the time of year and your flight schedule.

Suggested Walking Itineraries

Days 1-4: Hanoi and Ha Long Bay (extension to Sa Pa – add three days). Explore the tree-lined boulevards and rest up from jet lag. Hanoi is a trove of scattered remnants of French Colonial architecture – perfect for a day's wanderings. Walk around Ho An Kiem Lake, and stop for pastries or ice cream along the way. Detour to the side streets on the west and north sides of the lake and visit the artisans, galleries, and craft shops. Make sure you visit Ho Chi Minh's mausoleum and the 11th-century Temple of Literature. There is also a great art museum across from the north end of the Temple of Literature – ask the guard to point it out. Allow a full day and night (two days is better) to sail across Ha Long Bay to Cat Ba Island. This will give you time to kayak, swim, and relax in a Vietnamese-style resort. The karst caves and formations in the bay are spectacular, especially at sunrise/set. You can even spend the night on a junk, swaying to the waves.

If you extend to Sa Pa, see the section on Sapa, page 127-28, for the logistics. You'll spend two nights on trains, so three to four days is a minimum time to allow.

Fly to Hué.

Days 5-6: Hué is one of the best parts of Vietnam, and ideally suited to explore on foot. You can take a taxi or trishaw to the main tomb areas and walk between several of the tomb complexes, then come back to Hué by boat, along the Perfume River. The Forbidden City is another full day of exploring, and well-worth every minute. Try to climb the main gate at sunset for a great photo opportunity.

You can extend your trip by going (by train or van) to the former DMZ area and walk part of the Ho Chi Minh Trail, visit the Vinh Moc tunnels, and climb Hamburger Hill.

Days 7-8: Travel by bus or train to Da Nang. Spend a few days at China Beach and exploring the Marble Mountain area. It's a fairly reasonable walk from Da Nang to the wonderful riverfront town of Hoi An, with its pastel Chinese shophouses and speedy, quality custom tailors. You can arrange a sail on the nearby South China Sea, or go kayaking or fishing. There are dozens of crafts shops and a great covered market for shopping.

Fly back to Hanoi, on to HCMC, or on to Cambodia.

Suggested Biking Itineraries

Days 1-2: Begin with a few days in HCMC (Saigon) to rest up from jet lag. See the HCMC section for ideas about what to see and do. Biking the old French Quarter can be a relaxing way to spend part of a day, stopping in a boulangerie for baguettes and cheese.

Days 3-4: HCMC to Da Lat. Fly from Saigon to Da Lat. Hire a bicycle (if you didn't bring one) and ride the narrow, winding roads through peaceful, fragrant pine forests and terraced farmland. If it's late fall/early winter, stop and smell the coffee beans drying on mats along the roadside. Park (and lock) your bike and spend a few hours strolling around Xuan Huong Lake and former Emperor Bao Dai's summer palace. There is supposed to be a nine-hole golf course on the grounds of the palace – let me know if it's any good. The course used to belong to the emperor. Da Lat has a wonderful climate and is often called the "City of Eternal Spring" – for good reason. Take some time to explore the many surviving buildings from the

French Colonial period. Spend a pleasant afternoon exploring the flower and produce market.

Day 5: Travel to Nha Trang. This will take several days by bicycle or most of a day by bus or mini-van. You can also fly with Vietnam Airlines.

Days 6-7: Nha Trang. There are lots of rides along the coast and inland from Nha Trang. You can ride past terraced fields and salt pans to the beautiful sandy beaches – a favorite R&R spot during the American-Vietnamese war years. Spend a day biking through the picturesque countryside, through banana plantations and rice paddies, to the historic city of Khanh Vinh.

Day 8: Travel by bus or mini-van to Da Nang/China Beach. This will take the better part of a day. You can also fly with Vietnam Airlines.

Days 9-11: Da Nang/Marble Mountain/Hoi An area. Lock your bicycle and take a morning to explore the ancient cave temples of Marble Mountain. The next day, bike to the UNESCO World Heritage Site of Hoi An, with its Vietnamese, Japanese and Chinese architectural styles. This will take most of the afternoon. Join the locals the next morning for a session of Tai Chi at sunrise on spectacular China Beach. Make sure to spend the afternoon at the Cham Sculpture Museum, home to the largest collection of Cham artifacts in the world. The Chinese shophouses are a riot of pastels. If you can take an extra day or two, make sure to get some silk and wool clothes custom made – you can always ship stuff home!

Day 12: Travel by bus or mini-van to Hué, or consider biking if you're up to an all-day ride (with more than a few hills en route).

Days 13-15: Hué and the Perfume River. This is one of the best cultural sites in all of Vietnam. The Forbidden City and tombs along the Perfume River are truly wonderful sites. These tombs are so peaceful and relatively uncrowded. It does get a bit expensive to visit them all. A bike is the perfect means of getting from Hué to and from the tombs.

Day 16: Take the night train or fly from Hué to Hanoi. If you've got a week to spare you can ride, but make sure you're in good shape – the ride will be rugged.

Vietnam

Days 17-19: See Colonial Hanoi. Walk or take a cyclo (bike-propelled cart) along tree-lined boulevards, viewing historic architecture and enjoying the capital's chaotic street life. Navigate the Old Quarter, which has contained Hanoi's pulsing markets for 1,000 years. Enjoy a guided visit of the city, from its French Colonial architecture to Ho Chi Minh's Mausoleum and Hanoi Hilton Prison. Enjoy a final evening of traditional culture at the Temple of Literature, founded in 1070 by Emperor Ly Thanh Tong as a school for the children of Vietnam's Imperial Mandarins.

See the Hanoi section for other ideas – chill out, explore, and get ready to move on to your next destination or head home.

Motorcycle Touring

 Vietnam is increasingly popular as a motorcycling destination. Many War veterans are returning as tourists, and a large number are doing so on motorcycles. If you have three weeks to spend you can easily see the highlights of the country from Hanoi to HCMC (or the reverse), with a bit of time in the central and northern highlands. The roads are generally good, but often narrow and winding, and drivers are rather reckless. Watch out for domestic animals crossing the road, and don't plow through the coffee drying on the shoulders. Bring your own helmet!

Laos

■ Introduction

The Country at a Glance

There are several main areas in Laos that are on most travelers' itineraries:

- ☐ Champasak/Pakse
- ☐ Luang Prabang and the hill tribes of the north
- ☐ The Plain of Jars
- ☐ The Boloven Plateau
- ☐ Vang Vieng and the Mekong River
- ☐ Vientiane
- ☐ The Mekong Islands

Champasak was a part of the Khmer Angkor empire between the 10th and 13th centuries. Champasak's heritage is best explored by river boat (both public ferries and private charters are available) down the

In this Chapter	
■ Introduction	189
■ Vientiane	204
■ Vang Vieng	216
■ Bokeo	219
■ Xiengkhuang	220
■ Savannakhet	222
■ Champasak	226
■ Pakse	231
■ Northern Laos - Luang Prabang	234

Mekong to sleepy Champasak town. From here, you can hire a three-wheeled tuk-tuk to nearby Wat Phu, the impressive hillside ruin of a temple complex that was once an outpost of Cambodia's Angkor civilization. You can then travel by boat or bus to Don Khong, a charming island of rural villages and Khon Pha Pheng, a series of impressive waterfalls just above the Cambodian border near Don Khong Island.

Luang Prabang has been declared a UNESCO World Heritage Site. It is one of the most amazing places in Laos. Attractions include dozens of historic Buddhist temples (wats), French-era houses and lots of opportunity for active travel.

You can hike up Phousi (a steep hill with wonderful views over the town), and visit the wats, many of which are 400-500

years old. Another impressive sight is the former Royal Palace – it's now a museum. This is where the last kings of Laos lived – and it's very art deco. Make sure to take a boat to the Pak Ou Caves. They contain about 3,000 wooden and other Buddha images.
The boats often stop at hill tribe villages along the way so you can buy handicrafts and sample the local liquor.

> **Tip:** Luang Prabang has plenty of hotels, ranging from rustic to fancy. These are often full during the peak tourist seasons of December and the Lao New Year in April so be sure to book early.

 **Muang Sing** is 360 km/22 miles northwest of Vientiane in Laos' far northwest corner, near the borders of Myanmar and China. Muang Sing is a good place to see some of the country's hill tribes. This area was once the largest opium market in the Golden Triangle (Laos, Burma, Thailand juncture). It still has a number of opium dens (but no matter what anyone tells you, opium is illegal in Laos). The area, especially in the markets in town, is a center of commerce for a large variety of ethnic groups. To get there, fly to Luang Nam Tha and then take a passenger truck (a type of local bus service).

The Plain of Jars, 160 km/10 miles northeast of Vientiane, is a vast green plateau named after the large, stone-like funeral urns found here. These jars date from the sixth century; their purpose is unknown. Local legend has it that they were used to ferment rice wine used during celebration of the overthrow of an Angkor ruler. The area was heavily bombed by the US Air Force during the Vietnam War, but many of the jars survived. One of the few buildings to make it through the bombings was the Xieng Khouang Pagoda. The new capital of this area, Phonsavan, has several small hotels for visitors (the old capital, Xieng Khouang, was destroyed in the War).

 Be aware there are a large number of unexploded bombs and other ordnance in the area. Always use a local guide if you travel outside the towns.

The highlight of Saravan Province is the **Bolovens Plateau**, a beautiful area of waterfalls and forests. It's 485 km/300 miles southeast of Vientiane. Because of its proximity to the Ho Chi Minh Trail (the North Vietnamese supply line running through Laos), the provincial capital, Saravan town, was almost completely flattened during the Vietnam-American War. Little of historic value remains.

Savannakhet is 280 km/175 miles southeast of Vientiane, just across the border from Thailand. It is the country's second-largest city and is the capital of Savannakhet Province. This is Laos' most populous region, a fertile, productive agricultural area. It's really not worth a special trip, but if you're in the area you might spend part of a day in the colonial-era Old Town.

Vang Vieng is an easy four-hour van ride (or six-hour bus ride) from Vientiane. The area is known for its limestone and karst formations (similar to those found in both Thailand and Vietnam). Vang Vieng lies 160 km/100 miles north of the capital, Vientiane. Tubing trips along the Nam Song River are one of the highlights of a stay in Vang Vieng.

 The current is very fast in places – make sure you have a life vest. Check river conditions locally before signing up for any trip.

Several spectacular caverns (some developed, some not) are within a few hours' walk from town. Vang Vieng also has a number of opium dens but visitors are advised to steer well clear of these. There is a zero-tolerance policy for any kind of drug use, and tourists have been framed before.

 CAUTION Although there have been occasional problems with buses and vans being held-up along the road in the vicinity of Vang Vieng, the problem seems to have died down. For the most part the target is locals, not tourists. On the other hand, tourists are the prime target of drug dealers and too many unsuspecting tourists have had drugs planted on them or their property, or have bought or used drugs and then been arrested. Most of the time all the authorities and locals want is cash, but a few people have ended up in a Laotian jail – not a pleasant place to be.

Vientiane is the capital of Laos. It is possibly the smallest, most laid-back national capital in the world. There are tree-lined avenues, decaying Colonial-era houses, and almost non-existent traffic. Rural tribes come in to shop and the all-day "Morning

Morning Market in Vientiane

Market" is the place to shop and see the tribespeople. Major points of interest include That Luang (the national symbol of Laos, built in 1566), Wat Sisaket, and Wat Haw Pra Keo. The National Museum (formerly known as the Revolutionary Museum) is stuffed with propaganda against the "running-dog" Western imperialists. Patuxai, Laos' concrete-and-rebar answer to France's Arc de Triomphe, stands at one end of town (rumor has it the gate was built with concrete stolen from an airport expansion project!).

One of the most enjoyable views in Vientiane is provided by nature – the sunset over the Mekong River. You may also be able to watch a performance of traditional Lao music and dance at one of the riverside *salas* (pavilions or halls for various activities).

A good time to visit Vientiane is in early November during the That Luang Festival, a week of candlelit processions, fireworks, and games. Also in late October or early November are the Awk Phansaa festival boat races, in which teams paddle traditional dragon-prow longboats on the Mekong.

You might also want to visit the Xieng Khuane Stone Garden (25 km/15 miles from Vientiane) for its unique collection of Hindu-Buddhist sculptures. You can hire a driver and car or a scooter and visit the Vientiane Plain and its 11th-century Khmer Buddhas at Vang Sang.

Currency: US$1 = 10,842 Lao Kip (LAK).

History

The Early Years

 The original inhabitants of Laos were Austroasiatic peoples, who lived by hunting and gathering before the advent of agriculture. They were skilled at river navigation using canoes, trading throughout the mountains, especially along the rivers. The most important river route was the Mekong because its many tributaries allowed traders to penetrate deep into the country, where they bought food and products such as cardamom.

A number of small kingdoms, based on wet rice cultivation and associated with the pottery and bronze culture of Ban Chiang, developed in the Middle Mekong Valley beginning in the first century AD. As a result, in the early years, no one kingdom had control over the Middle Mekong Valley, which is present-day Laos. These small kingdoms (or power centers) are often referred to as *mandalas*.

In the meantime, the Khmers set up an outpost at Xay Fong near present-day Vientiane, and the Champa expanded again in southern Laos, maintaining its presence on the banks of the Mekong until 1070.

Khun Cuang, a warlike ruler, probably reigned from 1128 to 1169. Under Khun Cuang, a single family ruled over a far-flung territory. At this time, Theravada Buddhism was subsumed by Mahayana Buddhism.

The Mongol Influence

The last major influence prior to the founding of the Lan Xang kingdom was from the Mongols, operating out of Yunnan province in China.

Obviously the early history of the region is convoluted. You can get more information from some of the material referenced in the *Recommended Reading* section at the end of the book.

The Lan Xang Kingdom – Modern Laos

During its history Laos has been a subject state to the Cham, Khmer, and Sukhothai empires. Each of these left imprints on the culture, food, art, and architecture.

The "modern" history of Laos begins in the 13th century, when the rulers of what is now Luang Prabang (Louangphrabang) controlled a large, indigenous kingdom. The rulers of this kingdom, the **Lan Xang**, actually controlled territory that included Laos, and areas far beyond its current borders, for about four centuries. It was not until the late 17th century that the Lan Xang internal power struggles caused the kingdom to split.

Prior to the founding of the Lan Xang kingdom there was a multi-ethnic state that existed in river valleys and among mountain tribal groups.

Fa Ngum was crowned king of Lan Xang at Vientiane in June 1354. Lan Xang extended from the border of China to Sambor and from the Vietnamese border to the western escarpment of the Khorat Plateau.

The Lan Xang kingdom was made up of Lao and Thai people and a number of hill tribes. It maintained its original (1354) borders for over 300 years and briefly reached farther across the northwest.

The Split of the Lan Xang Kingdom

In 1690 the Lan Xang ruler was involved in a series of power struggles. The result was the splitting of the Lan Xang kingdom into three smaller kingdoms: Luang Prabang, Vientiane, and Champasak.

The Siamese (Thai) captured Vientiane for the first time in 1778-79, making it subject to Siam. Vientiane was finally destroyed in 1827-28 following efforts by its ruler, Chao Anou, to retaliate against the Siamese.

The 19th Century & the Influence of the French

The Siamese continued to control much of present-day Laos until the arrival of the French in the second half of the 19th century. During this time there were many conflicts between the Siamese and the various Lao kings, resulting in the destruction of Vientiane and the flight of the king of Vientiane to Hué in Vietnam. The Siamese army actually pursued the fleeing king to Vietnam; this did not sit well with the Vietnamese.

In the late 19th century the French imposed a treaty on Laos, essentially allowing the Thais to handle administrative functions in Laos but refusing to acknowledge any form of Thai political or military control in the area.

The arrival of the French probably prevented the political disintegration of Laos. Major elements of the country's population were at risk of being absorbed by adjacent countries.

Laos was far down in the pecking order of French Indochina. The good jobs and training went to the Vietnamese; they were encouraged to migrate to Laos in large numbers to handle the administrative functions as mid-level civil servants and militia officers. Laos never got the railroads and other infrastructure France provided to Cambodia and Vietnam. This left the country ill-prepared for independence and difficult to defend when the Japanese came calling in the 1940s.

World War II

The French were able to keep relative peace in Laos until 1940, when the Japanese forced France to sign a treaty allowing Japan access to much of Indochina, although nominally leaving France in control. In 1945 the Japanese entered Laos and began imprisoning French officials and attempting to take control of the country. French rule was effectively over.

When French control collapsed, the Vietnamese immigrant population tried to derail the actions of the "Free Laos" (**Lao Issara**) government. Vietnam continued to try to dominate Laos throughout the post-independence era, as evidenced by the armed insurgency called the Pathet Lao.

After the War

After 1945, the authority of the Lao Issara provisional government was extremely limited outside Vientiane.

In January 1946 the Lao Issara again lost Xiangkhoang and the control of the Lao Issara government began to decline. The monarchy was briefly reestablished in 1946, but this also didn't last long.

In 1947 a constitution was developed and accepted, making Laos an independent state within the French Indochina Union. At the same time, the French and Vietnamese began a war that evolved into the American-Vietnamese War and led to the departure of France from Vietnam in 1953. This gave rise to conditions that allowed the Pathet Lao and their Vietnamese communist backers to grow and eventually take over the country.

During 1959 the battles escalated all along the Laos/North Vietnamese border. Both the Lao King and the viceroy died in 1959, further extending the chaos that was starting to take over in the country. Over the next few years the controlling entities seesawed wildly. Then the war in Vietnam escalated, and things went downhill fast.

Negotiations in Paris in the autumn of 1972 between the United States and North Vietnam made a cease-fire agreement possible in Laos. The two sides signed the peace agreement in Vientiane on February 21, 1973. The ceasefire went into effect the next day.

By the time the cease-fire began, US aircraft had dropped almost 2.1 million tons of bombs on Laos, approximately the total tonnage dropped by United States air forces during all of World War II. Most bombs were dropped on the Laotian part of the Ho Chi Minh Trail (in the vicinity of the Plain of Jars). It is amazing that so many of the Jars remain intact – they were often used as targets by US pilots to off-load unused bomb loads before returning to their bases in Thailand.

The Provisional Government of National Union (PGNU), Laos's third and final experiment with coalition government, was finally constituted on April 5, 1974. It, too, was short-lived.

In 1975, after the fall of Cambodia and South Vietnam, the **Pathet Lao** (supported by the now-communist country of Vietnam) came to power in Laos. On March 27, 1975, North Vietnamese-Pathet Lao forces launched a strong attack against Vang Pao's Hmong defenders. On August 23, 1975 the Pathet Lao completed its seizure of local power with the takeover of the Vientiane city administration by a revolutionary committee.

The **Lao People's Democratic Republic** (Lao PDR) was established by the National Congress of People's Representatives at their meeting in the auditorium of the former United States community school on December 1, 1975.

> **Note:** Even though Laos is a communist state, the royal family is still revered and respected. Please do not make negative comments about either the government or the royal family.

Under the Pathet Lao

Since the 1980s, Laos has become a more approachable country but the trappings of communism/socialism are everywhere. The improved relations between Laos' chief supporter

– Vietnam – and the rest of the world have helped, too. At the same time, Laos remains a Third-World country in many respects, dependent on other countries and non-Governmental Organizations (NGOs) for much of its technology, infrastructure, farm improvement programs, and the like.

> **Tip:** Although the presence of communism is everywhere in Laos, it is not domineering and oppressive as can sometimes be the case in northern Vietnam. Still, this is a communist country and the people know it. Trying to engage people in conversations about their government, their history, or world events calls for diplomacy and tact.

Climate

 Laos enjoys a tropical climate with two distinct seasons – the rainy season from the beginning of May to the end of September and the dry season from October through to April. The yearly average temperature is about 28°C/82°F, with a maximum of 38°C in April and May. In Vientiane, the low temperature of about 19°C/66°F occurs in January. In mountainous areas, however, temperatures can drop to 14-15°C/the high 50s°F during the winter months, and at night drop to freezing or a bit lower.

The average precipitation is highest in southern Laos, where the Annamite Mountains receive over 3,000 mm (10 feet) annually. In Vientiane rainfall is 1,500-2,000 mm (five to almost seven feet) annually, and in the northern provinces only 1,000-1,500 mm (three to five feet) annually.

Physical Adventures

 The following gives you an idea of some of activities you might want to try while you're in Laos. The *Country Websites* section, page 313, has links to tour companies and other sites that can help in your planning. Laos is a country that is changing rapidly, so new companies appear and familiar ones disappear with amazing speed and frequency. It is always a good idea to do an online keyword search right before you leave home and print out the information you find useful. Then remain flexible since new options may be available once you arrive.

Bird watching. Laos does not have many interesting large animals, but it does have a profusion of birds – in fact, it is one of the few countries where you may find an as-yet undiscovered species or two! If bird-watching is on your list it is worth bringing binoculars and your own book. Many birds use Laos as a migratory stopover.

Canoeing. There are a few companies operating tours along the Mekong, Xekong, Nam Ou, and other rivers. You may be able to rent just a boat from some of the tour companies, but it is better to go with at least a guide, if not on a tour.

Climbing. Climbing in Laos is a mixed bag. While there is good quality limestone (karst formations around Vang Vieng, for example), free access to crags is still an issue. Many climbers have managed to climb near Luang Prabang and in around Vang Vieng and Vientiane. There are tour companies that may be able to help with arrangements and permits. Many hotels can also help.

Elephant trekking is easily arranged in the Luang Prabang area. You may also be able to do it in the Plain of Jars area.

Fishing is possible in many rivers and streams or along the coast. Bring your own tackle and gear with you. Some hotels offer rods, reels, and the like on loan (or for rent) to guests.

Horseback riding can be arranged through some hotels but the animals are usually in poor condition and poorly treated.

Kataw is a traditional game that uses a small rattan (or plastic) woven ball about 12 cm (five inches) in diameter. This ball is kicked around by players who stand in a circle (the size of which is determined by the number of players) and the goal is to keep the ball airborne by kicking it, soccer-style, from one player to another.

Laos

Motorcycling. Travel specialists can help arrange these trips, or your hotel may be able to help. The terrain is rugged and the quality of the roads is poor. Make sure you or the trip-arranger has proper tools, helmets, and other maintenance and safety equipment.

Mountain biking can be a great way to see the country, but it is a good idea to have a guide if you are going truly off-road. You might want to bring your own bike, but if you use the tour arranger's equipment make sure you can determine that it is in good shape and bring your own repair kit and helmet. You should be able to rent bikes and arrange guides in Vientiane, Luang Prabang, Vang Vieng, and Champasak.

Spelunking or caving can be fun since there are numerous caves across Laos. It is a very good idea to bring your own caving gear and hire a guide. Bring lots of extra batteries, too – they are hard to find outside the main cities.

Swimming and tubing are possible in some rivers, especially around Vang Vieng. Be careful not to swallow the water, though!

 There are a number of water borne parasites in fresh water in Southeast Asia. Enter the water at your own risk.

Tennis courts can be found at some of the top-end hotels. Bring your own racquet since the local equipment is questionable at best.

Trekking is one of the best activities in Laos. There are many outfitters and tour providers, especially in the Luang Prabang area. A trip to see the traditional village life in the hill tribes is not to be missed. Check in each town for a local guide to the nearby hill tribe areas.

Walking is an excellent way to see the countryside and meet the people. Laos is one of the safest countries in the world. The Mekong area referred to as the 4,000 Islands is great for canoeing, kayaking, walking, and biking.

Whitewater rafting is possible on many rivers, especially around Vang Vieng.

Cultural Adventures

Much that is historically or culturally interesting in Laos was damaged during the many wars and power struggles in the 19th and 20th centuries. Still, the UNESCO World Heritage Sites of Luang Prabang and Champasak are not to be missed.

The wealth of temples and remnants of French Colonial buildings in Luang Prabang are highlights of a visit to Laos. The for-

mer **Royal Palace** is a living history museum offering insights into Lao history and culture in the first half of the 20th century.

The temple ruins in **Champasak**, above and left) are not nearly as impressive as those in Bagan or Angkor Wat, but are still worth a day or two of your time. They are similar to, but different from, other complexes in Southeast Asia, and far more peaceful and less crowded, too.

Getting There & Around

By Air

Lao Aviation is the primary carrier for internal flights and many flights to adjacent countries. The airline codeshares with Vietnam Airlines. Many Lao Aviation aircraft are not up to Western standards. Always check to see which airline is actually flying your flight. The Lao Aviation website is www.lao-aviation.com. You can book online as well as find schedule information.

> **Tip:** I've flown with Lao aviation a number of times and always found the level of safety and service to be quite high. The food isn't so great, though, and the seats are often dirty.

Lao Aviation's schedule is subject to revision without notice, so you are well advised to reconfirm your flight(s) the day before and a few hours before your scheduled departure time. An easy way to do this is on the following website: www.mekongexpress.com/laos/schedule.

Lao Aviation normally flies to the following internal airports, with more are being added each year: Hoeuixay, Luang Namtha, Luang Prabang, Oudomxai, Pakse, Samnuea, Savannakhet, Sayabouly, Vientiane, and Xiengkhoung.

Flights go from Vientiane to/from Luang Prabang and Savannakhet at least daily and to/from Pakse almost every day. There are flights to most other towns in Laos, but they are infrequent. Still, flying beats most land transportation.

> **Note:** North-south flights almost always stop in Vientiane, so you may find yourself with an unplanned overnight in the capital. Flights also tend to leave very early or very late, and many city pairs do not have daily service.

Flights are very reasonably priced and take a fraction of the time a bus does to cover the same distance. Domestic flights generally cost $50 to $100 per leg.

By Road

Renting a car is not really an option.

It is possible, but not advisable, to rent scooters for trips outside the "major" metropolitan areas. The roads are not the greatest, although they are improving every year. Drivers are not skilled or concerned with proper passing, and banditry has been an occasional problem along some roads. Safety equipment, such as helmets, is dirty, poorly maintained, and rarely available.

Buses and private vans go almost everywhere. A major organizer of tours in private vans and buses is **Diethelm** (a Thailand-based company). Their Laos office is Diethelm Travel (Laos) Ltd., Setthathirath Road, Namphu Square, PO Box 2657, Vientiane, Lao PDR, ☎ (856 21) 213 833, 215 920, fax (856 21) 217 151, 216 294, ditralao@laotel.com. Their website is at www.diethelmtravel.com.

The tour bus company drivers are far better trained than the public bus drivers, and far less likely to pick up unscheduled passengers.

You can ride a bicycle, which is not a bad idea. Just keep in mind that others out there are not good or aware drivers.

By Boat

There are a number of ways to get around Laos by boat. As the roads expand and improve, the availability of boats is decreasing, but it is still possible to spend part of a day or several days floating or power-boating down the many rivers. Some are passable only in the monsoon season; others are impassable then due to flooding.

By Rail

There are no rail services in Laos. This is one of the many ways the French colonization period shortchanged the Laotians.

The Weather & When to Visit

Like Vietnam, Laos is a long, narrow country, but unlike Vietnam, Laos is completely landlocked.

The climate is tropical, with two distinct seasons – the rainy period, from the beginning of May to the end of September, and the dry season from October through to April. The yearly average temperature is about 28°C/82°F, with a maximum of 38°C/100°F in April and May. In Vientiane, the low temperature of about 19°C/00°F occurs in January. In mountainous areas, however, temperatures can drop to 14-15°C/the 50s°F during the winter months, and at night drop to freezing or a bit lower.

The average precipitation is highest in southern Laos, where the Annamite Mountains receive over 3,000 mm (10 feet) annually. In Vientiane rainfall is 1,500-2,000 mm (five to almost seven feet) annually, and in the northern provinces only 1,000-1,500 mm (three to five feet) annually.

What to See & Do

Laos is the true jewel of Southeast Asia. It is still under-visited, so people haven't yet become weary of tourists. No other place in Asia makes you feel more welcome than Laos. Don't be put off by the travelers who tell you there isn't anything worth stopping for. Laos is a historical and cultural treasure, and an eco-tourism destination waiting to be discovered. Before the rest of the world finds its wonders, this is the time to trek through the hill tribe areas, cycle the backroads, explore the temples, and paddle or float down Laos' many rivers and lakes.

It has been less than 10 years since Laos opened its borders to foreigners, so the impact is not yet as great as in adjacent and nearby countries. Having been closed for so many years, the agricultural and rural areas of the country are largely intact. The pace of life is very slow – in fact, it may be too slow for some of you! Go prepared to truly chill out. The Internet is available, but slow, the food is good but never rushed, and the roads are mediocre for the most part, so you can't rush there, either.

■ Vientiane

History

Vientiane was almost totally destroyed by the Thais in 1828. Under the French, many buildings were restored or rebuilt, and Vientiane became the administrative capital of Laos.

As major international capitals go, Vientiane is as small as you're ever going to find. There's not much to do, and little of historical significance, but still the city is worth a stop. There are remnants of French Colonial architecture, a bizarre triumphal arch, a few temples, a few markets, peaceful gardens, sunsets on the Mekong River, and decent restaurants along the water.

Where to Stay

Vientiane has a reasonable selection of three- and four-star hotels. The standards are good, but not up to Western equivalents. Most of the better hotels offer airport transfers and include breakfast.

The majority of Vientiane's hotels are within walking distance of both the City Center and the River. They are also close to the Nam Phou area and its central fountain and restaurants.

Laos

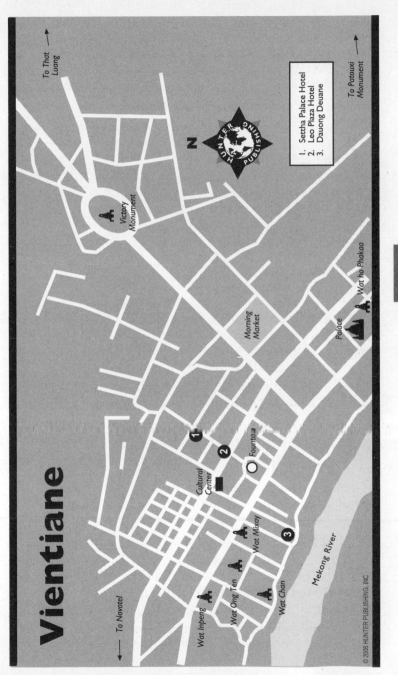

Vientiane

To That Luang →

To Patouxi Monument →

To Novotel ←

Victory Monument

Morning Market

Wat ho Phakao

Palace

1. Settha Palace Hotel
2. Leo Plaza Hotel
3. Dauong Deuane

Cultural Center

Fountain

Wat Inpeng

Wat Ong Teu

Wat Mixay

Wat Chan

Mekong River

© 2006 HUNTER PUBLISHING, INC

Tip: If your flight leaves early in the morning – and many do – your hotel may offer to pack your breakfast. I suggest taking them up on their offer since the food on short-haul Asian flights is rarely appetizing, even on Thai Air.

Pre-Paid/Pre-Booked Hotel Options

$$$$ **Accor/Novotel**, Unit 9, Samsen Thai Road, Vientiane. Ideally located within three minutes of Wattay International Airport by car, the hotel is perfect for in-transit tourists. The major commercial and financial district of the city is reachable in five minutes by car and the Mekong River

HOTEL PRICE CHART	
Rates are per room based on double occupancy.	
$	Under $12
$$	$12-$25
$$$	$26-$40
$$$$	$40-$80
$$$$$	Over $80

is just a 10-minute walk. There are 168 rooms ranked as Standard, Superior and Executive Suite. Both the Standard and Superior have a king-size bed or twin beds. The Executive Suite has a king-size bed. All rooms can accommodate an additional bed for a third person. Restaurants on-site.

Internet booking rates: $60 (S)/$69 (D) Standard, $63/$71 Superior (2004-2005). Rates subject to change and do not include 10% tax or breakfast.

$$$ **Asian Garden Hotel**, 379 Samsenthai Rd., Vientiane. A humble three-star hotel that has 40 rooms offering Superior Deluxe rooms and Asian Suites. Simple and comfortable budget accommodation. Rooms are fully equipped with deluxe amenities such as air-conditioning, mini-bar, satellite TV, shower, bath, and telephone. Restaurants on-site.

Internet rates are $25/$27 for rooms and $35/$40 for suites. Booking direct with the hotel is slightly more expensive. Rates include taxes, breakfast, and airport transfer.

General Hotel Options

$$$$-$$$$$ **Lao Plaza Hotel**, 63 Samsenthai, ☎ 218800, fax 218808, lph@laoplazahotel.com, www.laoplazahotel.com. This hotel is the top choice in Vientiane. During the late-2004 ASEAN conference many foreign dignitaries stayed here. It is

also centrally located. All rooms have A/C, satellite TV, and nicely appointed rooms. There are three restaurants and a health club (open to non-guests for a small fee). If your idea of roughing it is an American chain hotel, this place will fit the bill. Otherwise there are many more choices that give a true taste of Laos. Credit cards are accepted; traveler's checks may not be.

$$$$ Settha Palace Hotel, 6 Pang Kham, ☎ 217581, fax 217583, settha@laonet,net, www.setthapalace.com. This hotel is far more in keeping with the traditional Colonial French architectural style. There is French Colonial décor, beautifully landscaped gardens, and period furniture, along with a great French restaurant. A stay here is definitely worth the cost. Credit cards are accepted.

$$$ Lani I, 281 Setthathirat, ☎ 214919, fax 215639. This is an older auberge-style hotel in a garden-like setting. The facilities are minimal and the rooms not really up to Western standards, but the owners are lovely people. There is a Chinese restaurant on site, but with so many good restaurants in the town, I wouldn't choose this place just for its food. No credit cards.

$$-$$$ Douang Deuane, Nokeo Koummane Rd., ☎ 222301, fax 222300, douanddeuane@pan-laos.net.la. This is one of the best hotels in its price range. It has the basic features of A/C and satellite TV, with wood floors and nice bathrooms. There is a restaurant and the hotel accepts credit cards. Good, central location.

Where to Eat

 There are dozens of good restaurants within a block or two of the Mekong River. My personal favorites are an Italian restaurant (Italian-operated) and the bakery at the circle by the fountain.

$$-$$$ Lane Xang Restaurant, Quai Fa Ngoum, overlooking the river. If you want to taste traditional Lao dishes (such as many kinds of river fish, baked moose or turtle), this is the place to go. You can also see traditional Lao dance programs.

$$ Nazim, Fa Ngoum, ☎ 223480. This is one of my favorites, serving food from across the Indian sub-continent.

$$-$$$ **Cote D'Azur**, 63/64 Fa Ngoum, ☎ 217252. Another personal favorite, especially when the urge for a pizza and glass of decent red wine hits. You can also get respectable French cooking here.

$$-$$$ **Scandinavian Bakery**, 74/1 Pang Kham on Nam Phou Circle. A great place to have a lingering breakfast. Yogurt, pastries, breads, coffee, fruit bowls, and more. You can pick up English-language newspapers here and chill out for a bit.

There are Italian, French, Vietnamese, Chinese, and vegetarian restaurants all along the river. There are also restaurants of decent quality in almost every hotel, and dozens of food stalls in the markets and along the river.

RESTAURANT PRICES	
$	Under $2
$$	$2-$5
$$$	$6-$10
$$$$	$11-$20
$$$$$	Over $20

Nightlife

Vientiane is not exactly hopping in the evenings. Some of the restaurants put on evening traditional dance programs (see *Lane Xang Restaurant*, above), and there are a number of pseudo-pubs, cabarets, and bars.

For discos, your might try **Anou Cabaret** on Heng Boun, or **Dao Vieng's disco** upstairs from the restaurant, also on Heng Boun. For bars, I like **Sala Basi**, on a deck built over the Mekong just down from the New River Hotel, or **Sunset Bar** at the end of Fa Ngoum (nice place and an expat hangout).

Shopping

Books and newspapers: If you need to buy or exchange a book, try the **Vientiane Book Exchange** (four locations including one at 54/1 Pang Kham Rd and one in the Lao Plaza Hotel).

Clothing and handicrafts: Ek Hor Boutique is one of my favorites. It's located on Pang Kham (☎ 517247 for directions) and they have both locally made clothes (silk and cotton) and a variety of handicrafts. The quality is good and the prices are on the high side.

Art galleries: There are many galleries in Vientiane – surprising for a town of its size. Try **Oot-Ni Art Gallery** (306 Samsenthai, not too far from the Lao Plaza Hotel), and their branch in the Morning Market.

Morning Market: Make sure to visit – the earlier the better. This is a huge shopping complex on two levels, and the place where both locals and tourists shop. The morning "parade" is fascinating. If you know gold and jade you can pick up some great bargains, but you can also spend a lot and buy junk.

Along **Setthathirat** (43/2-43/3) there are several shops worth a visit.

Western food: If you have a hankering to picnic, or just want a break from restaurant food, try the **Phimphone Supermarket** on Samsenthai. You can buy Western-style bread and cheese, wine, cold cuts, and similar items.

Tours & Travels

You can easily cover all of the highlights of Vientiane on your own in two or three days, but the services of a good travel specialist never hurt. These agents can also help arrange visas, flights, hotels, and onward travel. Make use of their services to reconfirm your intra-Asia and return flights!

The premier travel and tour arranger in this part of Asia is **Diethelm Travel**, Nam Phou Circle, ☎ 213833, www.diethelmtravel.com. Contact them at ditralao@laotel.com. They maintain a fleet of comfortable mini-buses and run small group tours. Also, they don't stop on the highway to pick up travelers.

On the more adventurous side, there's the Asian Trails group of travel specialists in Vientiane. Try **Lao Asian Trails**, Unit 5, Baan Sokpaluang, ☎ 351789, or visit their website at www.asiantrails.com. There are additional tour operator websites at the end of this book.

Getting Around & Away

Vientiane is compact. There are few places you can't easily bike or walk to. Taxis are easy to find. If you are going about on your own, make sure you get a card from the hotel so you can show it in order to get back, and ask the hotel staff to write down the places you want to visit (in local script) for the driver.

Short-Haul/Local

Walking around Vientiane is very pleasant unless it's raining or hot. The city is small, and the traffic is still quite light. Keep in mind that many people just decide one day to get a scooter and start driving – training is optional. Drivers are not good about watching for you, so be sure to watch for them.

You can rent a **bicycle** at almost any hotel, as well as at street stalls and some bars. The cost is a few US$ per day. The quality of the equipment is hit and miss, and I recommend having your own helmet – they are almost never available in Laos.

Buses usually leave from the bus station next to the Morning Market. Some leave from Talaat Sao. If you are booking bus travel on your own, get your hotel to help so you get to the correct station and on the right bus! It is a short bus ride to the Friendship Bridge, and the cost is well under US$1. There isn't a city bus service – just buses to other parts of the country and the Thai border. Local buses and drivers are not the greatest. If you are going farther than the Friendship Bridge I suggest using the transport services of a tour operator.

You can **rent a car**, but if you are in an accident it is always your fault. Better to hire a car and driver or use the services of the tour operators.

You can rent a **scooter** for about $10 per day for a small engine Honda; double that for a more powerful machine. The best place to rent a motorbike is your hotel. If they don't rent them they will send you to a place that does and tell you what the rate should be. Remember that most local drivers are not very skilled.

Taxis don't circulate; they wait at the markets, bus stations, and major hotels. It costs about $1 (8,000 to 10,000 Kip) for the flag drop and then about the same again for each extra kilometer. You can order a taxi at ☎ 350000.

Long Distance

By Air: The best way to get around Laos is to fly. While the countryside is lovely it can get monotonous pretty quickly and the roads, drivers, and equipment often leave much to be desired.

The **Wattay International Airport** is six km/four miles west of town. It costs about $5 to take a taxi, but many of the better hotels provide free transfers if you book ahead.

The details on travel by air are in the initial *Getting There and Around* section, page 201-202.

 By Bus or Truck: Beat-up buses and over-crowded trucks are the mainstay of travel for most local people and many tourists. If you really want to travel this way, go to the bus station next to the Morning Market at least a day before you want to leave and check on trip details. Many buses leave only once a day and that can be at 4 or 5 am. Checking ahead ensures you know the cost, time, and departure location. Prices are dirt-cheap – a few dollars to go almost anywhere in the country.

You can take a bus to Vietnam, as long as you don't mind leaving between 4 am and 6 am. The trip takes all day over rough roads, and you end up in Lak Sao – not exactly a hot spot of tourism. The cost is about $6 (60,000 Kip) and the trip is quite uncomfortable. Ask your hotel which bus station to go to – these buses do not leave from the main station.

 By Boat: Long-distance boat travel is fast disappearing in most of Southeast Asia. If you want to take a boat upstream to Luang Prabang, you need to go to Kao Liaw village, located about eight km/five miles west of town. Boats don't leave every day, and when they do go, they leave pretty early in the morning (figure 8 am). Fares are negotiable and depend on whether you are on a fast or slow boat. The slow boat is going to cost close to $20 (200,000 Kip) and the trip takes four-five days. Sleeping accommodations are normally hammocks on deck. Check to see what, if any, food is included. At a minimum you'll want to bring lots of water and other beverages, as well as non-perishable snacks.

There are speedboats to the north, but they are noisy and incredibly dangerous. Wear a helmet and life jacket. If you aren't a good swimmer I suggest sticking to the slow boat or dry land. The trip takes a full day and the boats also leave from Kao Liew village. You will pay $30-50. Go light on the luggage – these boats are small.

Boats rarely go south from Vientiane any more – it's fly or go by road.

What to See & Do

Vientiane was almost totally destroyed by the Thais in 1828. The "city" itself is probably the smallest, sleepiest national capital in the world. It still shows the impact of many years of French occupation and control. The French influence is still evident in the wonderful baguettes, coffee, bits of architecture, and layout of the streets. Don't miss the several street and indoor markets. One of the indoor markets is a great place to buy jade, 18-karat through 24-karat (yes, really) jewelry, silks, and other local crafts.

Just walking the streets is pleasant, especially if you've recently come from Hanoi or Saigon. The roads have not been overrun with cars and scooters, you'll almost never hear a horn tooted, and you can even cross the streets in relative safety!

The Wats

Wat Sisaket, right, is the only temple that survived the 1828 invasion by the Thais. It is one of the most interesting temples in Laos, its walls covered with 6,840 Buddha images in niches and on shelves. There are also Buddhist inscriptions from the 18th century.

Wat Ho Phakeo was originally built in 1565 by King Setthathirat when he relocated the Lao (Lane Xang) capital to Vientiane (from Luang Prabang). The king built the temple to house the Emerald Buddha he brought from the Kingdom of Lanna.

Monuments

That Luang, shown at left, is the symbol of Laos. It is the most significant monument in Vientiane and was originally constructed in 1566 by the aforementioned King Setthathirat.

Patouxai was constructed (in 1958) entirely of cement and is centrally located. You can climb to the top for a great view of the city. Rumor has it that the monument was built with the cement provided by the US for constructing the new airport.

Day-Trips from Vientiane

The **National Ethnic Cultural Park** is about 20 km/12 miles south of Vientiane on the road to the Friendship Bridge and the crossing to Thailand. It is certainly worth a stop, especially if you can arrange it on the way to or from the border crossing. The park, called Suam Vatthana Tham, has walking paths, sculptures of important Lao heroes, and a zoo. You can see across the Mekong all the way to Thailand.

A bit farther south you will come to the **Buddha Park**. This is a statue garden with enshrined Buddha statues and images of Hindu gods. Keep in mind these two places contain many images that are holy to Buddhists.

River Trips

The **Mekong River** provides many boating opportunities, both in power boats and canoes or kayaks. Local travel agents or your hotel can help you make arrangements. Be aware it may not be possible to enter Thailand by boat. You may have to disembark before the Friendship Bridge, cross, and pick up a Thai boat on the other side. If you are coming from Thailand, the same consideration applies. It is possible to get your Laotian visa at the Friendship Bridge – another reason why the boats stop here.

Laos

The Mekong is placid and slow-moving; floating downriver can be a delightful experience.

Hiking, Cycling & Walking

 The country around Vientiane is even less hilly than around Luang Prabang. Since there are so few vehicles, you can cycle or walk around safely. There are temples and parks outside of town that make a pleasant day trip, but be sure to take a map. Several places rent bicycles – just stop at the kiosks along the street or ask your hotel to arrange a rental. A decent bike should cost only $2-$4 per day, but bring your own helmet.

Cars & Motor Scooters

 You are very unlikely to be able to rent a car in Laos, although you may be able to rent a scooter. If you have a scooter you might take self-guided tours to the parks and monuments outside the city. You might also enquire about hiring a car and driver. It's a great, but expensive, way to see the entire country quickly and on your terms. A local travel agent is your best source of information.

Useful Information

Airlines

 Lao Aviation, 2 Pang Kham (near the intersection with Fa Ngoum), ☎ 2122050 (international), 212057 (domestic). laoaviation@lao-aviation.com. There is also an office at the airport.

Malaysian Airlines, in the Lao Plaza Hotel, ☎ 218816.

Silk Air (Singapore Air), in the Royal Dokmaideng Hotel, ☎ 217492.

Thai Air, right by Lao Aviation on Pang Kham Rd., ☎ 216143.

Vietnam Airlines, 225 Saylom Rd., ☎ 222370, plus an office in the Lao Plaza Hotel.

> **Note:** Most airlines are open from 8-noon and 1-5 pm, Monday to Friday, and mornings on Saturday. Always reconfirm your flights. Lao Aviation is the agent for Air France and China Southern Airlines.

Banks/Money Exchange

Unless you need money wired you may never need to go to a bank in Laos. There are plenty of moneychangers offering better rates, and most hotels and guesthouses will also change money. You can actually pay many expenses in US dollars. Euros, yen, Australian dollars, Singapore dollars, and Thai baht are fairly easy to exchange, but take a few US dollars just in case.

If you need to cash traveler's checks, a bank may be your best choice. There are banks along the main streets and one is about the same as another. If you need to wire money you might want to stick with a bank from a more developed Asian country (such as the Thai Military Bank at 69 Khoun Boulom).

Embassies/Consulates

Australia, ☎ 413600.

Burma (Myanmar), **☎** 314910.

Cambodia, ☎ 312584.

China, ☎ 315103.

India, ☎ 413802.

Japan, ☎ 4144000.

Malaysia, ☎ 414205.

Thailand, ☎ 217158.

UK, no embassy – call the Australian Embassy.

USA, ☎ 212580.

Vietnam, ☎ 413400 (takes three days and $50 to get a one-month visa).

Call ahead to verify locations and ability to issue visas. Consider registering with your country's local office.

Internet/Communications

Internet cafés are everywhere. Expect to pay US$3-$6 per hour. Most connections are less-than-reliable and few connections are high-speed (no matter what the sign outside says). Many of these cafés have international calling facilities. The International Telephone office is just off Nam Phou Circle and is open from about 8 am to 9 pm.

Medical Facilities

There are a number of clinics and hospitals in Vientiane. It is advisable to check with your embassy before going to any medical facility in a Third-World country. The Australian Embassy has a clinic, as does the Swedish Embassy. If you need treatment beyond what these clinics can handle, go to Thailand!

■ Vang Vieng

History

Also referred to as Viang Vieng, Van Vieng or by similar variants, Vang Vieng is not a spot of any great historical significance. It earns its spot on the tourist map by virtue of its location as a convenient stop-over going between Luang Prabang and Vientiane, its scenic beauty, and the proximity of many active vacation options. If you are looking for culture or museums, you might want to give Vang Vieng a miss.

However, there are a number of nearby 16th- and 17th-century monasteries and a some of limestone caves that might entertain the intrepid visitor for a day or so.

Where to Stay

Vang Vieng is not known for its accommodations. This is a town favored by backpackers because it is cheap. It is also a hit with those interested in illegal drugs, especially hashish and opium.

There are a number of guesthouses, including **Amphone**, ☎ 511180, **Dokkhoun**, ☎ 511032, near the bus station, and **Erawan**, ☎ 511093, erawan_van@hotmail.com, English spoken. Few of these places have air conditioning, and none has television. They are all between $10-$15 per room.

Where to Eat

 The food choices aren't much better. **Nazim's**, ☎ 511214, is open for lunch and dinner and serves Indian and Halal food. For pizza and French food try **Phonephachan Bistrot** or **Sivixay** (this one has satellite TV at last report).

All these restaurants are very inexpensive. Figure less than $5 per person.

Nightlife

Watching the tourists is one of the highlights. The restaurants and bars in town are about your only option for evening activities.

Shopping

The **Morning Market** offers a variety of goods, but not much to write home about.

Tours & Travels

See the Vientiane and Luang Prabang options (pages 209 and 248) – you are better off booking with them. Otherwise, to arrange local activities (tubing, rafting, caving, trekking), check with your guesthouse or a local restaurant – they are the tour operators and arrangers here.

Getting Around & Away

Local

 Vang Vieng is very walkable – the town is just a strip along the Mekong River. You can rent bikes at most guesthouses for a few dollars a day. Motorbikes can be rented at the café near the telephone office at a cost of $10-$12 per day.

Long Distance

The only way out is by bus, truck, or private (tour company) van. Go to the Morning Market to arrange transportation. It takes three-four hours to get to Vientiane and seven-eight hours to Luang Prabang. If you go by private (tour company) transport, these times will be significantly less. The bus to Vientiane leaves five or six times a day, starting at about

5 am, and costs about 80¢ (8,000 Kip). The bus to Luang
Prabang leaves by 9 am and costs about $5 (50,000 Kip).

What to See & Do

This sleepy town actually has a number of nearby
sites worth a few days of your time if your schedule
allows.

Unfortunately, one of Van Vieng's major attractions, in certain circles, is the ready availability of illegal
drugs at the many bars, discos, and guest houses along the
main road through town. Backpackers come here in droves to
sample the wares, and many of them get far more than they
bargained for. Van Vieng has also been the site of various incidents of unrest in the past few years, so it is worth checking
the current political situation before planning a stopover.
Drugs are illegal and users could find they have been set up.

The main activities for most visitors involve either getting on
the river or going caving. You can rent a bicycle for 60-80¢
(6,000-8,000 Kip) for the day and ride/wade across the river,
then cycle to a number of caves and local villages. You can also
go tubing, canoeing, or rafting if it is not the rainy season.

Useful Information

Airlines

None

Banks/Money Exchange

Check at your hotel and around the Morning Market.

Embassies/Consulates

See *Vientiane*.

Internet/Communications

There are a few cafés in town with very slow connections.

Medical

Go to Vientiane or better yet, to Thailand. Beware needles of
any sort.

■ Bokeo

History

This is the heart of the infamous Golden Triangle. As a result, the area has a history that is less than savory, but the setting is beautiful and the tribal cultures fascinating.

Where to Stay

Again, this is an area not known for its accommodations. There are a number of basic, $10-$12-per-night guest houses with basic facilities. People come to this part of Laos for one of two reasons – to arrange a trek through the hill tribe villages and/or to see the Plain of Jars. The main town is Xiengkhuang – see the next section.

Where to Eat

Many of the guesthouses in the Bokeo area have small associated restaurants. There are also small cafés and food stands in the area.

What to See & Do

Bokeo is the smallest of Laos' provinces, but it is the best starting place to explore the local tribal areas and cultures. Home to a large number of ethnically and culturally diverse minority tribes, it's directly across from Chiang Rai province in Thailand, and also borders Burma. This tri-border area is the fabled "Golden Triangle," home to one of the largest opium poppy-growing and heroin-producing operations in the world. It is also a major source of **precious stones** such as sapphires ("Bokeo" means Land of Sapphires), and a lesser source of **gold** and other gemstones.

In the markets in various towns in Bokeo you can buy Laotian sapphires, Burmese rubies, and other precious and semi-precious stones and jewelry, but you need to know what to look for. Beware the flawless, low-priced stone – it's probably colored glass, a look-alike stone, or a stone created in a laboratory. That being said, if the price seems fair (and you assume it is not the real thing!), the gold setting is stamped with the 18-karat gold mark, and you like the piece, buy it.

Ask around and you might find a local who is going panning for gold in the Mekong or its tributary rivers, digging for precious and semi-precious stones, or undertaking other interesting activities. You might get to go along. Beware of the rough and tumble attitude toward life – this is not the safest area in Indochina.

Your hotel or guest house staff can almost certainly help you arrange a trek into the tribal areas. There are travel agents in most towns, regardless of how small, and they are very experienced at packaging customized trips. For more details, prices, and options, see page 252-55.

■ Xiengkhuang (Xieng Khoung)

The area was once home to many important temples but these were casualties of the American bombing. The French had a significant presence here and remnants of Colonial architecture can still be seen in a few places.

Where to Stay

There are few choices of accommodation here. The only reason to stop overnight is if it is not possible to get back to Luang Prabang for some reason.

Where to Eat

There are a few basic cafés and street stalls. If you are here for the day on a tour from Luang Prabang (the logical way to see the Jars) your tour operator will arrange lunch.

Getting Around & Away

Most people come on an organized day trip from Luang Prabang. If you come on your own you will likely arrive by morning bus from Luang Prabang.

What to See & Do

This is the town closest to the fascinating plateau called the "Plain of Jars." There are hundreds of stone jars, many of them several times the size of a person. These jars are in an area that was used as a dumping ground by flight crews returning from bombing runs in North Vietnam – they jettisoned unused bombs here. In some cases the US crews deliber-

The Plain of Jars

ately bombed the area. Amazingly, the vast majority of the jars survived unscathed. The Vietnam War (called the American War of Aggression by the Vietnamese and the Second Indochina War by others in Southeast Asia), wasn't the first time the area was savagely attacked; Chinese soldiers looted the area in the 19th century but were unable to seriously damage the jars. Over the centuries, many other invaders have tried to move or destroy the jars, but none have succeeded so far.

There is an ongoing debate about the jars – who made them, how they were moved and placed, when they were made, and what they were used for. It is generally agreed the jars are man-made, but the rest of the questions remain unanswered. Many experts believe they were actually funerary urns, probably for royalty, but they pre-date recorded history, so little is actually known about them. Anything of value left with the Chinese looters well over 100 years ago. Nonetheless, the jars are well worth seeing. Since travel around Laos is slow and difficult, you may want to plan a day excursion through your hotel or a travel agent in Xiengkhuang.

Day-Trips from Xiengkhuang

The Meuang Kham district is the site of the **Baw Nam Hai Nyai hot springs**. There is a very basic, low-key resort/spa here. It's a great place to relax and unwind after a day traipsing around the Plain of Jars. You should be able to arrange transport to the Plain of Jars, on to the hot springs, and back to Xiengkhuang through your hotel or a travel agent in

Laos

Xiengkhuang. While you're coordinating that trip, check into adding on a side-trip to the **Tham Pui cave**. This is the cave where villagers sheltered from the American bombs. It has become a pilgrimage site for many local Laotians.

Useful Information

Airlines

None.

Banks/Money Exchange

Check with your guesthouse or go to the local market to find a moneychanger.

Embassies/Consulates

None.

Internet/Communications

There might be an Internet café in the near future. Ask at your guesthouse.

Medical

Go to Vientiane or Thailand.

■ Savannakhet

History

Opium poppies

Savannakhet is strategically located on an ancient trade route connecting Vietnam and Thailand. As a result it has long been visited by traders and merchants. It was only natural for the French to set up a major business and governmental center here. Being in the far south of a semi-tropical country, Savannakhet has the additional advantage of being more temperate and fertile than the rest of Laos.

It was from this town that the French controlled the Lao opium trade, so it has a large number of Colonial French buildings in the former French Quarter, along with a large, European-style Catholic cathedral (St. Theresa's).

Where to Stay

 There are no high-end hotels in Savannakhet. However, there are several comfortable auberge-style options and a number of guesthouses and restored Colonial-era villas.

$$$-$$$$ **Auberge de Paradis**, next to the Old Market, ☎ 212445. This restored Colonial villa has only five guest rooms so reservations are a must. The furnishings are wood and rattan and all the rooms have attached bathrooms and A/C. No credit cards or restaurant. Probably the best choice in town.

$-$$ **Mekong**, Tha He Rd., ☎ 212249. Another restored Colonial villa, this time right on the Mekong River. Some of the rooms have A/C, others have fans, and all are large and airy with attached facilities. No credit cards or restaurant.

$ **Saisouok**, Makhavenha Rd., ☎ 212207. This is quite a bargain for the price. The guesthouse is new, and rooms are large and bright. Some rooms have A/C, but none has private facilities. No credit cards or restaurant.

Where to Eat

 All the local restaurants fall into the cheap category. One is much the same as another, although the **Happy Café** (about two km out of the center, by the market) is probably the best of the bunch. For the most part, the places look run-down so it pays to give the kitchen a look-see.

Nightlife

Not much to speak of – the local restaurants are about it. There is a disco at the **Hoong Thip Hotel** (Petsalath Rd.).

Shopping

There is the **central market** and a **Lao Cotton shop** on Ratsavong Seuk Rd.

Tours & Travels

Book your tours in Vientiane – local operators speak little or no English. You might try **Sabanbanhao Tourism Com-**

pany on Senna Rd., ☎ 212944. And maybe your guesthouse staff can help you make arrangements.

Getting Around & Away

Local

It is possible to rent bicycles at most guesthouses for a few dollars a day.

Long Distance

The only way in or out is by uncomfortable bus, private van, or by plane. There are three-times-weekly flights to Vientiane (about $70) and four-times-weekly flights to Pakse (about $50).

Buses leave from the government terminal on the northern edge of the town. Plan to take a tuk-tuk to the terminal for 50¢ (5,000 Kip or so). There are five or six buses a day to Vientiane, taking about eight hours, costing $3 (30,000 Kip). The first bus leaves at around 5 am and the last about noon. There are two buses each day to Pakse and these take six-seven hours, cost about $2.50 (25,000 Kip), and leave at 6 am and 2 pm. There is also a private bus service – similar prices and better equipment. The departures are early in the morning. Ask your guesthouse staff for help arranging the private bus.

You can also get buses to Thailand and Vietnam. There is a daily bus to Lao Bao in Vietnam from the government station (6 am) and private buses at 7 am and 11 am. The trip is over rough roads and will take close to 10 hours. The trip to Thailand takes the same amount of time.

There are also boats to Thailand.

I highly recommend flying out of town. The boat and bus information I just gave is the best available at the time of writing, but schedules are unpredictable, equipment is poor, and roads can be impassable.

*Above: Family-run restaurant overlooking the falls
in the 4,000 Islands area, Southern Laos*
*Below: Your ride has arrived – transportation
outside Vientiane, Laos*

Above: Laotian girls on the Mekong in Luang Prabang
Below: Approaching Angkor Wat, Cambodia (©Jack Scott)

Above: Girl in Angkor Wat (©Jack Scott)

Above: The 12th-century Bayon Temple at Angkor Thom, north of Angkor Wat (©Jack Scott)

What to See & Do

Wandering through the remnants of another era makes for a fascinating morning. Then, for contrast, you can spend the afternoon visiting the stupa of **That Ing Hang temple** – a 16-km/10-mile trip from Savannakhet. This stupa is one of the most important and revered Buddhist monuments in all of Laos. If you happen to be there for the annual festival in February, it will be crowded but worth the visit.

Laos

Useful Information

Airlines

Lao Aviation has a local office in Savannakhet. The office is at the airport.

Banks/Money Exchange

The best places to exchange money are the booths around the market or at your hotel. If you must have money wired, try the **Lao Mai Bank**, ☎ 212226, on Khanthabouli Rd. This bank also has a branch in the post office and one in the new market.

Embassies/Consulates

There is a **Thai** consulate in the Nanhai Hotel.

The **Vietnamese** consulate is on Sisavangvong Rd. You need the usual photos, about $50, and the ability to wait for three days for a visa.

Internet/Communications

As with most places in Laos, Internet cafés are sprouting like weeds. There is a place near the post office that doubles as a travel information center – the **River Net and Computers shop**. The post office itself is a place to make international calls.

Medical

Go to Thailand.

■ Champasak

History

If you're interested in UNESCO World Heritage temple sites, Cambodia isn't the only place to visit. Plan on spending a few days relaxing and exploring in Champasak. This is the location of the renowned Wat Phu, a collection of Khmer ruins constructed between the sixth and 12th centuries. There are ongoing restoration and preservation efforts, but these are far less obvious than at other Khmer sites in the region. Being so far off the beaten tourist track, you can wander and imagine what life was like 1,500 years ago, without having your reverie interrupted by a bunch of tourists piling off a bus (shades of Angkor Wat). There is a small, ever-changing admission fee, and it's worth every penny.

The province itself has a history going back almost 2,000 years. There are a few other sites of note. Some of the best, and certainly the largest, waterfalls in Laos are in Champasak province. I highly recommend a visit to at least one of the falls: Selabam, Khonphapheng, or Liphi (the largest in Laos).

Where to Stay

Pre-Book/Prepay Hotel Options

Tad Fane Resort, Ban Lak 38, Paksong, Champasak. This overlooks the Tad Fane waterfalls, thundering down a 200-m/600-foot deep gorge. Beyond the waterfalls stretches the extensive jungle of Dong Hua Sao, one of the 18 National Biodiversity Conservation Areas in the country.

The Tad Fane Resort is nestled on one of the most scenic spots in Southern Laos, the Boloven Plateau. It is located 38 km/23 miles west of Pakse town and the airport. Less than 10 km/six miles from the resort is the provincial town of Paksong. Along the road to Paksong are several villages of minorities, such as the Alak and Lawen.

HOTEL PRICE CHART	
Rates are per room based on double occupancy.	
$	Under $12
$$	$12-$25
$$$	$26-$40
$$$$	$40-$80
$$$$$	Over $80

The resort has 14 spacious and comfortable bungalows built in traditional Lao architecture. The rooms each have a private bathroom with hot and cold shower and a spacious veranda.

Internet rates are $22 (S)/$24 (D) for standard rooms and $26/$29 for deluxe rooms in high season (May to November), a few dollars less in the off-season. Rates include tax and breakfast. Booking directly with the hotel is $35/$35 for a standard room and $40/$40 for a deluxe room. Restaurants on-site.

General Hotel Options

There are dozens of guesthouses along the main road just in from the river. Many are quite new with A/C, private bathrooms, balconies or patios looking over the river, satellite TV, and breakfast included in the price. They can usually arrange tours and often rent bicycles (for the princely sum of $1-$2 per day). New places are cropping up monthly, so the list that follows is just to give you an idea of your options.

$$-$$$ **Auberge Sala Wat Phou**, ☎ 213280. Along the river road. There are 10 nice rooms with hot water and private bathrooms. Some of the rooms have balconies. There is an attached restaurant. No credit cards.

$$$-$$$$ **Champasak Palace Hotel**, Number 13 Road, Pakse District, PO Box 718. No phone.

$$-$$$ **Pakse Hotel**, Street Number 5, Bane Watlouang, Central, Pakse. No phone.

Laos

Where to Eat

Champasak is not known for its restaurants.

Your guesthouse is likely to have a small eatery, and that is where most people eat. There is a restaurant at the **Auberge Sala Wat Phou**, and you will see occasional places to eat along the river road.

Getting There & Around

Most people arrive on the **bus** from Pakse or the Mekong Islands in the south. You may also be able to snag a ride with a private van or one belonging to an NGO (that's how I got from the south to Champasak). Buses run several times a day to and from Champasak – you just flag the bus down in front of your guesthouse and pay on board. You and the bus get to take a ferry to the main road and proceed from there. You may have to change buses once you get off the ferry. The buses going from the Mekong Islands to Pakse will let you off along the main highway (Hwy 13) and then you have to catch a bus to the ferry and into town. It's not as hard as it sounds. Just plan on an early start – by 7:30 am or so – to catch a bus going south.

There are more choices going north to Pakse, unless you plan to go all the way into Thailand the same day (in which case plan on an early bus). Pakse is only 45 km/27 miles to the north but the trip takes close to two hours and costs about $1.50 (15,000 Kip). The trip south to the islands takes several hours and costs about $ (30,000 Kip).

Many people prefer to make this trip by **boat**. It takes about two hours to Pakse ($1/10,000 Kip) and five or so to the Mekong Island area ($1.50/15,000 Kip). I found the boats to be seriously overloaded and completely lacking in both safety equipment and seat padding. Nonetheless, the river air is quite cool and pleasant even when the weather is hot.

To catch the boat, figure on an 8 am departure; go to the river and ask where the boats are.

A **bicycle** is the best way to get around the Champasak area. The temples are too far from town to walk to them.

What to See & Do
Champasak Temple Complex

This is a great alternative to the frenetic pace of Angkor Wat. I actually rented a bicycle at my guesthouse for the grand sum of one dollar and rode the eight-10 km/five-six miles to the complex. You can't take bicycles inside, though, so entrust yours to the watchful eyes of the men who just hang around outside the entry. Make sure you stop at the museum on the way out, too.

Once you have your fill of the temple complexes, Champasak is a great place to buy traditional, quality Lao crafts and goods. Check out the silks and cottons – they are made from hand-woven, hand-dyed thread.

❖ Wat Phu

This is the reason to go to Champasak. The Mekong River setting is great, and the complex is stunning. The complex is about eight km/five miles south of Champasak. If you're not riding a bike, you can always flag a local bus – the driver will know where you are going.

The admission fee is about 50¢ (5,000 Kip, but will probably go up soon). There is a museum at the entrance area and admission is included in the complex fee. The hours are flexible, but generally from 8 am to 5 pm. Make sure to get the guide and map so you can relate the descriptions that follow to what you are passing by.

Laos

Most of the ruins date from the fifth and sixth centuries and are not in good repair. Since Angkor Wat wasn't even started for another 200 years or so, you can get a good feel for the architecture that came before. The complex is more Hindu than Buddhist, from Linga Parvata in the background to the style of the remaining buildings and the overall layout.

Very little is known about the history of Wat Phu or the people who built the complex. It is suspected the sixth-century Chenla capital was based here.

In addition, there are remains of walls and a **palace** in the area. These date from the mid-12th century. It is possible the buildings are the work of the Khmer King Suryavarman II – the founder of Angkor Wat.

You enter the complex along the **grand causeway** (late 11th-early 12th century) and walk around a number of buildings and a moated area. There are two sandstone buildings on either side of the causeway; these are probably the most intact buildings in the complex.

If you continue up some stairs behind the two sandstone buildings you will come to the **Nandi Pavilion** and more temple remains. Nandi is Siva's bull (Hindu). At one point each chamber of the pavilions contained statues, but these disappeared many years ago. Continuing on you will come to the ruins of six small temples made of brick.

Walk farther up the hill and you will come to the **main temple** sanctuary. This temple was dedicated to Siva and parts of the building date from the sixth century. Note the Buddha statue and sacred linga. Walk around the sanctuary and you will encounter more sixth-century ruins – a possible library, a statue of Siva, and the holy spring.

Take care while walking. The ground and steps are uneven and safety is not a concern of the local authorities.

Day-Trips from Champasak

There are other temple complexes in the Champasak area, many dating from the same time as Wat Phu. One that is worth a day-trip is called **Oum Moung** (Um Muang). Most people coming down the river from Pakse make this stop, but you may be able to find a boat going upriver and get off at Ban Noi. Just make sure you know how you are getting back! You can also take the Pakse-bound bus and get off at marker 30 at Ban Thang Beng and follow the track to Ban Noi and on to the Oum Moung site. This road is vehicle-accessible so you might want to hire a tuk-tuk to take you there, wait, and take you back to Champasak (or Pakse).

The highlight of this complex is a sixth-century temple complex surrounded by jungle. The complex is open from about 7 am to 4 pm every day, and admission is around 30¢(3,000 Kip).

Useful Information

Champasak is very limited in services. It is hard to change money or find Internet access.

■ Pakse (Pakxe)

Pakse is a pleasant town with a few remnants of Colonial architecture, an interesting market, and a much better selection of hotels and restaurants than in Champasak. Many people make Pakse their base and day-trip to Champasak and the surrounding temple complexes.

Since there is an airport here and decent road and air connections to Thailand, Pakse is a useful place to handle housekeeping details such as reconfirming or arranging flights, arranging bus, boat, or van travel to the south (Mekong Islands), and resting up if you've just returned from the oouth.

Historically Pakse is of little significance, so there aren't any sights worth your attention. A museum displays a few relics from Wat Phu and other nondescript wats in town. The Morning Market is worth a visit, but that's about it.

Places to Stay

There are a number of good, three-star hotels, and a few guesthouses in Pakse.

$$$$ **Champasak Palace**, No. 13 Rd, ☎ 212781. This was built as a palace, but it never got used as one. Now it has been turned into what passes for a luxury hotel in central Laos. There are 55 rooms of varying sizes and degrees of comfort. If you need access to a health club, satel-

lite TV, and an international restaurant, this is the place to be. Rumor has it the management is planning to open a golf course – the first ever in Laos – but don't hold your breath. Ask about credit cards.

$$-$$$ Champa Residence, No. 13 Rd, ☎ 212120, champare@laotel.com. This is one of the best places to stay in Pakse, but it's a bit out of town. It has A/C, hot water and private bathrooms, satellite TV, and a terrace. Credit cards accepted.

Places to Eat

$-$$ May Kham, with Vietnamese and Lao food, No. 13 Rd, right near the bridge over the Don River.

Several of the hotels in town have decent restaurants, but it may be hard to get a seat since there are numerous tour buses unloading at these places. If you crave Western-style food, the hotels are your best bet.

Nightlife

Pakse is not known for its nightlife. Hotel bars are your best option. Otherwise you can always watch the people and activities along the river.

Shopping

The **Morning Market** is pretty comprehensive, but doesn't have much in the souvenir department.

Tours & Travels

Sodetour is one of the better-known and most reliable agencies. It is conveniently located next to the Vietnamese Consulate on No. 13 Rd (☎ 212122).

Getting There & Around

Pakse is a regional hub, so there are options here not found in nearby Champasak or in the south.

Local

The town is small enough to walk almost everywhere. A bicycle (available at most hotels and guesthouses for a small charge) is another good

option. You can also hire a tuk-tuk –
especially for the trip to the long-distance bus station or the boat quays.

Tuk-tuk

Long Distance

For **bus** travel, make
sure you go to the right
station – there are two. If
you are going north, you
need to go to the station at KM 7 on Highway 13. The other
terminal is at KM 8 on the south side of town. Take a tuk-tuk
(40¢/4,000 Kip) to get to the station. Tell the driver where you
plan to go so you end up at the right place!

The buses operate on a schedule (in theory), but in reality
many don't leave until they are fully loaded (some would say
over-stuffed) with passengers and cargo. Our bus to the
Mekong Islands was quite dilapidated. It left over an hour
late and was loaded down the center with a double layer of
bags of concrete. The late arrivals had to sit on the concrete.
Baggage went on top – no guarantee it wouldn't fall off or be
taken by someone else. The alternative was an overloaded
boat that took longer than the bus.

Fares are about $4 (40,000 Kip) to Vientiane (12-15 hours,
leaving every few hours beginning at 7 am). To Champasak,
plan on leaving at 9 am (two hours, $1.50/15,000 Kip). To Don
Khong (the main Mekong Island) plan to leave about 9 am
and spend four five hours en route ($1.60/16,000 Kip).

If you are going to Thailand you need to take a **ferry** across
the river (at the end of Rd. No 11) to the village of Muang Kao.
Then you can get a mini-bus or share taxi to the Thai border
at Chongmek. From there you get a share taxi or bus to Ubon
Ratchathani. The cost is about $2 (20,000 Kip) plus 200 Thai
Baht ($4), and it takes five hours altogether.

> **Tip:** Having done this before, I think next
> time I will fly to Vientiane then go by road
> across the Friendship Bridge!

Right now you can't get to Vietnam or Cambodia by road from
Pakse (unless you go to Vientiane). This is changing, but not
yet. **Van/mini-bus** is the way to go to Vientiane (about $20) or

Don Khong ($10). Check with the better hotels for vans going your way. Sodetour may also be able to help.

 By **boat**, you'll find the boats are rickety (unless you arrange one through a private company) with no safety vests or padding. Still, the people I traveled with who took the boat trip south enjoyed it. The ride to Don Khong takes six-seven hours and costs about the same as the bus. The ride to Champasak takes about two hours and is also on par with the cost of the bus. Boats leave from the jetty at the south end of town.

Going north by boat (to Vientiane) is not really feasible any more.

By **air**, Lao Aviation has daily flights to Vientiane and three-four flights a week to Savannakhet.

Useful Information

Airlines

 Lao Aviation has an office at the airport, and may still have one near the boat departure area (☎ 212252).

Banks/Money Exchange

There are money changers at hotels and the Morning Market. Banks are few and far between.

Embassies/Consulates

The **Vietnamese** consulate is on No. 13 Rd, by Sodetour.

Internet/Communications

There are a few Internet cafés on the edge of town away from the river.

Medical

You are only a couple of hours from Thailand. Charter or hire a car and go there.

Northern Laos

The northern part of Laos is an adventurer's dream. Wild rivers, waterfalls, caves, elephant camps, trekking, hill tribes, ancient temples, mountain biking trails, and former royal palaces. You could spend the entire trip in and around Luang Prabang, wander into the hill tribe areas, go to the Plain of Jars, or to the Pak Ou caves, and on and on. By far my favorite place is Luang Prabang and the activities accessible from there.

■ Luang Prabang

Luang Prabang (LP) is a city that always seems to be calling my name. Whenever possible, I try to include a stopover in LP – at least yearly, if I'm fortunate. It is a town that is truly deserving of its designation as a UNESCO World Heritage Site. Change is coming to LP, faster than I'd like, but some-how the town is coping with a move into the 21st century without giving up all the charms of the past.

During my first visit, among the charms and yet most nega-tive aspects of LP were the dirt alleys running down to the Mekong – often filled with mud, garbage and dead critters in the rainy season. Under the auspices of a UN-French pro-gram, the alleys are changing, but without losing their unique charm. The open gutters and dirt paths are being replaced with interwoven brick surfaces and covered gutters. No lon-ger is crossing in the dark or during a torrential downpour a risk to life and limb. The houses look almost the same, although many have sprouted large satellite TV dishes, and the chickens still peck in the gardens along the sides of the brick work.

Luang Prabang is a place to relax, recharge, see Southeast Asia as is should be, and experience the charms of a people and culture that maintain their roots while moving onto the future. Take at least a few days – a week is better – and you'll return to your work-a-day world refreshed, with a greater appreciation for a seriously unique part of a wonderful country.

History

Luang Prabang was the capital of Laos for about 200 years, beginning with the rule of Fa Ngoum (or Ngum), the king of The Land of a Million Ele-phants, or Lane Xang. When Fa Ngoum chose this

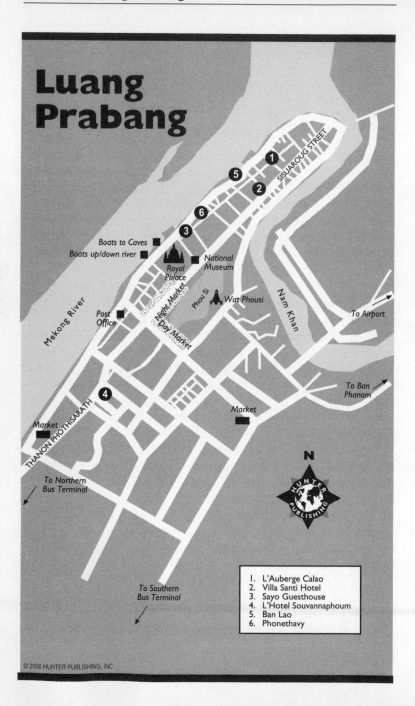

Luang Prabang

Boats to Caves
Boats up/down river

Royal Palace

National Museum

Phou Si · Wat Phousi

Mekong River

THANON PHOTHISARATH

Post Office

Night Market / Day Market

Nam Khan

To Airport

To Ban Phanom

Market

Market

SISUAROUG STREET

To Northern Bus Terminal

To Southern Bus Terminal

N

1. L'Auberge Calao
2. Villa Santi Hotel
3. Sayo Guesthouse
4. L'Hotel Souvannaphoum
5. Ban Lao
6. Phonethavy

area as his cap-
ital in the 14th
century, it had
already been
the capital of
local rulers for
at least the
previous 600
years.

There used to
be as many as
65 or 70 wats

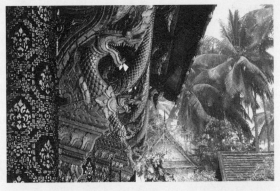

in LP – during the heyday of the late 18th century – but now
there are *only* about 30 left – quite a few, considering the
"city" has only about 10,000 residents.

Luang Prabang was a great prize, fought over repeatedly. As a
result, virtually every wooden building has been destroyed,
but the wats remain.

The capital was moved to the area of present-day Vientiane in
1563, and the importance of LP as an administrative center
diminished greatly over the next 300 or so years. Nonetheless,
LP remained the seat of the royal family until the communists
took over in 1975.

The French had primary control over Laos from about 1886
until the 1950s, although they continued to have some influence until the monarchy fell. The end result is remnants of
French influence – in the coffee, bread, and pastries, at least.

Luang Prabang was once the capital of an ancient kingdom
known as Lane Xang. The entire village is now a UNESCO
World Heritage Site (1995). The city is almost overrun with
beautiful temples and historical monuments, and is well
worth several days of your time. It's also a good place to
arrange tours in other cities or to the hill tribe areas, arrange
flights, and plan onward itineraries if this is close to your last
stop in Laos.

Luang Prabang is located on the east bank of the Mekong
River, about 500 km/300 miles upriver from Vientiane and
200 m/600 feet above sea level. It is the oldest Laotian town
still in existence.

This is the capital of Luang Prabang Province, as well as being the ancient capital city of the Lan Xang Kingdom (Kingdom of a million elephants...which by the way, have long since disappeared, as visitors will quickly see). Luang Prabang was founded around 1354 and was an important religious and cultural center. During its original heyday Buddhism became the main religion. Luang Prabang remained the capital of the Lan Xang kingdom until 1545 when King Photisarat moved it to Wieng Chan, now called Vientiane.

THE LEGEND

According to legend, the town was first named Muang Swa (Sua), after King Khun Xua around the eighth century and was later known as Xieng Dong and Xieng Thong. During the reign of King Fa Ngum between 1354 and 1372 the town was renamed Luang Prabang after the golden image of Buddha, the Phrabang.

Even after the Lan Xang period ended, Luang Prabang was considered the main source of royal power. It wasn't until the Pathet Lao took over in 1975 that the monarchy was finally dissolved.

Luang Prabang is well maintained. It was a major trade center with people from upper Laos, Thailand, Vietnam, southern China and Burma but there was little contact with non-Asian countries until the French arrived in the mid-19th century.

Today Luang Prabang is both a port on the Mekong River and a trade center for agricultural products and handicrafts of silk, wood, and silver. It is also developing as a massage/spa center.

Getting There & Away

 I highly recommend flying to almost all destinations in Laos. The roads are generally poor, and the drivers are, to put it mildly, undisciplined. There are occasional outbreaks of banditry, but generally only along a small stretch of highway between Vang Vieng and Vientiane. However, since this stretch is one of the few road trips I would even suggest you consider, always ask local tourist offices in LP and Vientiane before booking the trip.

By Road

Tourist buses ply the main road between Vientiane and LP. The company I am familiar with is called **Diethelm** (www.diethelm-travel.com), and any quality travel agent can help you arrange a seat. The cost is about double the same trip on a local bus or mini-van, but the drivers are much better, the vehicles top-notch, and the trip is quicker since few if any stops are made along the way. I don't believe the drivers on the Diethelm buses are supposed to pick up passengers en route, but they do anyway. You can complain to the company, but there is little they can, or will, do. Laos is desperately poor, so if someone can make a bit extra, he or she is going to try. Expect to pay $10-$15 for the one-way trip. It will take any-where from six to about 10 hours.

Some people come overland from Chiang Mai in Thailand – more power to them. It takes 25-28 hours and costs $25-$30. The buses are so-so, the road is tortuous, and the risks, extra 24-26 hours, and discomfort are not, in my opinion, worth the few dollars you save. If you do choose this route, you MUST get your Laotian visa in advance. The visas are not issued at the border, and don't believe anyone who tells you otherwise. You will be turned back and have to wait hours for the return bus, pay a duplicate fare, and end up losing about 36 hours, most of it on a bus.

Driving yourself is not really an option. I doubt there is a place that will rent you a car, and the roads are poorly marked and dangerous. You can, however, rent a scooter or motorbike – there are dozens of travel agencies and tourist offices that will be glad to help. Figure on about $15 per day for a decent bike, and bring your own helmet. Ask the agent to draw a strip map and show you where you can get fuel en route. Many times fuel is simply sold from 50-gallon drums or small bottles at shops along the side of the road. It is worth asking your agent to write down the information you need to get gas, and what the price should be per liter.

It may be possible to hitchhike, but that is also not an option I can endorse. You may, however, be able to arrange a ride with someone from a Non-Governmental Organization (NGO), but that is usually only possible from within the country. From Vientiane it is a real possibility, though.

By Boat

It is possible to travel within Laos by boat, but connections are disappearing as the roads improve. You can go between Vientiane and LP on the Mekong River. The boats are not luxurious, and some offer better accommodation than others. At a minimum you should be able to get a room with a door and sleeping mats. Ask around at the various travel agencies in Vientiane and LP to see what is available. Cargo boats are going to take several days to reach Vientiane, and longer to LP (upriver). There are faster boats, but you should still allow two days. Either type of boat may include overnights on the boat or in small villages – it pays to ask. Figure on $25-$50 for the entire trip, including meals, but make sure to bring some snacks and water, just in case.

You can also go to and from LP and the Thai border area (Ban Houei Xai near the Thai border) if you're feeling really adventurous.

By Air

Lao Aviation and **Thai Air** fly several times a day between Luang Prabang and Chiang Mai. Thai Air also flies from Bangkok to LP several times a day. Other carriers may fly from their home countries – for example, Vietnam Airlines flies from LP to Hanoi, and the regional Chinese carriers may have flights. Check with the carriers. It is difficult to book Southeast Asian countries' national carriers from outside the region. Thai Air can be booked from overseas, however.

The flight from Bangkok to LP is about 90 minutes; from Chiang Mai it's about 60 minutes. It takes 60 minutes to fly to Hanoi from LP.

Within the country you can get almost anywhere on Lao Aviation. However, there are three things to keep in mind:

□ Flights are often overbooked, sold-out, canceled.

□ Flights do not go to the places you want to go as often as you would like. Many flights are only once or twice a week, so plan accordingly.

□ Other than a few places in the north, there are no direct flights from LP to the rest of Laos. Plan on overnighting in Vientiane.

Lao Aviation, as mentioned earlier, flies French-made ATR-72 props and has a decent safety record to date. You can get almost anywhere (except the far south of the country) by air.

Getting Around

 Luang Prabang is made for walking and biking. It is a compact town with a few hills and almost all the local attractions are within a few km of the center of town.

Bicycle: You can rent bikes at almost any guesthouse, travel operation, or independent rental shop in LP. Expect to pay $3-$5 per day, depending on the quality of the bike. High-end hotels will likely charge more, but the equipment may not be any better.

Motorbikes: There are places up and down the main street that rent scooters for $10-$15 per day.

Tuk-Tuks: These are everywhere. You can hire one for a short ride or for the day to go to outlying temples. Prices are fluid, so bargaining is required.

Boats: If you go down to the river behind the Royal Palace/Museum you will find several places that hire boats for short trips or longer ones to the Pak Ou Caves and local villages. A boat for several hours will cost about $15-$20.

Van/Mini-Bus: This is the means the travel/tour operators generally use. As long as you don't mind organized tours and are in a small group, this can be the best way to see the local sites.

What to See & Do

 Wats, wats, and more wats. More than 30 of them, to be precise. That's what Luang Prabang is all about. Some, like Wat Phousi, are better known for the spectacular views, while others are quite historically significant, in addition to being beautiful. Since there are so many wats, it is worth choosing the ones to inspect closely with some care – otherwise you will quickly overdose and all the wats will start to look very much alike.

The "Must See" Wats

Wat May. Next to the National Museum, parts of this structure date from the late 1700s, making it one of the oldest buildings in the area. The building is heavily gilded, and the gilt is embellished with red inside. Make sure to take note of the heavily carved central beam inside – the figures are all from Hindu mythology, not Buddhism.

Mount Phousi (Wat Pa Huak and Wat Chom Si). This is one of the best known landmarks in all of Laos. The "Mount" itself is not all that high – a bit over 300 steps brings you to the top – but it has a commanding position in LP. Its location, almost directly across the street from the former Royal Palace, and the views at sunrise and sunset, make it easy to find and a must-see site. The hill is right in the middle of LP, and many visitors never make it to the top, let alone around to the other side. You can go up one side and down the other, and walk back around the "Mount." **Wat Pa Huak** is in poor repair. There is a fee (about $1) to go up from the Royal Palace (western) side, but not from the eastern side. Unfortunately, the eastern side is not well marked, so it is better to pay on the west side and either return the same way, or wend your way down on the eastern side. At the top, **Wat Chom Si** is worth a quick peek. Note – there is a Red Cross-run Internet center and massage/sauna facility very close to the exit point on the eastern side – you can kill two birds with one stone, if you're so inclined.

Wats Along Phothisarath

Some of these wats charge admission and some don't.

Wat Sene lies upriver along the main road. It is built in the highly ornate Thai style, and dates from 1718. The outside borders on gaudy, and the interior is only slightly more understated – lots of red and gold here, too.

Wat Xieng Thong is a bit farther upriver, and you have to climb a flight of steps to get there. This wat is actually a compound with a number of buildings, mostly in the usual red and gilt. This wat is known for its tiled roofs, painted

scenes, carvings, and mosaics, and is probably the single most essential wat to visit during your stay in LP. It is also quite historic, having been built in 1559, and having survived both Chinese raids and the communist takeover. Unlike Wat Sene, Wat Xieng Thong is built in the less ostentatious Luang Prabang style. Admission charged.

There are other, less impressive and less important wats lining Phothisarath, and they all make for a pleasant day's meandering. Some of these include **Wat Phra Maha That** (near Hotel Phousi), **Wat Phra Bath** (behind the market), **Wat That Luang** (behind the stadium), and others farther out of town. If you want to visit all the wats, allow at least two days, and hire a bicycle or scooter.

Other wats close to town that are worth a visit include **Wat Vixoun** at the south end of Mount Phousi. Although the original building dated from the early 1500s, it was destroyed by the Chinese and rebuilt in the late 1800s. It is noteworthy for the large collection of religious art, ancient steles, even older stupas, and Buddha statues.

Wat Aham is right next to Wat Vixoun, and its interior is worth a look.

The National Museum

This living history museum, the Former Royal Palace, is easy to find, and absolutely not to be missed. It's right off the main street (Phothisarath), on the Mekong River side. The building only dates from 1904, but it is significant since it is one of the few buildings used by the former royal family that was not destroyed after the 1975 communist takeover. Although the building was a "gift" from the French, it is classically Lao in style. The museum is filled with mementos given to the king by dignitaries, heads of state, and other royals from all over the world, and has more than its share of ancient Buddhas. However, perhaps its most interesting aspect is the glimpse it gives into the day-to-day life of a citizen-king. The tour takes you through the royal chambers, living areas, kitchen, and more.

Suggested Walking Tour

Luang Prabang is meant to be seen on foot. The best way to orient yourself is to bring a map of the town and climb to the top of **Mount Phousi**. Then head back down the west (river) side, and visit the **Royal Palace**. Take a break for a leisurely lunch along Phothisarath. Then choose a selection of the wats described above and explore them during the afternoon. You can duck in and out of the many shops along your route.

The next day, head to the south end of Phothisarath (near the Post Office), then down to the **Mekong**. You can walk along the river, looking down at the dhows and other boats that are so important to community life, and eventually you'll end up at the far northern reaches of Phothisarath again – the river curves around so subtly you may not even notice. Spend the afternoon enjoying a **massage** with herbs and hot stones. This will get you ready to rent a **bicycle** the next day and ride east of LP to explore some of the outlying wats.

Where to Stay

There are literally dozens of reasonably-priced B&B accommodations within walking distance of Mount Phousi and the sights in LP. In addition, there are hotels of all sizes and standards, although none come close to four-star.

Most people stay close to the center of LP, so that's where you'll find the majority of the top-end hotels and many B&Bs as well.

Pre-Book/Prepay Hotel Options

If you want true luxury and a wonderful setting, here is a great one.

$$$$-$$$$$**Villa Santi Hotel**, the former residence of a Lao princess, on Sakkarine Rd., Ban Wat Nong Village, Luang Prabang. The Villa Santi Hotel Luang Prabang is situated in the heart of the

HOTEL PRICE CHART	
Rates are per room based on double occupancy.	
$	Under $12
$$	$12-$25
$$$	$26-$40
$$$$	$40-$80
$$$$$	Over $80

World Heritage Site conveniently positioned close to many historical sites such as the former Royal Palace, ancient temples, Mont Phousi and shopping areas. The hotel is 10 minutes from the airport and right in the town itself.

There are 25 luxurious boutique rooms and suites, all elegantly decorated in a charming Royal Lao theme. The rooms are decorated with authentic Lao rosewood furnishings and silk textiles, using only genuine local natural products appropriate to the theme and comfort. Rooms are fully equipped with deluxe amenities such as air conditioning, mini-bar, satellite TV, hot water shower, bath and telephone.

Internet booking rates range from $78/$78 for single/double in low season (summer) to $96/$96 the rest of the year for deluxe rooms (pre-paid) to $100/$100 summer and $130/$160 the rest of the year for Internet booking (non-prepaid). Rack rates are at least double or triple the pre-paid rates. All rates include taxes, breakfast, and airport transfers. Highly recommended. Worth the money.

General Hotel Options

$$$$ **L'Hotel Souvannaphoum**, Phothisarath, ☎ 212200, fax 212577, sunaphum@laotel.com. This hotel takes VISA

credit cards, which is unusual for this part of Laos. The hotel consists of two French Colonial-era villas that have been restored and filled with statues set in gardens. There is an on-site restaurant. It's conveniently located right on Phothisarath (at the north or upriver end). Although pricey, the hotel falls far short of luxury status. There are many pleasant choices that cost far less.

$$$ L'Auberge Calao, on the River Road, ☎/fax 212100. The views over the Mekong River make this hotel worth the slightly high price. It is small (four rooms), friendly, and relaxed. There is also an on-site restaurant.

$$-$$$ Sayo Guesthouse, Sotikoumman Road (close to/above Wat Xieng Muang), ☎ 252614. This place is one I highly recommend if your budget allows. It's decorated in local fabrics, lots of wood, and has 10 cosy rooms. If you have children, this is a great place since it is well designed for them.

$$ Ban Lao, Souvannaphum Road (south of Phousi), ☎ 252078, banlao@laotel.com. Another good choice, especially for the cost-conscious. The rooms are large and airy. The building is an old mansion with wooden floors and a white-washed exterior. It's one of the few places in town with satellite TV, if that's important. An attached restaurant serves French and Asian specialties. Most of the rooms have en suite bathrooms.

$ Phonethavy, Chaotonkham Road (center of town), no phone. Tile floors, some en suite bathrooms, and owners who speak very good English.

Where to Eat

The River Road and Phothisarat are lined with dozens of restaurants, and the quality varies greatly. You can get a beer, a baguette sandwich, pizza, a few Lao specialties, French dishes, or any number of

RESTAURANT PRICES	
$	Under $2
$$	$2-$5
$$$	$6-$10
$$$$	$11-$20
$$$$$	Over $20

Southeast Asian options at most places. In addition, there are wonderful seafood offerings in the River Road places. I have never had a bad meal in Luang Prabang.

For quality Lao/French foods, your best choices are the better hotels or the places along the main street.

For ethnic (non-Southeast Asian) food, try the following:

$$ **Nazim Indian Restaurant** (there's also one in Vientiane along the river). It's on the east side of Phousi, close to the Red Cross massage and Internet center. The food is good and the prices very reasonable. I always have at least one meal here when I'm in LP.

$ **Visoun**, Visunnarat Road, across from the Rama Hotel, no phone. Serves a variety of Chinese and Thai dishes, intermingled with French options.

$ **Yong Khoune**, close to Visoun, no phone. Serves a mix of Chinese and Thai dishes. A good choice for Mekong River fish.

For cafés try **Healthy and Fresh** or **Luang Prabang Bakery** – both on Sisavangvong.

Nightlife

Bar- and café-hopping make for a pleasant evening. There are English-style pubs (**Maylek**), and a few good bars (**La Villa**, **Visun**, **L'Auberge Calao**). People-watching is always fun, and most restaurants have either a terrace or patio along the street.

The **Royal Theater** at the National Museum hosts dance and other cultural events at a cost of about $7 (70,000 Kip).

Shopping

The main street is a shopper's paradise. You can buy native crafts (there is a shop run by a pseudo-government entity that sponsors local tribal women and their work), spend a day getting spa-quality treatments at low prices, and buy the usual tourist kitsch. The **Day Market** at the south end of town is a great place to buy crafts, but bargain *hard*. As the Day Market closes down, the main street is closed off and the Night Market opens. A shopper's dream!

The **Night Market** offers lengths of silk, carved items, antiques, and silver, among other things. The colors of the silk are marvelous – warm reds, yellows, golds, and oranges, with the occasional cooler blue/green piece. These make great scarves or table runners and are easily packed for your return trip.

On the main road (Phothisarath/Sisavangvong) you will find galleries (**Baan Khily Café** and **Paper Gallery**, **Nora Gallery**), and handicrafts shops galore.

Tours & Travels

Luang Prabang is filled with tour operators. For those seeking active, managed adventure trekking with quality materials and very experienced guides and European ownership, see the later section on Tiger Trails.

You can find **Tiger Trails** on Photisarath near the post office, or check their website at www.tiger-trails.com. The operation is owned by a German who has been in LP for years.

Another tour operator is **Diethelm Travel**, far up on Photisarath – Namphu Square (PO Box 2657), Setthathirat Road, Vientiane, Laos PDR, ☎ 21 213833, 215920, 215128, fax 216294, 217151, www.diethelm.laopdr.com, ditralao@laotel.com.

Day-Trips from Luang Prabang

The west, or right, bank of the Mekong River is a paradise of small villages and monasteries. It's easy to get there – just head down to the river below the Royal Palace area and you'll come to the boat landings. You can hire a boat for a half-day ($8-$10 for the boat), or arrange with a ferry operator to take you across to Wat Chom Pet, and pick you up about four hours later. This should cost about $5 or so, but make sure to agree on the price as well as the pick-up place and time in advance.

> **Tip:** You should not pay the ferry operator until you are on the boat for the return trip!

Boat tours can also be arranged, but the distance to be covered is easily walkable, and probably faster than getting on and off a boat numerous times. The main wats, going upstream, are: **Wat Chom Pet**, **Wat Long Khoun**, and **Wat Tham**. There are admission charges of $1-$2 for each wat, and Wat Long Khoun is actually a cave, so bring a flashlight.

You can also go downstream from Wat Chom Pet to **Wat Xiang Men**, and another four km/2.5 miles to the pottery village of **Ban Chan**.

To really see these wats and nearby villages, chartering a boat is an excellent idea – and the cost is quite reasonable if shared. Local travel agents can arrange this and make sure you are not left in some unplanned place quibbling about fees and payments.

East of Luang Prabang are some handicrafts villages specializing in weaving and knife-making. If you rent a bicycle, these villages are easy to visit. **Ban Phanom**, the weaving village, is about three km/two miles east. The villagers are from a minority tribe – the Lu – from southern China. Close by is the tomb of Henri Mouhot – the Frenchman who is credited with "discovering" Angkor Wat. Ask for directions in Ban Phanom – it's only about two km/1.2 miles. The second village, **Ban Hat Hien**, is on the road to the airport. Bear to the right just before the terminal and go to the end of the road. This village has put the shells from Vietnam-American War big guns to good use – as bellows for the fires used to make knives and bullets!

Pak Ou Caves – Upstream

 This is the most popular excursion from LP. The caves are about 25 km/16 miles upriver from the town. Any travel agent in town can arrange the boat trip and caves visit for you. These caves are supposedly filled with over 4,000 Buddha statues of all sizes in the series of caves. Bring a flashlight or candles and matches. If you want, you can charter a boat for about $20, but the tours are so well-organized that it makes sense to go that route. Besides, you are almost guaranteed a stop-over at **Xang Hai** village on the way back. This is the village where the local whisky (lau-lao) is brewed.

It is possible to rent kayaks or canoes – ask at the travel agents in LP. Note that overnight accommodation, should you need it, is very basic, as is food.

Khouang-Sy Waterfalls – Downstream

These scenic waterfalls are about 30 km/20 miles south of LP. Again, the local travel agents are usually the best source of travel arrangements for the trip. The falls are more like cascades than actual free-falling "falls," but still quite lovely. You can swim in the pools above the falls, but not in the lower pools. You can charter a boat for $10-$20, or let a travel agent make the arrangements ($5-$10 per person, usually including lunch). There are also buses, but they are slow and uncomfortable. Finally, you can hire a tuk-tuk for a few dollars, but the driver may abandon you.

As above, it is possible to rent kayaks or canoes.

Caving

There are dozens of hotels, guest houses, and travel agents that can arrange trips to explore some of the many caves in the area. Check out the equipment and ask around with other travelers to choose a trip that suits your needs.

River Trips

The Mekong wends its way south to Vientiane. If you have the time, and/or you don't like frantic bus rides over hilly, bumpy, winding roads, a sedate float down the Mekong may be just your cup of tea (or coffee!). The trip generally takes about two days and one night, so arrange a boat and accommodations that suit your style and temperament. As always, your hotel or a local travel agent is the best source for arrangements, but other travelers are the best choice for quality assurance.

River excursions also allow you to visit some of the temples that are not too far from Luang Prabang, if you aren't "templed out" already. These trips are easy to arrange in the village.

Cycling

The area around Luang Prabang has a number of interesting temples that can be reached by bicycle, often combined with a bit of hiking. There are several places in Luang Prabang that rent low-tech bicycles to tourists. Take a good map with you. The riding is easy, but if you plan to ride here, or anywhere else in Asia, a lightweight cable lock and a helmet are worth packing. They are in short supply in this part of the world. Rental rates should be only a few dollars a day and there are several street-side vendors with bicycles for rent.

Walking & Hiking

As a major walker and hiker, I found Laos to be a great place. You can easily and safely walk almost anywhere. There aren't many cars or scooters (yet), and those that are around generally yield to pedestrians (unlike Vietnam). Most of the terrain around the main sights and destinations is flat or gently sloping so it's easy to walk. Walking also puts you closer to the people, architecture and commerce. In fact, it was because I walked so much that I found the Red Cross Internet Café, massage center, and body scrub salon – a great place to relax and contribute to a good cause!

Useful Information

Airlines

Lao Aviation is on Visunnarat, not far from the Rama Hotel, ☎ 212172. It has a small office at the airport too.

Bangkok Airways has an airport office.

Thai Air may soon be flying into Luang Prabang. You can contact them at www.thaiair.com, or through the Star Alliance website (www.staralliance.com).

Any of the tour operators in town can help arrange flights.

Banks/Money Exchange

Exchanging money in LP is easy. There are money changers all along the main streets. You may pay a hefty commission for travelers checks, so be careful.

Embassies/Consulates

There aren't currently any offices in LP.

Internet/Communications

Internet cafés are everywhere. The service has improved dramatically over the past five years and is approaching high speed in a few places.

The Post Office at the south end of the main street can handle international calls.

Medical

If you need medical assistance get to Chiang Mai or Bangkok – it's only an hour or so by air.

■ Adventures in Northern Laos

Northern Laos is a truly beautiful, laid-back, adventure-filled place. Most people base out of Luang Prabang, so that's the area of focus in this book. Some of the favored activities are:

☐ Hiking

☐ Trekking

☐ Mountain biking

☐ Rafting

☐ Kayaking

☐ Rock climbing

☐ Elephant safaris

☐ Mekong River trips (slow and fast boats)

Luang Prabang is literally swarming with tour organizers. Every guest house and hotel has someone who can make arrangements, and the main street is lined with travel agents. Some agents are actually representatives for other agents, and some are specialists. My personal choice is **Tiger Trail** (www.tigertrail-laos.com), owned by an expatriate German and staffed by locals and other expatriates, all speaking excellent English. The equipment is top-notch, and helmets are standard. They offer both small group and cus-tom-designed tours, tailored to your abilities. For more gener-alized tours (to the Pak Ou Caves, Plain of Jars, along the Mekong River, or to nearby temples) there are dozens of arrangers in town, and one is much like the other. For spe-cialty tours with an active, adventurous twist, most tour oper-ators sent me to Tiger Trails.

Hiking & Trekking

Someone asked me once what the difference is between hiking and trekking. In Laos a hike is for one day or less (no overnight stay) and trekking is two or more days, normally involving camping.

Either way is perfect for reaching waterfalls, caves, jungle trails, and rugged mountains that are off the beaten path. In Laos you may not see waterfalls on the main path – you have to get off the road. You are also likely to see wonderful plant and bird life (but not much wildlife – the local people have eaten most of it!).

Locally arranged treks and hikes tend to run from a few dollars a day to $15 or so, but can run more if you want to have all the amenities included on overnight trips.

Some of the highlights of treks include:

□ Visiting hill tribes such as Hmong and Khmu.

□ Sighting waterfalls and taking a cooling dip in the pools.

□ Riding an elephant.

□ Rafting or canoeing down a river.

□ Visiting the Pak Ou and other caves.

□ Padding along a jungle path.

□ Trading experiences with other travelers.

□ Seeing how other people live.

Recent sample prices for the Tiger Trails hiking and trekking trips were:

Full-day hike/trek for two people: $25-$28 each.

Two-day trekking for two people: $54-$59 each.

Four-day trekking for four people: $115 each.

These are trips that include meals, gear, transport, and almost all other costs. This is not always the case with other arrangers, so check carefully. Information for other tour arrangers is included at the end of this section.

What can you expect on a trek or combination of trek and other activities? Most one-day treks (or hikes, if you prefer) visit two hill tribes: the Hmong and Khmu. They leave from your hotel or a central location about 8:30 am in a four-wheel drive or mini-van and return about 5:30 pm. You can expect to hike for six hours or so over fairly steep terrain at moderate altitude.

The trips may also be extended to include stays in one or more hill tribe villages. In these treks you normally get to the Tad

Sae Waterfall and get a boat trip on the way back. You may visit more than one tribe, depending on the route.

On a three-day trip you can visit two of the three hill tribes (overnighting with each one), the Kuang Si Waterfall, and the Pak Ou Caves (where families leave their old Buddhas). This involves bus or jeep and river transport the first day, then about seven hours of trekking spread over the next two days. If you are interested in a more challenging trek, you can choose an option that is still three days but includes much more difficult trekking all three days, visiting the Tad Sae Waterfall and Hmong and Khmu villages, with overnights in each village. The Hmong village is at 1,400 m/4,700 feet, so it is a bit of a climb the first day. This option includes about 14 hours of trekking, almost half on the first day.

There are longer trips. You can spend several days on the 2,200 m/7,300-foot Phou Phabang (a high plateau, also called the Phou Pavie). This option is pure trekking – you probably aren't going to any caves or waterfalls – and you can expect to hike for at least 18 hours over four days. The altitude can be a problem for some people, so avoiding alcohol is an excellent idea.

The better tours, as mentioned before, include all meals and admissions, as well as equipment and transportation. Many tours do not include equipment such as mosquito netting and sleeping bags, or safety gear like helmets. Find out so you aren't surprised when you reach camp.

THE HILL TRIBES

The three hill tribes you are most likely to encounter in northern Laos are the Hmong (a tribe belonging to the High Lao or Lao Suung), the Lao Lum (Low Lao), and Khmu (a tribe belonging to the Upland Lao or Lao Theung).

The **Hmong** are very warlike and were ideal as CIA-trained special forces during the 1960s and 1970s. Following the 1875 revolution, overthrow of the monarchy, and take-over by the Pathet Lao, many Hmong fled, settling in large numbers primarily in the United States. The Hmong are farmers, growing dry rice and corn using slash and burn techniques. They also raise various domestic animals such as cattle, pigs, chickens, and water buffalo. The Hmong are the major growers of opium among the ethnic groups in Laos. They are called the High Lao because they live at altitudes of at least 1,000 meters/3,300 feet above sea level.

Hmong women

The **Lao Lum** have traditionally lived in the vicinity of or in the Mekong River valley. They are related to the Thai-Kadai – a group that lives all over Southeast Asia as well as in southern China and the eastern part of the Indian subcontinent. They tend to live at 200-400 m/650-1,300 feet of elevation and are subsistence farmers who grow wet rice. Unlike many other hill tribes, they are Theravada Buddhists.

The **Khmu** are the poor cousins in northern Laos. They tend to live on slopes between 300 and 900 m/1,000 to 3,000 feet above sea level. They have the lowest standard of living among the hill tribes in the north. They either work as laborers for other hill tribes or are farmers growing rice, cotton, tobacco, and coffee.

All three tribes live in houses with dirt floors and wood beams.

Elephant Rides

Riding an elephant is something everyone should experience at least once. Riding one as part of your trek is far more interesting than if you ride one at a big tourist attraction, and the cost will be far more reasonable. Most elephant rides are two people to a "hoodah" (the wicker basket/seating area). You can only put one foot on top of the elephant, so the other foot keeps slipping down the side. An hour

or two is probably long enough, so make sure that is agreed upon before you get on. Elephants don't mind getting muddy, so it's a great way to follow a stream and stay relatively clean and dry. It's also a less strenuous way to head up into the hills than doing it all on foot. The rolling motion is rather nice once you get used to it.

> **Tip:** Try to ride the lead elephant. Elephants like to dip their trunks in mud, dirt, water, and other runny or gooey substances, and then spray the concoction over their backs to cool off. If the lead elephant decides it's time to give you a shower, you could be in for an unpleasant surprise!

You can ride an elephant for half a day along jungle tracks, visit the Tad Sae Waterfall, pass teak plantations and rice paddies, and come upon wonderful valley and hill views around every corner.

Elephants are easily trainable and able to move incredibly heavy objects. They are also interesting, if not always comfortable, to ride. The view from up high is great.

Many tour operators offer half- or full-day elephant rides, using jeeps or similar vehicles to get you to the villages where the elephants are maintained. Costs vary depending on outfitter and duration, but expect to pay anywhere from $25 to $40 for a day's ride, including end-to-end transportation from

Luang Prabang. Overnight trips and combination trips (with mountain biking, hiking, or rafting/kayaking) are available, too. The higher-end trips will cost about $37 for a half-day elephant ride for two people or $46 per person for a full-day elephant ride with mountain biking or trekking.

Rates vary widely from operator to operator, as do group sizes, amenities, and quality of equipment and guides. You probably can't check out the elephants ahead of time (they don't come to town!), so you'll need to ask other travelers, check out the rest of the equipment, and take your chances.

> **Note:** Do you know how elephants are trained not to run away? When they are very young, the babies are taken away from their mothers, but kept in sight, and a heavy leg iron and chain or rope is placed around the baby's leg. The chain is staked to the ground, and the baby keeps straining to reach its mother. When it continually can't reach her, it gives up. Then the trainers can replace the chain with a very light rope or harness, and the elephant never tries to get away. It has "learned" that something around its leg keeps it tied in place!

Most elephant rides out of Luang Prabang leave from the tour operator's office or other central location about 8:30 am. Some tours actually pick you up at your hotel. The prices I gave assume hotel pick-up and drop-off. You are normally taken by a four-wheel-drive vehicle to the elephant staging area. Your elephant ride may or may not return to the same staging area. Some rides end at the Mekong River and you return to the camp by motorboat and then to Luang Prabang. That is usually the end of the bargain rides. The higher-end tours usually include lunch, a trip to the Tad Sae Waterfall (with admission fees paid), and return to Luang Prabang by boat or four-wheel-drive vehicle, arriving around 3;30 pm.

If you combine the elephant ride with a mountain bike excursion or some trekking, you could spend the rest of the day biking or trekking and get back to Luang Prabang about 5:30 or 6 pm – a pretty full day, so many people choose to extend their trip to two or three days, with overnight stays at a camp or hill tribe villages. On the trek you naturally can't cover as much ground as on the mountain bike, but you should expect to get to the Tad Sae Waterfall and a Khmu village. On the bike extension you can get farther afield, visiting Ban Phanom (a weaving village), Wat Pa Phon Phao (a temple), and the Henry Mouhot gravesite, plus the waterfall.

By extending your trip another day and combining biking, trekking, and the elephant ride you can add a visit to a Lao Lum village, a Hmong village, and a Khmu village.

If you like the sound of two days, you may like three days even better! By adding the third day you can include all the preceding, plus a river trip on a raft or in a kayak.

Mountain Biking

Mountain biking has finally arrived in northern Laos. Tiger Trails was the only operator I found in early 2004 that offered trips, but that has changed by now. Look for quality bikes and helmets or it will be a very hard, very dangerous ride. Most day-trips run 30-50 km/20-32 miles. You will visit a variety of villages, maybe a waterfall, and spend some time on single track in the jungle. Part of your trip will likely be by motorboat.

Keep in mind there can be significant elevation gains on these biking trips, and the trails are minimally maintained at best. A helmet is absolutely essential. You are a long way from medical facilities, and ambulances can't reach you. You should consider having an extensive medical/first aid kit with you and not rely on the trip organizers.

Rafting, Boating, Canoeing & Kayaking

Most tour operators offer river trips of one day, and may offer combinations with trekking, biking, or riding elephants. These trips are usually by raft, but some places are now offering kayak trips as well. The options include visiting villages, waterfalls, and the Pak Ou Caves. These are normally set up to be easy, down-stream paddling trips. For more challenges, a few places are offering whitewater trips, too. For rafting, per person prices for one day/two people average $28-$30, depending on difficulty level.

RIVER SAFETY

Make sure you feel the equipment is waterworthy, and if you think the rafts are overloaded, don't get on. Boats in Southeast Asia are not known for their stability or quality, and overloading is a way of life. A quality tour should have good equipment in good repair, never overloading or taking on passengers who are not part of the tour, and with one life vest per passenger and crew member.

There are three main rivers in the Luang Prabang area that offer opportunities for whitewater rafting: the Nam Suang, Nam Ou, and Nam Pa. Trips on each river should allow you to visit a Lao Lum village. All trips involve four or five hours on the river, and all are of moderate difficulty.

Canoeing/kayaking prices with tour organizers that include everything and use quality equipment (one day, per person) average $45-$50.

Canoeing is not yet easily available despite the relatively placid rivers in the Luang Prabang area. This is probably going to change very soon.

Tubing

Tubing is another activity that is just beginning to show up in Luang Prabang, although it has been available in Vang Vieng for years.

Venturing Farther into Luang Prabang Province

If you want to go to even more remote sites, you might try trekking in and around Muang Ngoi. These trips are usually at least three days since it takes several hours to get there. The treks visit the Hmong and Khmu tribes, and include a stay in a village, a stay in Muang Ngoi, plus a motorboat ride.

The same trip is possible with a combination of trekking and/or biking and/or rafting. You can cover a bit more ground.

The pure trekking option includes eight hours of moderately strenuous hiking. The other options include four or five hours of trekking as well as several hours of biking and/or rafting.

Recent prices for the Muang Ngoi options in US dollars:

☐ Per person, three-day trek, $160

☐ Per person, three-day trek/raft, $180

☐ Add another $10 per person for a biking add-on

Another option is to go to Muang Khua in the far north of Thailand. These trips usually involve extensive trekking and several other activities. The trips tend to be between seven and 14 days. Shorter trips (five days) are possible, but it's a long way to go for such a short time. Most of the activities are at least moderate in difficulty, and the sheer length of the trip adds to the strenuousness. But this excursion gives you the opportunity to visit hot springs, mountain bike to remote villages, visit additional tribes, raft down some new rivers, and see a rarely visited part of Laos. This trip costs anywhere from $50 to $60 per person, all-inclusive.

Other tour operators may be a bit less expensive, but the group size and equipment may not be to your liking. It is very worthwhile to run through all the steps in this section before handing over your money. You may not want, need, or expect the level of service of a Tiger Trails excursion. In Southeast Asia you almost always get what you pay for – that is both good and bad – and this is probably the trip of a lifetime, so scrimp with care.

Tour Operators & Arrangers

Author's note: Adventure travel is just beginning to take off. While the people at Tiger Trails are ahead of the game in many ways, including having their own base camp and European equipment (such as bikes and helmets), things change. By the time this book is available you will likely find there are several competitors offering similar services and quality. We need to hear from you so we can provide the most current information. Please e-mail us at comments@hunterpublishing.com with any updates.

Do a web search for other tour arrangers in Luang Prabang. You can also arrange tours from Vientiane, Vang Vieng, Pakse, and other cities, but you lose the chance to pre-certify the equipment and guide.

Trekking

Most treks to this area can be arranged from Luang Prabang, either through your hotel or a travel agent in town. Just ask around, and help will come pouring out of nowhere! Ask fellow travelers, too – this is the best way to get a handle on features, prices, and trek quality.

If you want to visit the tribal areas, and I highly recommend doing this in all of the Southeast Asia countries, there are a few things you should do to make the trip as interesting and safe as possible.

First and foremost, make sure you talk directly with the person who will be guiding your trek, and meet the rest of the trekking group before you hand over your money. If your group is all in their 20s and you're in your 40s or 50s, you may have very different ideas about the pace, sights, etc., that interest you. The price for a quality trek should include sleeping bags, accommodations, your meals (you have to buy your bottled water and liquor), your guide (except a small tip or gift such as a CD), admissions, and extras you might want. Bring DEET (at least 30% strength).

If you expect to ride an elephant, take a motor boat, canoe, or kayak on the Mekong River, be driven back to your start point, or indulge in other activities, make sure you have negotiated these activities in the price of your trek.

One more thing...your guide should speak several local Lao/tribal dialects and English. Get someone with a good ear for languages to listen to your guide talking to local people and tribal people before you hand over your money.

On the Mekong River

Many treks to the tribal areas include a fast (power) boat ride up or down the Mekong River or one of its tributaries. Ask around at some local travel agencies or your hotel or guest house and you can probably find someone who arranges canoe or kayak rides on a nearby river. This is a great way to see the way people live in small villages along the rivers. It is incredibly relaxing since there are few, if any, rapids. Just look over your craft for leaks or signs of leaks. If you don't want to paddle both directions, make sure you negotiate your return ride. If you're not sure you managed to get return transportation included, I highly recommend you insist on paddling upriver first – it's much easier to float back when you're tired than paddle back against the current! Besides, if your return ride is included, your guide is probably going to insist on a downstream departure.

Cambodia

■ The Country at a Glance

The main attractions, hands down, are the temple complexes at **Siem Reap** – **Angkor Wat**, **Angkor Thom**, and the surrounding temples and monuments.

In this Chapter	
■ History	263
■ Weather & When to Visit	276
■ Phnom Penh	277
■ Siem Reap/Angkor Wat	290
■ Battambang	309
■ Sihanoukville	310
■ Bokor Hill Station - Kompot	312

Next is **Phnom Penh** with its **Silver Pagoda**, **National Museum**, and remnants of Colonial architecture.

Finally, there are the beaches and park at **Sihanoukville**, the **Tonle Sap**, and nearby **Battambang**.

Currency: US$1 = 4,262 Cambodian Riel (KHR).

■ History

Cambodian history can be divided into several main periods:

☐ Pre-Angkor period

☐ Angkor period

☐ Post-Angkor period

The highlight of Cambodian history has always been the Angkor Period, with a confusing multiplicity of kings and influences.

The following is a timeline.

☐ Funan (1st century-613 AD)

☐ Chenla (550-8th century AD

☐ Java invasion (8th century)

☐ Birth of Angkor (802-834 AD)

☐ Angkor era (834-1431 AD)

☐ Angkor sacked by Thai Army; glory of Ankgor ends in 1431

- ☐ Through the mid-1800s, dark period of Angkor (few historical accounts found)
- ☐ 1863 Cambodia became a French colony
- ☐ 1975-1979 reign of terror by Khmer Rouge
- ☐ 1990 Modern Cambodia

Prehistory/Early Kingdoms

Archaeological evidence indicates that parts of the region now called Cambodia were inhabited during the first and second millennia by peoples with a Neolithic culture. By the first century AD, the inhabitants had developed relatively stable, organized societies. The most advanced groups lived along the coast and in the Lower Mekong River valley and delta regions, where they cultivated irrigated rice and kept domesticated animals.

The Indianized Kingdom of Funan

Indian religion, political thought, literature, mythology, and artistic motifs gradually became integral elements in many Southeast Asian cultures. Fortunately, the caste system was never adopted in this region. Funan was the earliest of the "Indianized" states.

By the fifth century, Funan controlled the Lower Mekong River area and the lands around the Tonle Sap. At the same time, much of the Funan culture was thoroughly Indianized.

The Chenla State

The people of Chenla were Khmer. Once they established control over Funan, they continued a three-century conquest of the region. At its height, the Chenla state included much of present-day Laos and Cambodia, as well as parts of Thailand and Vietnam. However, in the eighth century disputes in the court resulted in the kingdom being split into northern (Land Chenla) and southern (Water Chenla) halves. Land Chenla was a relatively stable country; Water Chenla was not. After a number of battles, Water Chenla was taken over by a Khmer ruler from an area north of the Mekong Delta. This marked the beginning of what was to become the huge Khmer empire.

What Caused the Angkor Empire's Rise?

Location, Location, Location. The strategic location chosen by King Jayavarman II made attack very difficult for over six centuries. Angkor was situated at the north end of Tonle Sap Lake, and the only way for invaders to bring in enough forces to fight against Angkor was by sailing upstream from the Mekong River. Geographically, Angkor was protected by rugged, thick forests on all sides. There were no well-developed roads so troops and weapons had to be delivered in a long, vulnerable line.

The Adoption of the Indian Concept of the God-King. As deities, the Khmer kings had the strength of the divine right and absolute power.

Control Over Water and Related Resources. The geographical location of the Angkor Empire results in two extreme seasons – heavy rainfall during the monsoon and the dry period during the off-monsoon season. The Khmer built numerous large reservoirs, dikes, moats and ponds to prevent floods during the monsoon season and to store water for the dry season. The efficient and extensive irrigation system of the ancient Khmer enabled them to cultivate crops two to three times a year, which led to a strong economy.

Why Did the Angkor Civilization Fall?

Many factors led to Angkor's ruin:

☐ The advent of Theravada Buddhism.

☐ Loss of control over water resources.

☐ Increasing external threats.

> **Note:** There is a reason Siem Reap is called that. It means Thai Defeated, and at one point that was a mainstay of Khmer existence – defeating the Thai.

The long waning of the Cambodian empire after the fall of Angkor is not well documented. Only the creation of the French protectorate (1863) prevented its neighbors from swallowing it completely.

Cambodia continued to decline under the French. In 1884 Paris imposed another unequal treaty that went beyond the original protectorate of 1863. This treaty limited the authority of the king, abolished slavery, stationed Colonial officials in the countryside, and codified land ownership.

In March 1945, the Japanese invaded and encouraged the young king to proclaim independence.

In the late 1940s and the early 1950s, the struggle for independence in Cambodia continued. Two political parties were formed under princes of the royal house. The Liberal Party, the more conservative of the two, advocated an evolutionary approach to independence. The Democratic Party, the more radical one, favored the rapid attainment of independence and the formation of whatever political alliances might be necessary. Left out of the political process, Cambodian guerrillas took to the jungles to fight the French.

During the Vietnam-American War the country became a supply area and safe haven for North Vietnamese and Viet Cong forces. Cambodia suffered air strikes from South Vietnam, aimed at destroying enemy installations and supply lines.

Next came the ill-fated Khmer Republic. Unable to defend itself, by 1971 it was on the defensive and losing ground steadily. Lon Nol's inept and corrupt regime suffered one military defeat after another. By early 1975, the situation of the Khmer Republic was so precarious that Phnom Penh itself was invaded. In the following months, the Khmer Rouge steadily tightened the noose around the capital until all escape routes were cut off, and resistance collapsed. The fall of Phnom Penh in April 1975 marked the end of the Khmer Republic.

The entry of the Khmer Rouge into the capital began the grimmest period in Cambodia's history. The Khmer Rouge rulers of Democratic Kampuchea, as the regime that supplanted the Khmer Republic was called, envisioned a totally self-sufficient Cambodia. This self-sufficiency was to be achieved by accelerated agricultural production, which in turn would provide the means to develop other sectors of the economy.

Self-sufficiency, however, was pursued with such ruthlessness that between one and three million people died from purges, beatings, malnourishment, and overwork. To head off opposition to economic and social restructuring, the new regime hunted down and executed virtually anyone who had served the former government.

Sometime in the fall of 1978, the leadership in Hanoi decided to mount a punitive expedition into Cambodia. The Vietnamese launched their military invasion of Cambodia in late December 1978 and Phnom Penh fell to Hanoi's forces in early January 1979.

Cambodia is slowly opening and recovering, but the infrastructure is a disaster, and the lot of the children is often miserable. There are orphans and children pressed into the sex trade or what amounts to slave labor. Education is hard to come by. There are no families who did not suffer the loss of loved ones during the Khmer Rouge rampage of death.

The country has a long way to go before it becomes self-sufficient in terms of food, exports, infrastructure, or basic services.

Highlights of the Angkor Kings

❖ Jayavarman II—the First Angkor King (802-834)

In 802, Jayavarman II crowned himself (for the second time), and thus began a period now considered the beginning of the Khmer civilization and the birth of the Angkor Empire. He was revered as a god-king with absolute power. He decided to place his capital at the northern end of the Tonle Sap (Lake) because of the area's military significance and defensibility. To reach his capital enemies would have to work their way upstream, a difficult task without motorboats.

Jayavarman II actively waged wars throughout Cambodia and expanded his territory. He built a temple devoted to god Shiva at Phnom Kulen about 40 km/24 miles northwest of Tonle Sap. King Jayavarman II reigned until 834. His name is significant in Angkorian history: "Jaya" literally means "victorious" and "varman" means "the protector."

❖ Jayavarman III (834-877)

After the death of Jayavarman II, his son Jayavarman III succeeded him and reigned for over 40 years. Little is known about him. He may have built the Prei Monti temple.

❖ Indravarman I (877-889)

He was the third king of the Angkor kingdom and regarded as the first great builder. Indravarman I was not related to the first two kings so it is not known what right granted him the throne. He built at least three primitive Khmer temples, the Preah Ko temple, the Lolei and the Bakong. Indravarman I also built a large reservoir named Indratataka.

Lolei

❖ Yasovarman I (889-910)

Yasovarman I built a new Angkor capital called Yasodharapura, located not far from Roluos on the vast plain of Siem Reap and about eight km north of the Tonle Sap. At the center was Phnom Bakeng Hill. Yasovarman I built one of the largest reservoirs in the Angkor Kingdom, called East Baray (Lake).

❖ Harshavarman I (910-923) & Isanavarman II (923-928)

After the death of Yasovarman I, his son Harshavarman I became the next king. The two monuments built by Harshavarman I were the Baksei Chamkrong, a laterite temple northeast of Phnom Bakheng, and Prasat Kravan, built of bricks and dedicated to god Vishnu. His reign was followed by his brother Isanavarman II.

Bakong temple

❖ Jayavarman IV (928-941)

When Isanavarman II died in 928, Jayavarman IV ascended the throne and moved the capital to Koh Ker, about 90 km/54 miles north of Angkor Wat. At his new capital, Jayavarman IV constructed obscure Rahal Baray (Lake), running in a non-traditional north-south direction, and difficult to engineer. Sandstone may have been first introduced as the building materials of the Khmer monuments during this time. Koh Ker remained as the capital for only about 15 years.

Harshavarman II (941-944) was designated crown prince. Harshavarman II ascended the throne by force with the help of his cousin who become the next king.

❖ Rajendravarman II (944-968)

As soon as Harshavarman II died, his cousin Rajendravarman II took power. He reinstated Angkor as the capital, and started to build the mountain-temple of Pre Rup which was sited on top of the ashramas built by Yasovarman I. Rajendravarman II had problems keeping his crown due to rebellions among his rivals.

Rajendravarman II had a strong military urge since he not only waged war with his rivals, but even sacked the Champa Kingdom located to the east in modern Vietnam and the Thai tribal states to the west.

❖ Jayavarman V (968-1000)

He was the son of Rajendravarman II and succeeded to the supreme throne after his father in 968. Jayavarman V had to fight vigorously with other princes in order to maintain his kingship. For some reason, he built a new capital at the vicinity of Angkor and named it "Jayendranagari," meaning "Capital of the Triumphant Monarch," which implied his victory over his many enemies. During his

Banteay Srei doorway

reign, two major complexes were constructed, Banteay Srei and Takeo.

❖ Udayadityavarman I (1001-1002) & Jyaviravarman (1002-1010)

When Jayavarman V passed away in 1000, the historical account of his rule ended with the crowning of the new king named Udayadityavarman I. He apparently became king through violent conflict. He ruled only for a few years before being ousted and killed in 1002. His rule was followed by a power struggle between two princes, Jayaviravarman and Suryavarman I. The first prince ascended the throne in 1002, but his regime was consistently challenged by his rival Suryavarman I, who successfully overthrew him in 1010. During this decade of civil war, no significant monuments were built.

❖ Suryavarman I (1010-1050)

His reign was long but not peaceful. Suryavarman I spent much of his time and energy defending his kingship. He was the first king who built his palace surrounded by a wall. His palace was situated in the vicinity of Angkor Thom (the Royal Complex). Suryavarman I claimed to be the descendant of Brahmin Kaundinya and princess Soma. Later, in 1022, Suryavarman I expanded his territory to the west up to Lopburi in modern Thailand. The major temples built by him were the Preah Vihear on the Dangrek Mountain and the Phimeanakas, a modest temple in a pyramidal style located near his palace. Suryavarman I also started to build the second Angkor reservoir, the West Baray, which is almost twice as large as the East Baray.

❖ Udayadityavarman II (1050-1066)

Udayadityavarman II ruled over the Angkor Kingdom during a time of war. He was not the son of Suryavarman I, but a descendant from the line of Yasovarman I's spouse. A stone inscription made during his reign praised one of his faithful generals, Sangrama, who put down several major rebellions. Udayadityavarman II built the renowned Baphoun Temple devoted to the god Shiva. He completed the construction of the West Baray started in the time of his predecessor, and built the West Mebon, an earthen island, in the center. A temple dedicated to the god Vishnu was constructed on the island, but has vanished. The West Baray reservoir is still in use today.

❖ Harshavarman III (1066-1080)

Harshavarman III was the former king's older brother. No monuments built by this king are known and there are almost no historical accounts referring to him. It is believed he died in a violent rebellion.

❖ Jayavarman VI (1080-1107)

Jayavarman VI did not seem to have any direct connection with the royal family of the preceding kings. The center of his power was to the west of Angkor in the area of Phimai, now in Thailand. Jayavarman VI claimed to be the descendent of legendary Kambu and Mera (from Mount Mera). During his reign, there were few monuments built, except the one at the center of his power – the Phimai temple.

❖ Dharanindravarman I (1107-1113)

Jayavarman VI died in 1107, and the throne was assumed by his elder brother Dharanindravarman I. He was ousted and killed in a civil war that lasted for only one day. His killer was his nephew, Suryavarman II, who later became one of the greatest kings of the Angkor Empire.

❖ Suryavarman II (1113-1150)

Apsara carvings, Angkor Wat

Suryavarman II was a highly ambitious Khmer king. He was the builder of the most impressive temple of the Angkorian Empire, the Angkor Wat. Angkor Wat is a mountainous temple dedicated to the god Vishnu. It has five towers linked by galleries to signify the heavenly residence of Hindu gods. It is 65 meters/182 feet high and the outer rectangular enclo-

Cambodia

sure measures 1.5 km by 1.3 km (close to a mile on each side) and is surrounded by a moat 200 meters/560 feet wide. In addition to its remarkable size, Angkor Wat also houses thousands of sculptures and stone carvings that showcase the delicacy of Khmer artworks. It took 37 years and over 50,000 workers to complete the construction of this temple.

Not only a great builder, Suryavarman II was also a great warrior. He sacked several Champa states to the east and even waged an unsuccessful war with the strong Ly Dynasty of Vietnam. To the west, he conquered the Haripunjaya Kingdom, one of the Mon tribal states in central Thailand, and extended his power as far north as the southern border of modern Laos and as far south as the border of the Grahi Kingdom on the Malay Peninsula. His territory expanded to the border of the Bagan kingdom (ancient Burma) in the West.

Other monuments built during the reign of Suryavarman II, in addition to Angkor Wat, are Beng Melea, Banteay Samre, Chey Say Tevoda, and Thommanon.

❖ Minor Reigns (1150-1181)

No records exist to explain how Suryavarman II died. The last inscription referring to him was carved in 1145, when he was preparing to invade Vietnam. It is likely he died sometime between 1145 and 1150 on a battlefield.

His death led to the decline of the Angkor Empire for a short time and the succeeding kings were both weak and tyrannical. The minor rulers were Dharanindravarman II (1150-1160), Yasovarman II (1160-1165), and Tribhuvanadityavarman (1165-1181). Yasovarman II seized power from Dharanindravarman II and, in turn, was ousted by Tribhuvanadityavarman.

In 1177, a Champa king, who was the bitter enemy of the Khmer, attacked the Angkor Empire by sailing his troops along the Mekong River. A fierce naval battle was fought on the Tonle Sap and resulted in the painful defeat of the Angkor Empire and its subsequent fall into the hands of the Champa. The Khmer king Tribhuvanadityavarman was under the subjugation of the Champa until 1181.

❖ Jayavarman VII (1181-1219)

Being a Khmer prince, Jayavarman VII ruled over a Champa province or vishaya, which was under the Angkor Empire's

Above: Banteay Kdei, built by Jayavarman VII in the 12th century
(©Jack Scott)

Below: Typical house, Siem Reap (©Jack Scott)

Above: Lolei "temple maiden," part of the Roluos Group, 10 miles southeast of Angkor Wat (© Jack Scott)

*Above: Girl washing along the river, Siem Reap,
north of Angkor Wat (© Jack Scott)*

Above: Buddha statues, Angkor (© Vaughan Acton)

Below: Reclining Buddha, Angkor (© Vaughan Acton)

Small figures at Bayon Temple

authority. When the Champas seized the Angkor Empire in 1177, Jayavarman VII fought against the intruders and was able to re-capture the capital of Yasodharapura, where he ascended the throne in 1181. The war with the Champa kingdom did not end immediately but continued for another 20 years. In 1203, Jayavarman VII won a final victory and conquered the Champa kingdom.

Jayavarman VII was the last great king of the Angkor. He liberalized and unified the country and built the new capital of Angkor Thom, which lies on the plain of Siem Reap north of Angkor Wat. At the center of Angkor Thom is the Bayon Temple, famous for its 50 towers, each bearing the large faces of Bodhisattva Avalokiteshavara (a lord Buddha) on all four sides. These faces are thought to be copied from the actual face of Jayavarman VII, and whose smiles are so gentle that it is often referred to as "the Khmer smile." This great king was a devout Buddhist of the Mahayana sect.

In addition to Angkor Thom and Bayon, Jayavarman VII also built other impressive temples and monuments such as Ta Phrom, Banteay Kdei, Neak Pean, and Sras Srang.

Jayavarman VII constructed an extensive road network throughout his empire and thus linked all the major towns to Angkor. This efficient road system facilitated the transportation of agricultural products and goods. Along these roads were built 121 resting houses to accommodate the travelers and officials, and 102 hospitals to accommodate the sick.

The reign of Jayavarman VII was regarded as the peak period of the Angkor Empire as well as of the Khmer civilization, which began to decline gradually after the death of this great king in 1219.

Cambodia

❖ Indravarman II (1219-1243)

Indravarman II, Jayavarman VII's son, took the throne in 1219. It is believed that many of the great works initiated by Jayavarman VII were continued and completed by Indravarman II. Interestingly, few historical records about this king remain. They were probably destroyed by his enemy, who was also his successor.

Now the Angkor Empire's power began to decline. In 1220, the Khmers retreated from many of the Champa states they had conquered earlier. At the same time, the Thais succeeded in driving the Khmer from the western frontier and established the first Thai kingdom of Sukhothai, whose descendants were to become the major threats to the Angkor Empire in the next two centuries.

❖ Jayavarman VIII (1243-1295)

Jayavarman VIII was a strong believer in Hinduism, and a brutal enemy of Buddhism. He was responsible for the massive destruction of the Buddha statues in the empire; the original number was estimated to be in the tens of thousands. The main Buddha statue in the central shrine of Bayon was found sliced into three pieces and was replaced with the Hindu god Harihara. Jayavarman VIII transformed many Buddhist temples into Hindu shrines.

During his reign, the Mongol troops of Kublai Khan attacked the border of the Angkor Empire from the east in the year 1283. Jayavarman VIII did not wage war with the Mongols. He decided to pay tribute instead and so his empire survived.

In 1295, Jayavarman VIII and his tyrannical regime were overthrown by his own son-in-law, Srindravarman.

❖ Srindravarman (1295-1309)

The first inscription engraved in Pali indicated that the royal family had adopted Theravada Buddhism as their main religion, and thus the king was no longer regarded as deva-raja or "god-king." Theravada Buddhism was introduced from Sri Lanka (Ceylon) and gradually influenced every level of the Angkor Empire.

In 1296, Chou Ta-kuan, the Chinese ambassador from the Yuan Dynasty (Mongols), visited the Angkor Empire and wrote an important historical document in the Chinese

Chronicles about the Khmer. It is this chronicle that gives the majority of the information known about day-to-day Khmer life in the Angkor area.

❖ Minor Reigns (1309-1431)

Following the reign of Srindravarman, there were very few historical records. The last stele engraved in 1327 was in Pali and no more inscriptions were found for the next two centuries. No more major temples or monuments were built during this period.

The Khmers were no longer able to maintain their vast irrigation systems efficiently. Various dikes and canals silted up. The rice crops, previously cultivated two to three times a year, dropped drastically since the Khmers could no longer prevent floods in the monsoon season. They also didn't have enough water storage capability in the dry season. As productivity dropped, the empire was weakened.

The first Thai kingdom of Suhkothai, emerging after the Khmers were driven out in the early 13th century, was later absorbed by another Thai state, established as the Ayuthaya kingdom in 1351 by Ramathibodi I. The Ayuthaya kingdom became a major threat to the Angkor Empire and in 1431 a large Thai army marched on the road built by King Jayavarman VII from Chao Phaya River Basin through Aranyapathet to attack Angkor and sack the city. This marked the end of the Angkor Empire.

Now the Angkor area began its own Dark Ages. There were few inscriptions found in later centuries.

The West knew nothing about the existence of the Khmer civilization until the French botanist Henri Mouhot published his description of this lost empire in 1861 (one year after he rediscovered Angkor Wat). He was amazed by the magnificence of Angkor Wat and Angkor Thom. His announcement aroused the interest of the Westerners and subsequently attracted explorers, historians, archaeologists, and thieves.

In 1863, Cambodia became a French colony. After annexing Siem Reap (Angkor) and Battambang from Thailand in 1907, the French established the Angkor Conservation Center in 1908 to conduct archaeological studies of the Angkor civilization as well as to restore the various Khmer temples. These

Cambodia

activities were abruptly ended in 1972 due to civil war, followed by the reign of terror imposed by the Khmer Rouge (1975-1979).

Angkor Wat and the other Khmer temples were named a UNESCO World Heritage Site in 1992. Archaeological activities have been restarted with funding from UNESCO in order to preserve this World Heritage for future generations.

■ Weather & When to Visit

Cambodia is largely landlocked, so the climate is not greatly affected by the ocean. The monsoon is significant, however, and the best time to visit is during the dry season.

SIEM REAP/TONLE SAP											
Temperature											
	Jan	Feb	Mar	Apr	May	Jun	Jul	Aug	Sep	Oct	Nov	Dec
°C	27	28	29	30	29	29	28	28	27	27	27	27
°F	80	82	84	86	84	84	82	82	80	80	80	80
Rainfall											
mm	15	3	13	43	221	330	315	269	335	269	114	56
inches	.6	.1	.5	1.7	8.5	13	12	10	13	10	4.4	2
Humidity											
%	61	56	58	60	71	78	80	78	80	80	75	68

THE HIGHLANDS											
Temperature											
	Jan	Feb	Mar	Apr	May	Jun	Jul	Aug	Sep	Oct	Nov	Dec
°C	17	18	20	24	28	30	30	29	28	26	22	19
°F	63	65	69	75	82	86	86	84	82	79	72	67
Rainfall											
mm	18	28	38	81	196	239	323	342	254	99	43	20
inches	.7	1.1	1.5	3.2	7.8	9.6	12.9	13.7	10.2	4	1.7	.8
Humidity											
%	68	70	76	75	69	71	72	75	73	69	68	67

	Jan	Feb	Mar	Apr	May	Jun	Jul	Aug	Sep	Oct	Nov	Dec
THE COAST												
Temperature												
°C	22	23	24	27	29	30	30	30	28	26	25	23
°F	72	74	76	81	84	86	86	86	85	79	78	74
Rainfall												
mm	102	3	12	18	47	42	99	117	447	530	221	209
inches	4.4	.1	.5	.7	1.9	1.7	4	4.7	17.9	21.2	8.8	8.4
Humidity												
%	86	86	85	85	81	77	78	77	84	85	86	86

■ Phnom Penh

Unlike most international capitals, Phnom Penh is not much of a gateway. It is very easy to see much of what Cambodia has to offer and never set foot in Phnom Penh. Until very recently it was actually pretty difficult to get there. Your choices were a few flights a week on Siem Reap Air, a long, rough bus ride from Ho Chi Minh City (HCMC) or Thailand, or a very long boat ride on the Mekong River – upstream from HCMC or downstream from Vientiane. Now the roads are much improved and the big international carriers like Air France are flying there. Vietnam Airlines has also expanded its services.

Nonetheless, many people give Phnom Penh a miss, preferring to spend their limited time and money at Angkor Wat or in neighboring countries. If you only have a few days in Cambodia, by all means spend them in Angkor Wat – you'll need at least two or three full days there. Then if you have a few more days, visit the Cardamon or Elephant Mountains and the Tonle Sap for a bit of activity. Finally, if time allows, spend a few days in Phnom Penh.

Phnom Penh is at the junction of three rivers—the Sap, Mekong, and Bassac. This strategic location has always ensured the city a place, both good and bad, in history. Cambodia has been at war, or the victim of others' wars, for many years, and it shows. The infrastructure is crumbling, the people look underfed, children are too often sold into slavery, and

Phnom Penh

1. Intercontinental
2. Le Royal
3. Juliana
4. Goldiana
5. Sofitel Cambodiana
6. Foreign Correspondents' Club of Cambodia

petty thievery at knife-point is all too common. In the 1950s only about 100,000 people lived in the city. Now the number is about 1,000,000.

Following the Paris Peace accords in 1991, the brutal regime of Pol Pot, the Khmer Rouge, and the killing fields was ended, but the coup in 1998 was "déjà vu all over again" and the fledgling capitalists and their international backers once again fled the country. The investors have been slowly returning, but few are willing to commit to the country's long-term future right away. As a result, Thai investors are filling the gap, and Phnom Penh is beginning to look like a small version of Bangkok. One way to see just how strong the Thai influence is? Take a look at the cars and ubiquitous pick-up trucks. Despite being surrounded on all sides by countries that drive on the right, with left-hand drive vehicles, the majority of vehicles are right-hand drive. This is both a safety issue and a legal one. Technically these vehicles are not legal, but the government looks the other way unless it is convenient **not** to do so.

 You probably can't (and don't want to) rent a vehicle in Cambodia. If you decide to rent one, make sure it is a left-hand drive. Don't give the under-paid, not-always-honest police an excuse to pull you over.

If you get sick or hurt, get out by any means possible. Don't go to a Cambodia hospital or clinic. If you have absolutely no choice, go to your embassy or consulate and throw yourself on their mercy. The electricity and plumbing also leave a lot to be desired. Make sure your hotel has a generator or you may spend lots of time in the dark with no running water.

Where to Stay

 The western four- and five-star hotels have arrived in Phnom Penh, and also in Siem Reap. Still, there are a wealth of three- and four-star Asian-style hotels – a bit on the cookie-cutter side but well-worth the stay. The cost difference is tremendous, allowing you to have access to CNN or the BBC, but still save significantly.

If it's Western-style luxury you're after, consider the Intercontinental or Le Royal. Both are international five-star hotels with all the expected amenities and great locations. Of course, all this luxury comes at a price – figure on $150-$200 per night, plus taxes and often a service charge.

HOTEL PRICE CHART	
Rates are per room based on double occupancy.	
$	Under $12
$$	$12-$25
$$$	$26-$40
$$$$	$40-$80
$$$$$	Over $80

There are several main areas for accommodations: Central, the Sisowath Quay area on the Tonle Sap, and the Boeng Kak Lake area.

Central

$$$$$ **Intercontinental**, 296 Mao Tse Toung Street, ☎ 424888, fax 424885, phnompenh@interconti.com. This hotel is very popular with business travelers. It's on the south end of the city, and tends to be a bit less pricey than the more elegant, traditional Le Royal. There are about 350 rooms, a business center, nice pool, and a Cantonese restaurant.

$$$$+ **Le Royal**, Street 92, just off Monivong Blvd., T981888, fax 9881168, www.raffles-hotelleroyal.com. As the website indicates, this is one of the several Raffles Hotels you'll find in Southeast Asia. It is a wonderful, restored Colonial building in a tree-shaded, sedate setting. The bookshop makes a great stop to pick up new reading material for the rest of your trip or the return flight. There's a pool, business center, and several restaurants. A bit more central than the Intercontinental.

For the more budget-minded, there are many hotels in the $15-$50 price range. At the higher end you're more likely to get CNN or other English-language cable services; at the lower end it's usually a French-language channel with an hour of English language news in the early morning.

$$$ **Juliana**, Number 16, Street 152, ☎ 366070, fax 880530, juliana@cqan.net.co.kh. This hotel may make you feel you wandered into a resort instead of a city hotel. The garden set-

ting makes a great retreat from the sometimes busy and noisy streets of Phnom Penh. You'll find a pool, decent restaurants, and even a beauty salon and massage center. A fabulous way to end the day.

$$-$$$ **Pallin**, 219 Monivong Blvd, ☎ 426375, fax 426376. A mid-sized (80-room) business hotel that is still a good bargain although a bit faded. You'll find satellite TV, several decent restaurants, and nice rooms with air-conditioning.

$$ **Goldiana**, Number 282 Street 10, ☎ 219558, no fax, www.goldiana.com. A good value for the money. I haven't stayed there, but it comes highly recommended. There is a pool on the roof and restaurants are close by.

Sisowath Quay

$$$$$ **Sofitel Cambodiana**, Number 313 Sisowath Quay, ☎ 426288, fax 426392, www.hotelcambodiana.com. This hotel was originally built for the guests of Prince Sihanouk. It has a prime location at the juncture of the Mekong, Tonle Sap, and Bassac Rivers. There are almost 300 superbly fitted out rooms, tennis courts, a pool, European (French) and Chinese restaurants, a business center, a fitness facility, and a bookstore (although many titles are in French).

$$$ **The Foreign Correspondents' Club of Cambodia** is at 363 Sisowath Quay, ☎ 210142, fax 427758, www.fcccambodia.com. It has three rooms available, although the facility is more desirable for its press connections than its rooms.

Beyond these hotels there are many budget and mid-range hotels, and more are popping up every month. Travel agents are often a good source of alternatives, but they may have an "arrangement" with certain places, so always take their recommendations with a grain of salt. It is certainly worth doing a search online a few weeks before your arrival to check options, prices, and availability. The online bargains can be quite good in many cases.

Boeng Kak Lake area is generally a backpacker's enclave. The quality of the hotels is more along the line of youth hostels and dormitories. It is also a 10- to 15-minute hike into the central area.

Where to Eat

 If the choices are too daunting or you want Western/European food, there are always the restaurants at the four- and five-star hotels. Otherwise, here are some other options to try. Don't pass up the bakeries with their wonderful bread and croissants, or the great coffee.

The best food is found in Thai, Chinese, Indian, and Vietnamese restaurants. There are few Khmer restaurants. Meals are quite reasonable – figure on $3-$8 (13,000-34,000 Riel) per person for dinner with a beer or glass of wine.

As with the hotels, new restaurants are cropping up regularly. Ask other travelers for their recommendations, try some of these, or take your chances with a place that looks good. Most places have English menus with fairly accurate translations so at least you'll know what you're getting.

Even if the restaurant is only a few blocks from your hotel it is an excellent idea to take a taxi or let your hotel arrange transportation. Even in groups it is not a good idea to walk around the streets of Phnom Penh after dark.

Central

$$ Baan Thai, Number 2, Street 306, ☎ 362991. Open daily from about 11:30 am to 2 pm and again from 5:30 to 10 pm. The building is an older, teak, Thai-style building with cushions and seating at low tables. Everything I tried was good – chicken with basil, tempura, spring rolls, and more. This is a traditional house, so plan to remove your shoes upon entering. Main courses tend to cost about $4. Recommended.

$$ Boddhi Tree, Number 50 Street 113, open daily from about 11 am to 10 pm. You eat in a beautiful garden. There are sandwiches, snacks, salads, and more for about $3 each. The kitchen closes an hour before the restaurant does. Recommended.

RESTAURANT PRICES	
$	Under $2
$$	$2-$5
$$$	$6-$10
$$$$	$11-$20
$$$$$	Over $20

$$ **Comme à la Maison**, Number 13, Street 57, ☎ 360801, open daily from about 11:30 am to 10 pm. This is one of the few good restaurants that delivers. It also has a regular restaurant. You can get sandwiches, salads, and a few French traditional dishes. I like the bakery/deli for breads and take-away picnic fixings. Similar in price to the other choices.

$$ **Mount Everest**, 98 Sihanouk Blvd., ☎ 213821. The place to go for Nepalese and Himalayan specialties, or so I've been told.

There are many other restaurants in the central area, including very cheap pizza and Indian restaurants and lots of mid-range to cheap continental and Chinese places. You can also hire a taxi (don't walk around after dark) and go a few km (about two miles) past the Japanese Friendship bridge to the group of restaurants located there. It's a bit of a fairyland with lights strung in the trees.

Sisowath Quay Area

$$ **Bali**, Number 379 Sisowath Quay (in the Bali Hotel), ☎ 982211, open from 7 am to 11 pm. A place to get breakfast if your hotel doesn't offer it. There's an upstairs balcony so you can watch the action on the river. The food choices are varied and generally about $4 or so.

$$-$$$ **The Foreign Correspondents Club of Cambodia**, 363 Sisowath Quay, ☎ 210142. The bar and restaurant are on the second floor of this noted hangout. The old Colonial building is worth a visit in itself. There are pizzas, a fabulous breakfast, and many local and international choices on the menu. A bit pricier than most places (figure $6-$10 per entrée) but a nice treat.

There are lots of other small restaurants along the quay – take your pick – most are decent values with more than acceptable food and river views.

What to See & Do

The most famous landmarks in Cambodia, after the temples of Angkor Wat, have to be the Silver Pagoda and the Royal Palace complex. The **Silver Pagoda** is so-named because of its floor of over 5,000 silver blocks. It is also often called the Pagoda of the Emerald Buddha because of the green (crystal)

Buddha statue inside. The **Royal Palace** has the early 20th-century Throne Hall and the Royal Treasury.

The location of this complex is stunning – along the Mekong River, with stupas and spires, green spaces, and bright colors. During the dark times it surely gave the people something to look back on with pride and forward to with hope. It's one of the few sites of note that the Khmer did not destroy. And they didn't fully loot the complex either; about 40% of the treasures are still there.

The Royal Palace

Between Streets 184 and 240. The main building is the Throne Hall, built in 1917. It is built in the Khmer style with a tower and multi-stepped roof. It is still in use as a reception and coronation facility. There are nagas (demi-gods) guarding the steps, French-style thrones, a sacred gong inside, and scenes from the Ramayana frescoed on the ceilings.

Take note of the nine-tiered umbrella or parasol behind the thrones. This is the Preah Maha Svetrachatr, the symbol of heaven. Notice also how the huge rug includes the same patterns found on the steps and tiles nearby.

There are several additional rooms for the king and queen and for keeping cremated ashes, but only the throne room is normally open to the public.

If you head south from the Throne Room you will quickly come to the Royal Treasury and the Napoleon III Pavilion. The Pavilion was actually built as an accommodation for the Empress Eugenie during the Suez Canal opening celebrations and then moved to Phnom Penh, under the Empress's orders, as a gift for the Cambodian king. The building is surprisingly delicate, stuffed with knickknacks and other small items.

The Silver Pagoda

This is out the north gate of the Royal Palace. The pagoda was built of wood in 1892, and rebuilt in 1962. It has marble steps leading to the 5,000+ silver blocks composing the interior floor. Housed inside is an emerald-colored Buddha made of Baccarat crystal. There is also a 200-pound (90-kilogram) gold Buddha, created in 1906, studded with almost 10,000 diamonds. This gold Buddha is accompanied by silver and bronze Buddha statues. There is another "jade" (actually jadeite) Buddha in the back of the Pagoda.

Take time to walk along the inside of the 2,000-foot (600-meter) wall around the Pagoda. It is covered in 100-year-old frescoes showing scenes from the *Ramayana*, as well as scenes of the Palace, Temple and daily life. To follow the stories, start at the east gate.

There is an admission charge for the complex of about $9, plus charges for cameras and videos. The lockers and "secure" storage facilities are not secure, so you are better off paying for your camera so you can keep it with you.

Other Sights Adjacent to the Royal Palace & Silver Pagoda

There is a statue of King Norodom on horseback just to the east of the Silver Pagoda. It is actually a statue of Napoleon III, but the Cambodians cut the head off and replaced it with a head of King Norodom. Right next to the statue is a stupa with the ashes of an earlier king. If you continue to the south wall you will come to a series of pavilions, one of which contains a footprint of Buddha. There are a number of additional stupas, as well as a mondap (library). The entire area is filled with urns, vases, flowering plants and shrubs.

The National Museum of Cambodia

Corner of 13 Street and 178 Street. Located in the reddish-colored building (1920) just to the north of the Palace, this museum houses a collection of Khmer art and a large number of bats in its attics. Open from about 7 am to 5:30 pm, closed for lunch from 11:30 am to 2 pm. There is an admission charge of about $3, plus charges for cameras and videos. As above, the lockers are not secure, so keep your camera with you.

The Riverside

Along the Mekong River is an array of Colonial buildings almost a mile long. These used to be merchants' offices, shops, private residences, and government buildings. Today they are shops, restaurants, bars, and guesthouses.

Although the Silver Pagoda is attractive, it is not the most famous wat in Phnom Penh. That honor goes to Wat Ounalom, shown at left. This is located just north of the National Museum at Street 154 and Samdech Sothearos Boulevard. It faces the Tonlé Sap. Prior to 1976 over 500 monks lived here, but their leader was killed by the Khmer Rouge and the facility was heavily damaged. Even so, this wat is the official headquarters of Cambodian Buddhism. At one time it housed a hair of Buddha.

Wat Phnom

Located at the end of Boulevard Tou Samouth at Street 96 (the north end of the city), this is one of the oldest wats in the city. It dates from 1372, although it has been rebuilt many times.

The Victory Monument

If you go south from the Royal Palace, between Street 268 and Preah Sihanouk Boulevard, you come to the Victory Monument. It was built in 1958 to celebrate independence from French Colonial rule. In the vicinity is a variety of good-quality Colonial architecture – mostly on Streets 53, 178, 114, Norodom Boulevard, and Samdech Sothearos Boulevard.

South of the Center of Town

There is a museum dedicated to the victims of genocide at the hands of the Khmer Rouge. This museum, the **Tuol Sleng**, is on Street 113, close to Street 350. It commemorates the victims taken to the Khmer interrogation and torture center at Tuol Svay Prey High School. More than 20,000 people passed through this school and were either killed and buried on the grounds or taken to the Choeung Ek (Killing Fields) and killed there. There are displays of photos and other paraphernalia – the Khmer were very methodical, taking photos and keeping historical records of all their victims.

There are numerous other wats and riverside sights if you have extra time to spend in Phnom Penh, but with so much else to see and do in the country and around the region, two days is just about enough for most short-term visitors. Following are some ideas for day-trips from Phnom Penh. For the longer jaunts to the mountains, Sihanoukville, Battambang, and, of course, Angkor Wat, see the other sections devoted to those areas.

Day-Trips from Phnom Penh

Travel agents are happy to arrange these trips for you, or you can hire your own transportation or moto, or let your hotel arrange everything.

Oudong

Oudong was the royal capital before Phnom Penh. It is about 20 miles (35 km) north of Phnom Penh. Although it was the center of power for about 250 years from 1618 to 1866 (the

Cambodia

arrival of the French), little remains but the foundation of the old palace. There are some memorials to the Khmer Rouge's victims, but little else of note. The views from the high points are spectacular, though.

Choueng Ek - The Killing Fields

If you have the time you really should go here. The killing fields are in a class with Dachau and Auschwitz. They have to be felt, not just looked at. There is a glass tower filled with the skulls of thousands of men, women, and children killed by the Khmer Rouge under the direction of Pol Pot and his cronies. There is an admission charge of about $3. The site is southwest of Phnom Penh, about 15 km/10 miles out along

Pol Pot

Monireth Boulevard. You can easily hire a moto for a few dollars to take you, wait, and bring you back.

Kirirom National Park

If you want to do some hiking close to the city, this park is about 50 miles (82 km) southwest of Phnom Penh. It is covered with beautiful pine trees, filled with hiking trails, and has very attractive picnic spots. It is not a good idea to bathe or swim here though – there have been ongoing problems with pollution in the waters. There is an off-chance you might see some interesting wildlife – a census about 10 years ago recorded deer, tigers, leopards, and other animals. It will cost $8-$10 to rent a motorbike or $30 for a car. If you want a motorbike and driver, expect to pay around $15 for the day. It is possible to stay overnight at the very basic Kirirom Guest House, but you are 10 km/six miles from the park.

Mekong River Cruises

A number of local tour operators are offering "cruises" down the Mekong. This is a great way to observe a fast-disappearing way of river life. You can also hire a boat at the quay for about $10-$12 per hour, bring your own food, and make a day of it, stopping wherever the spirit moves you.

Cambodia is a wonderful place, but is not one of the safer places in Asia. There are many tips, recommendations, and other suggestions to help make your trip as care-free as possible, but Cambodia is not a place for the unwary traveler. Nowhere is this more true than in Phnom Penh. Still, a bit of caution goes a long way.

Transportation in Town

Try the local motor scooter entrepreneurs, or rent a bicycle. You might also enjoy walking.

Hiking, Cycling & Walking

You can cycle, but you are taking a big risk. Still, many hotels and street-side kiosks will rent bikes for $2-$10 per day.

Cars, Scooters & Cyclos

You can rent cars for about $25-$30 per day. Ask at your hotel. Vehicles are not well-maintained and your fellow drivers are nuts.

Scooter drivers are glad to offer you a lift for a few dollars.

Car hire to the airport is about $10. Metered taxis cost about the same but you'll only find them outside the big hotels.

Buses & Taxis

Buses are cheap, but make sure you get on the right one. Ask at your hotel to get the bus number and tell the driver where you need to go.

Taxis don't want to use meters.

Useful Information

Airlines

All travel companies should be able to handle flight confirmations and reservations for you.

Cambodia

The main airline addresses and telephone numbers are:

Air France, 389 Sisowath Quay, ☎ 219220

Bangkok Airways/Siem Reap Airways, Number 61 Street 214, ☎ 720022

Lao Aviation, 58C Sihanouk Blvd., ☎ 216563

Silk Air, Mi Casa Hotel, 313 Sisowath, ☎ 426808

Thai Air, 294 Mao Tse Tung Street, ☎ 214359

Vietnam Airlines, No 14 Street 214, ☎ 36339

Embassies & Consulates

Australian, No 11 Street 254, ☎ 213470

Canada, No 11 Street 254, ☎ 426000

Laos, 15-17 Mao Tse Tung Blvd., ☎ 983632

United Kingdom, No 29 Street 75, ☎ 012-802992

United States, No 27 Street 240, ☎ 216436

Vietnamese, 426 Monivong Blvd., ☎ 362531

Internet/Communications

You can go to most post offices and make international calls at a steep price. Better is to buy a calling card and go to one of the many calling centers popping up all over.

Some hotels let guests use high-speed Internet for free. There are also dozens of Internet cafés now, and the cost for high-speed is about $3-$5 per hour. Most connections are likely to be dial-up speed, however.

Medical Facilities

It is best to try to get to Thailand if you need serious care. Pharmacies will dispense almost anything here (such as antibiotics) without a prescription. Make sure you know what you are taking and that it is not expired.

■ Siem Reap/Angkor Wat

Although this area has been inhabited for many years, the glory days were the ninth to 13th centuries. During that time the royal capital was located at various sites in the region and hundreds of temples were built. The area was irrigated through a number of water entrapment schemes (using Barays – lakes) and several crops could be grown each year, making the Khmer Empire self-sufficient in food production. The water entrapment system also reduced the devastating effects of the annual flood and drought cycles.

The remote, upstream location of present-day Siem Reap and Angkor Wat/Angkor Thom made the area difficult to conquer and subdue, but eventually (in the late 14th to early 15th centuries) the Thai managed to gain control, ending the Angkorian Khmer Empire.

Now the area is a UNESCO World Heritage Site and one of the top destinations in Southeast Asia. The hassles of getting there are far out-weighed by the sight of Angkor Wat.

Getting There

Getting to Siem Reap is much easier than in the days of empire, and much improved over just a few years ago.

By Air/From the Airport

 From Thailand you can fly in on Bangkok Airways or Siem Reap Airways, several times a day. Lao Aviation may fly from Vientiane in Laos, and Vietnam Airlines flies from both HCMC and Hanoi. Figure $100 or so for the flight.

You can also fly from Phnom Penh – a short hop on Siem Reap Airlines – and given the poor condition of many roads this may be $60 or so well-spent.

There are few taxis but lots of scooters to give rides to your hotel. If you have more than a small bag, consider hiring two scooters – one for you and one for your bags – so you don't have to balance a huge suitcase on the back of a motorbike! Scooters only cost a few dollars. If you are staying at a higher-end hotel you may well have a car picking you up at the airport.

Overland

There are so-called express mini-buses between Khao San Road in Bangkok and Siem Reap, with a change of buses at the border. The limiting factor is the roads, which are still terrible (especially in the rainy season). Allow at least seven-eight hours for the trip.

You can also come by bus from HCMC, via Phnom Penh in many cases. Allow six-eight hours for this trip. The cost is only $10-$12 or so.

There is no viable train service, but that may change in the next few years.

Where to Stay

New truly international standard luxury hotels are appearing monthly, or so it seems. Check www.asia-hotels.com for the latest additions. I've listed a few top-end hotels here.

Pre-Paid/Pre-Booked Options

Angkor Century Resort and Spa. Komay Road, Khum Svay Dangkorn, Siem Reap. The Angkor Century Resort and Spa Siem Reap is ideally designed to accommodate both the business and leisure traveler. The 190 stylishly, elegantly appointed rooms and suites provide guests with accommodation of an international standard. Strongly inspired by the local culture, it is conveniently located in the heart of Siem Reap, only a short distance from the international airport and a few minutes from Angkor Wat. There are a wide range of services to meet all dining, business and recreational requirements. Amenities include satellite TV, phone, dataport, minibar, massage, pool, airport transfers and more.

Angkor Century Hotel is a four-star international hotel in a resort setting with lush tropical garden covering an area of eight acres. Angkor Century pays tribute to Siem Reap's 800-year ethnic, artistic, and cultural heritage. Located in the heart of the city and 15 minutes drive to Siem Reap International Airport, it is less than a mile to the town center.

Internet rate at press time: $82-$95 with breakfast and tax.

Angkor Diamond Hotel. Vithoi Achasva Road, Phum Watbo, Khum Sala Kamroeuk, Siem Reap. Located near the river, in the central part of town. Ten minutes drive to the Angkor historic sites. $29-$32 pre-book, pay at hotel, plus 20% tax. Includes airport transfer and breakfast. For a higher price there are luxury suites. Rooms have private bath and may have satellite TV.

Angkor Saphir Hotel. 82 National Highway Route 6, Siem Reap. Centrally located. Forty elegant rooms complemented by useful features and amenities to cater to international business and leisure travelers visiting Siem Reap. Good location for Siem Reap town and the temples of Angkor beyond. Fifteen minutes to the airport.

Internet rates at press time: $20-$25 for a standard room, $30-$35 for a deluxe room. Rates drop in the first half of 2006. Rates include breakfast and taxes.

General Hotel Options

$$$$$ Grand Hotel d'Angkor, ☎ 963888, raffles.grand@bigpond.com.kh. This is the grande dame of hotels in Siem Reap. It is impressive on the outside, but reports from other travelers say the inside is not worth the big bucks.

$$-$$$ Secrets of Elephants Guesthouse, Airport Road, ☎ 016-901901. This is my favorite. It's small (only eight rooms), family-run, and very traditional in its construction (teak, silk, antiques). The setting is a mini-jungle. Breakfast is included and you can order dinner if you want. Not all rooms have the bathrooms inside, but none of the facilities are shared. Not all rooms have air conditioning.

Beyond these choices, the Airport Road, center of town, and River Road are stuffed with guesthouses and two- to three-star choices that are quite pleasant, if uneven in quality and amenities.

Where to Eat

All the four- and five-star hotels have decent restaurants and fair prices. Many of these restaurants serve three buffet-style meals a day. Along the river there are many acceptable restaurants, and some even serve my favorite traveling food – pizza!

Near the River

$ **Bayon**, an old standby, on Wat Bo Street. Eclectic and cheap.

$ **Chiang Mai**, Wat Bo Street, serves Thai food.

$-$$ **Kampuccino**, on the river. Eclectic, with pizza and sandwiches.

$-$$ Swiss Centre d'Angkor, near the river. Great sandwiches and chips/fries.

Near the Old Market

$-$$ New Delhi has standard Indian fare – with excellent curries and tandoori.

Entertainment

There are a few bars, and most of the riverfront restaurants stay open late. Many of the fancier hotels have ethnic and local artists to entertain at and after dinner.

Markets & Shopping

The **Old Market** (Psar Chars) has some interesting items and shows the daily life of the people who live in Siem Reap. The market is surrounded with tourist-oriented shops. We actually found an antique Rolex pocket watch for $125 – it works and is the real thing.

There is a school for orphans just off Sivatha Street. It teaches them to make various handicrafts and the wares are sold in the shop called **Chantiers Ecoles**.

Tours & Travels

Apsara Tours is one of the main agencies here. You can reach them at ☎ 380198 or through apsarasr@camintel.com. They can arrange tours, tickets, and the like. Another option is **Diethelm Travel**, at ☎ 963524.

What to See & Do

The Angkor Complex – UNESCO World Heritage Site

Angkor and its numerous wats formed the seat of power for the Khmer people for much of what corresponded to the Middle Ages and early Renaissance years in Europe. From the beginning of the ninth century until well into the 13th century this was the place to go in Asia – for learning, culture, and the arts. Even the destructive Khmer Rouge left the area largely alone.

As an "upriver" city with few roads, Angkor's inaccessibility was both its source of power and the reason for its ultimate demise, as the historical portions of this book detail. As outsiders accessed the Angkor complex they took away ideas for their own architecture and arts, but nothing copied ever came close to the glories of the Angkor temple complex. The buildings are incredibly detailed, constructed on a massive scale, yet retaining an impressive delicacy, despite the ravages of time, war, and people.

> **Note:** When you walk through the Angkor complex, consider this. It was built in large part at the same time as Paris's Notre Dame Cathedral, but with far fewer resources in a remote location. Even so, it is much larger and just as intricately carved.

To truly appreciate the complex, you need to see it in many lights and moods. Take time to see the temples at sunrise, at sunset, on your own, with a guide, under the full moon, on foot, and by bicycle. Note the detailed carving, the fig trees slowly shattering the facades of many buildings, the peaceful atmosphere of the less-touristed temples, and take time to absorb the other-worldly feeling that surrounds you.

> **Tip:** You can buy one-, three-, or five-day passes. One day is not quite enough, so I advise spending the extra bit of money to get the three-day pass. You can always chill out in Siem Reap and explore the nearby countryside – the break allows you to reflect on the sights of Angkor and gain some additional perspective.

The Angkor complex is too far from town to walk to, so you should consider catching a ride on a scooter – many times the driver is a decent guide (for an additional fee). Expect to pay $7-$10 for the ride, and more if you want the driver to actually do more than drop you off and pick you up at the entrance. Don't pay the driver the full amount until he returns to take you to your hotel. You can also hire a car for about $25, and

Cambodia

the same again for a guide. Hotels can arrange the car and guide. It really is worth having a trained guide for at least one day, and you need a car to see the "best" temples at sunset or sunrise. Finally, you can hire a bicycle for $5-$7 per day, or arrange a ride in a three-wheeled tuk-tuk-style vehicle for $10 or so.

❖ Seeing the Temples

The tourist trade has split the temple routes into three so-called circuits: The Petit Circuit, the Grand Circuit, and the Rolous Group Circuit.

The **Petit Circuit** is the quickie, one-day trip around the highlights of Angkor. If you are on an excursion from Phnom Penh this is probably the trip you will make. Unfortunately you miss many of the most interesting and unique sites, but you do see the three main temples and the Terrace of the Elephants.

The **Grand Circuit** is more involved, including many of the smaller temples – the little gems of Angkor.

The **Rolous Group Circuit** goes to outlying temples.

By combining the Rolous and Grand Circuit routes you will see the vast majority of the popular temples in two days. Having the third day on your pass allows you to go back and revisit your favorite temples (or the ones that were too crowded the first two days) and visit at least one temple at sunset or sunrise.

● The Main Temples & Sights:

- ☐ Angkor Wat – Petit and Grand Circuit
- ☐ Bayon – Petit and Grand Circuit
- ☐ Baphoun – Petit and Grand Circuit
- ☐ Terrace of the Elephants – Petit Circuit
- ☐ Ta Prohm – Grand Circuit
- ☐ East Mebon – Grand Circuit
- ☐ Neak Pean – Grand Circuit
- ☐ Lolei – Rolous Group Circuit
- ☐ Preah Ko – Rolous Group Circuit
- ☐ Bakong – Rolous Group Circuit

The main temple cluster, including the ever-popular Angkor Wat, is about seven km/4½ miles north of the town of Siem Reap. You have to buy a photo admission ticket to enter the complex, so make sure to allow half an hour or so on the way in. The ticket sales office is about two kilometers outside the complex.

> **Tip:** While prices are subject to change, the three-day admission ticket to the Angkor complex has stayed at $40 for many years. Since the US dollar has fallen in value so steeply in the past few years it is possible this fee may rise, and/or other currencies may be accepted.

You must have a visa-sized photo for your photo ID entry pass. Bring two photos in case the ticket office needs to keep one. It is not currently possible to get on-site photos.

You can usually go into the complex for free after 5:15 pm – great for viewing some of the temples at sunset.

The fee for admission may seem steep, but once you have seen how much needs to be restored and kept up you may think the fee is too low. Make sure to buy your ticket from the official station outside the main complex, and don't give away your pass when you are done. Too many places in Siem Reap sell recycled passes. That leads to problems. First, it is illegal and you could get into trouble. Second, the money doesn't go to the upkeep of the sites.

If you want to get the most out of your visit you really should hire an official guide for at least one day, and hire a car and driver, too. Angkor Conservation trains guides and you can hire them from the Angkor Guide Association right across from the Grand Hotel D'Angkor (☎ 063-964347). These guides cost $20-$25. You can also hire an unofficial guide at many places – the airport, your hotel or guesthouse, other hotels, and so on. If you do this, you need to quiz the person to make sure he (almost all guides are male) speaks your language in an understandable manner, and ask questions based on what you've read in this book and learned from other travelers to make sure he knows the site.

If you go to the temple complexes on your own you are likely to be surrounded by children wanting to show you "their" temple and wanting you to give them a small tip and/or buy their postcards and souvenirs. You will also be dogged by scooter drivers wanting to take you around; ditto tuk-tuk drivers.

Cambodia has been heavily mined – landmined, that is! – by various groups over the past half-century. Although great effort has been made to locate and destroy the mines, they still exist all over the country, even around Angkor. **Stay on well-trodden paths!** Don't head off into the jungle, even with a guide, unless the path is clearly well-used. If you see pieces of metal or plastic sticking out of or lying on the ground, get away!

Cambodia has several poisonous snakes. The most deadly one, found all around Angkor, is the nasty green *Hanuman* snake. It is most prevalent during the dry season but can be encountered at any time.

There are also thorny bushes and other dangerous nuisances, so use care. Don't pick the flowers, pluck the leaves, or otherwise disturb things.

Cambodia's treasures have been plundered for many centuries by invaders, locals looking to make a fast bit of cash, the Khmer Rouge, the French Colonials, and collectors from all over the world.

Throughout its history invaders came seeking treasure. Since much of the Khmer people's riches were hidden inside towers or otherwise buried at or around Angkorian temples, many of these were destroyed in the treasure hunt.

However, none of this thievery, or the insidious destruction by the fig tree roots and branches, came close to the damage inflicted by the Khmer Rouge (and other guerrilla groups). They plundered the remaining treasures and destroyed hundreds of buildings.

Don't even think about trying to take out souvenirs from Angkor, or any other banned items or antiquities. You will find yourself in a very unappealing jail so fast your head will spin, and Cambodian jails are very detrimental to your life expectancy. They are also hard to get out of. Sentence commutation or reduction is virtually unheard of. Your embassy can't do much for you, either.

● **Angkor Restoration**

From the time of its rediscovery by Henri Mouhot in 1860, there were attempts to restore the Angkor temples. Part of this "restoration" involved removing many treasures (mostly statues) to France in the 1870s. To date few if any of these statues have been returned to the Cambodians.

As part of their efforts to find and remove the best statues from the Angkor complex, the French began a "restoration" effort in 1898 under the auspices of the École Francaise d'Extreme Orient (the French School of the Far East). The scholars cleared the jungle, mapped the complex, and inventoried much of the site. They found about 400 temples, walls, and tombs.

In the mid-1980s, while the communist Vietnamese held sway, they decided further restoration of Angkorian temples was in order. Although their intentions were noble, the contractors they hired did an incredible amount of damage to the entire site. A group of Indian archaeologists was hired to clean and restore a number of buildings and galleries at Angkor Wat. They used the same techniques applied so disastrously in much of Incan Peru – chemical stripping and concrete for repair work. As a result much of the wonderful patina of the old stone was removed, fine carvings were scrubbed almost out of existence, and damage was patched with concrete rather than laterite and sandstone.

Only after a number of years of this haphazard, destructive "restoration" did the rest of the world wake up to the possible damage being done. Of course hindsight is always 20-20. At the time the Indian restoration experts were brought in, much of the Western world was boycotting Cambodia and its Vietnamese overlords.

Following the signing of the Paris Peace Accords in 1991 an international group, overseen and coordinated by UNESCO, began working on the newly-declared World Heritage Site.

● Angkorian Culture & Lifestyles

Not much is known about the heyday of the Khmer empire that was centered on the Angkor complex. There are bits and pieces of written material scattered across Southeast Asia, carvings and bas-reliefs on temple walls depicting day-to-day and religious life, and one fairly comprehensive written record.

The written record is interesting, but it comes from near the very end of the Angkorian period. In 1296, Chou Ta-kuan came as an emissary from the Chinese court. He kept detailed records of the lifestyles and people he encountered, and from his impressions it seems the Angkorian court was an impressive and very sophisticated society, even as it was rapidly declining.

● The Art & Architecture of Angkor

The dominating influence at most of the Angkor sites is Indian. Although they did not attempt to colonize the area known today as Cambodia, their widespread trading network and the appeal of the Hindu beliefs spread their influence to much of Southeast Asia. The influence on the architecture is clear, but this influence didn't spread to the culture and art forms. Toward the end of the Angkorian period the influence shifted to Mahayana Buddhism. In fact, it was this Buddhist influence that was a major contributor to the fall of the God-King and the Angkorian (Khmer) empire.

● The Temples of Angkor

The influence of the Chenla predecessors can be seen in the temples of Angkor. Since these temples were modeled after Indian ones, the influence carried over to the Angkorian temples.

The first temples at Angkor were simple designs, but over time they evolved to the elaborate pillars, galleries and features seen at Angkor Wat and other wats in the complex today.

● **Common Elements**

Many of the temples in the Angkor complex share features ofIndian Hindu and Buddhist structures. The domed or hipped appearance is intended to symbolize Mount Meru's peaks, and most of the temples are surrounded by a wall representing the earth, with moats to represent the oceans. The central area in a temple was the residence of the god-king (devaraja).

The central tower was the keeping place for the images of the Hindu gods to which the temple was dedicated. These statues are largely gone – to museums and collectors in France and other parts of the world. Very few are still in their original sites, or even in Cambodian museums. Also kept within the central temple structures were sacred scriptures and other materials. These temples were not for worship but rather places to store and safeguard the images of the gods. Only priests entered them; the common people stayed outside in long-vanished wooden structures.

As you walk around and through the Angkor temples you will quickly discover almost all the windows and doors are false, so there is little light inside the temples. After all, why bother providing light in a place almost no one ever got to visit?

Mortar was not used and the concepts of the arch and flying buttress (integral to Angkor Wat's contemporary – Notre Dame) were unknown. Instead, the temples use a technique called *corbelling* – a primitive form of vaulting that severely limited the height of buildings and the load-bearing ability of the walls.

As the shift from Hinduism to Mahayana Buddhism occurred (12th century), the building styles didn't change much, but the gods inside did. A good example of the changes can be seen at Bayon.

● **Statues, Carvings, Bas-Reliefs & Sculpture**

As the temples evolved from their simple Chenla period precursors into ornate monuments, so did the ornamenting change and become more intricate. Carvings progressed from

Cambodia

simple figures to ornate lintels, carved columns at doorways, to elaborate bas-reliefs depicting Hindu stories. Baphoun is an excellent example of some of these allegorical Hindu stories in bas-relief. A good guide is invaluable to explain what you are seeing and how the carvings (and buildings) evolved.

Although early buildings (Preah Ko) are largely built of brick, the next iteration of buildings was made of the soft sandstone found in the area. Sandstone was much easier to carve and inscribe than brick, so the bas-reliefs and other carving and statuary became ever more elaborate. Moats and foundations were laid with laterite, a stone easy to cut and shape, and common to the area around Angkor.

As the Angkor period ended, buildings were increasingly constructed from wood. This wood was ornately carved, but very little survives today – the humid climate is not conducive to long-term survival of anything made of organic matter.

● Visiting the Temples of Angkor

Angkor Thom: The royal capital city, built by Jayavarman VII (12th century), is called Angkor Thom. The entire city was walled and surrounded by a moat that was several hundred yards wide. It may have been populated with alligators to help discourage marauding invaders. Much of the complex was destroyed by invading Chams, and the site was rebuilt. A few temples in the area (Baphoun and Phimeanakas) survived the destruction and became part of the new city.

There are five gateways into the city – one facing each compass point and one (the Victory Gate) that leads from the Royal Palace to the East Baray (a baray is an artificial lake or reservoir). As you stand there, try to imagine parades of elephants with their howdahs passing through, bearing the royal family and their cortege. Elephants were highly venerated and valued in a culture with no other way to do the heavy work or get from place to place.

There are five causeways that pass over the former moat. They are lined on one side with demons and on the other side with gods.

● **Bayon**

This is one of the temples Jayavarman VII built when he restored his royal city. It is in the center of Angkor Thom. As you walk around the Angkor Thom site, keep in mind that no walled European city of the time came close to this size, nor were the walls anywhere near as high (eight m/24 feet) or their moats as wide (100 m/300 feet).

The Bayon is one of the most impressive sights in the entire area. You can get a much better perspective on this wat than many others because it was not built within the traditional wall – Jayavarman VII must have decided the outer walls were enough.

It is shaped like a pyramid with four towers that are actually carved heads of Jayavarman as a Bodhisattra. There are additional carvings on each head of lotus flowers and numerous smaller towers with heads that look to the compass

Cambodia

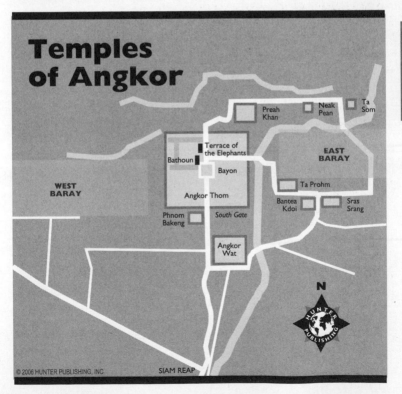

Temples of Angkor

Preah Khan

Neak Pean

Ta Som

Terrace of the Elephants

Bathoun

Bayon

EAST BARAY

WEST BARAY

Angkor Thom

Ta Prohm

Phnom Bakeng

South Gate

Bantea Kdoi

Sras Srang

Angkor Wat

N

HUNTER PUBLISHING

© 2006 HUNTER PUBLISHING, INC.

SIAM REAP

points. The all-seeing god-king, perhaps? The walls of the building are decorated in bas-reliefs, but the ones at Angkor Wat are much more impressive.

● The Royal Enclosure

The site built upon by Jayavarman VII was actually already in use. An earlier emperor, Suryavarman I, had laid it out; Jayavarman made additions and improvements.

One of the top sites in the Royal Enclosure is the **Terrace of the Elephants (the Royal Terrace)**; another is the **Kleangs**, believed to have provided accommodations for foreign ambassadors and dignitaries. All of these buildings pre-date Jayavarman VII.

Terrace of the Elephants (courtesy itravelnet.com)

Tip: The Terrace of the Elephants is a must-see.

Phimeanakas (Celestial or Flying Palace) was renovated by Suryavarman I. At one time (according to Chou Ta-kuan) this entire structure was sheathed in gold. Now it is a ruin, but you can still see the lions that used to guard the four entrances to the central tower.

Until the construction of the Phimeanakas the Angkor site buildings had square bases. Now, for the first time, a rectangular base was used.

The Baphoun

The **Baphoun** is one of the most important temples to see at the Angkor site – one of the few buildings to survive the sacking by the Chams. It is not in a good state of repair, so it is more noteworthy for its builder (Udayadityavarman II) than its architecture. In its heyday only Bayon was a larger temple.

● Phnom Bakheng

As you head south from Angkor Thom you will come to the "temple mountain" – Phnom Bakheng. There is a Buddha footprint and great views of the surrounding area – especially Angkor Wat – from the 60-m (200-foot) hill. You can climb the hill or ride an elephant. The elephant rides are over-priced ($15 or so) but the elephants need the work if they are going to eat.

● Angkor Wat

In addition to being the symbol on the Cambodian flag, this is the temple that people most want to see. In fact, most people think the entire site is called Angkor Wat.

Angkor means "city" or "capital," and a "wat" is a temple, so Angkor Wat is the temple city or city temple for the royal city of the Angkorian kings.

The Angkor Wat is probably the largest religious complex ever built. Pictures don't do it justice. The site covers about 200 acres.

As is typical with most Khmer temples, the outline of Angkor Wat, with its stylized domes, is meant to symbolize a religious story – in this case the home of gods, Mount Meru. The gods reside at the top – the main tower. The other five towers represent the five peaks of the mountain.

Angkor Wat is in surprisingly good condition for two main reasons. First, it was used as living and working quarters by Buddhist monks for much of the time since the demise of the Angkorian Empire. Second, even the Khmer Rouge stayed away in their rampages.

Around the wat is a huge moat and a high retaining wall covered in bas-reliefs. The bas-reliefs are some of the greatest cultural treasures in Cambodia. They are probably in such good condition because of the former resident monks – their presence discouraged thievery.

There are 12 towers that can be reached via steep stairways.

> **Tip:** Trekking up and down stairways in Khmer monuments and temples is not for the faint of heart. The steps are uneven and steep.

Cambodia

The best way to see Angkor Wat and the other complexes around the area is to buy an English-language guidebook. You'll get all the details, maps, and suggested routes to suit your interests.

> **Note:** Khmer culture didn't begin with Angkor. Not too far from the Angkor complex is the seventh-century complex of Sambor Prei Kuk. It is a Chenla-era complex of over 100 temples, about 35 km/22 miles north of the town of Kompong Thom. Local travel agents or your hotel can arrange an excursion.

Around the Area

To the east of Angkor Thom are several monuments and wats of interest.

Chau Say Tevoda and Thommanon are just outside the east gate. **Chau Say Tevoda** has a fair number of carvings in good condition. Most are of Vishnu, although the temple is dedicated to Shiva. The other temple is largely in ruins.

Ta Keo is a huge edifice is to the east of the complex. It is over 50 m (165 feet) high, and was never completed. It is built largely of sandstone – one of the earliest buildings made this way.

Ta Prohm is south of Ta Keo. It still stands largely surrounded by jungle. The experience of the jungle makes the side-trip worthwhile. Cambodia used to be covered by jungle, but only a few sections of it remain.

Bantay Kdei is another huge temple complex, also to the east (about three km/1.8 miles) from Angkor Thom. Little is known about what appears to be a hodge-podge of buildings and towers.

Carving from Chau Say Tevoda

One of the oldest buildings in the area is **Prasat Kravan**. It dates from 921 and is unusual because it is built of brick, at a time when laterite and sandstone were the materials of choice.

Pre Rup is also nearby, and its claim to fame is as the first building to use the five-tower (Mount Meru) motif as its central theme, 150 years before Angkor Wat was built.

The **Eastern Baray** (Lake) is also in this area. It is dry now. In the middle stands the East Mebon with its five towers, dating from 952.

To the north of Angkor Thom are several buildings of interest.

Preah Khan is about four km/2.4 miles from the Bayon. It is a 12th-century walled complex and was the capital immediately preceding the move to Angkor Thom.

To the west of Angkor Thom is the **Western Baray** (lake) with the **West Mebon** in the middle. The bronze statue of Vishnu (in the national museum in Phnom Penh) was found here. The lake is still in use today.

Ak Thom is also to the west and is noteworthy as the oldest surviving temple in the region.

Outlying Temples

The main group of outlying temples is the **Roluos Group**, about 16 km/10 miles to the southeast of the main temple groups. The three main temples are the **Preah Ko** (879), **Bakong** (881), and **Lolei** (893). All three temples are Hindu sites and made of brick with stone entries.

There are additional complexes in the area – **Banteay Samre**, **Bantey Srei**, **Phnom Kulen**, **Beng Mealea**, and **Preah Vihear**. All have certain appeal, and a comprehensive guidebook

Roluos Group statue

bought in Siem Reap is your best way to decide where else to visit.

Transportation in Town

You might really enjoy walking.

Hiking, Cycling & Walking

You can cycle, but you are taking a big risk. Still, many hotels and street-side kiosks will rent bikes or scooters for $2-$10 per day.

Scooter drivers are glad to offer you a lift for a few dollars.

Useful Information

Airlines

All travel companies should be able to handle flight confirmations and reservations for you.

The main airline addresses and telephone numbers are:

Bangkok Airlines/Siem Reap Airlines, Airport Road, ☎ 380191.

Lao Aviation, opposite the provincial hospital. No phone. Normal business hours.

President Airlines, Sivatha Street, ☎ 964338.

Vietnam Airlines, Airport Road, ☎ 964488.

Embassies & Consulates

None

Internet/Communications

You can go to most post offices and make international calls at a steep price. Better is to buy a calling card and go to one of the many calling centers popping up all over.

There also lots of Internet cafés now, and the cost for high-speed is $3-$5 per hour. Big hotels really rip you off – they charge for every bit you send or receive, in addition to charging upwards of $20 per hour.

Medical Facilities

It is best to try to get to HCMC or Thailand if you need serious care. Pharmacies will dispense almost anything (such as antibiotics) without a prescription. Make sure you know what you are taking and that it is not expired.

■ Battambang

Battambang is a sleepy town on the western end of the Tonle Sap. There are a few temples, and not a lot else. However, if you arrive by fast boat from Siem Reap or mini-bus and then truck from Bangkok you may appreciate the break in your journey.

The main sights are the market and the largely intact Colonial buildings that fill the town.

Getting There

There are three main ways to arrive and depart – by air, truck, or speedboat.

There are daily flights from Phnom Penh. This is the way I recommend making the trip if you must go to Battambang. The cost is about $100 on President Airlines.

From Thailand you take a mini-bus and then switch to an overcrowded truck at the border. The truck ride, combined with the rough roads (potholes the size of VW Beetles and bridges that are terrifyingly beat up – you can see the rivers below, right through the bridge base), is not fun.

From Siem Reap (or Phnom Penh) you can take a speedboat across the Tonle Sap, swamping villages as you pass by. You can also go by road in another overcrowded pick-up truck.

In theory you can take a train from Phnom Penh but it is slow and unreliable.

The truck trip from Siem Reap to Battambang costs $5-$10, depending on whether you sit inside or outside. The trip from Battambang to the border is about the same.

The speedboat trip from Siem Reap to Battambang costs $15-$20. It takes three to four hours; the trucks are much slower.

Where to Stay

There are no hotels of note, and not all that many guesthouses. Many of the places to stay have unreliable hot water and shared facilities, and rarely include breakfast.

$$ **Teo Hotel**, Road 3, ☎ 015-535067. This is a new hotel with air conditioning and private bathrooms. It's a bit out of the way, but nothing is far in this small town.

Where to Eat

There are a few cafés near the river. You could try the **White Rose**, near the Angkor Hotel, or the new and nice **World Café** (on the river).

There is little in the way of services except for a few Internet cafés. The market is interesting for an hour or so. If you need medical help, get to Thailand or HCMC.

■ Sihanoukville

If you want to check out the Cambodian beaches Sihanoukville is probably your best bet. You can also continue onward to catch a boat to Thailand. Note that if you arrive from Thailand at any border crossing, including this one, you need to have your visa first.

The town is an alternative royal seat, founded in 1964 by Prince Sihanouk as a deep water port. It is incidentally just about the only seaside resort in Cambodia.

Getting There & Away

Most people arrive by bus or mini-bus from Phnom Penh or Siem Reap, and depart the same way. The buses are cheap and reliable. Expect to pay $3-$5.

Since this is an alternative royal seat the road from Phnom Penh is pretty well-maintained.

You can also fly in on **President Air** from Phnom Penh for about $50 each way.

Finally, you can come and go by boat from Koh Kong (Koh Island) for about $15.

Where to Stay

The level of accommodation is improving rapidly. Although not all places are up to Western standards, there is plenty to choose from.

A few places to try:

Ochental Beach

$$ Orchidee Guesthouse, ☎ 9333639. Filled with orchids, friendly and well run. Clean, with private baths and air conditioned rooms. Only a five-minute walk to the beach.

Victory Beach

$ Chez Mari-yan, Sankat 3, Khan Mittapheap, ☎ 933709. Adequate, with nine wood bungalows, no hot water. Has its own seafood restaurant.

Where to Eat

There are small seafood restaurants all along the coast. Try the restaurant at **Chez Mari-yan** at Victory Beach or **Les Feuilles** at Ochental Beach.

Entertainment

Sihanoukville is not known for its nightlife. You will find a few bars in town and that's about it.

You can also try sport fishing for day-time excitement. **Condor Marine** at the Marlin Bar and Grill can set you up.

What to Do & See

The town sits on a peninsula that juts into the Gulf of Thailand. The beaches are lovely, the water is still clean, and the temperature is pleasant most of the year.

The three beaches are:

☐ Victory Beach

☐ Park or Independence Beach

☐ Ochental Beach

Ochental Beach is the farthest south and generally considered to be the best.

Close by (a 30-minute drive) is **Preah Sihanouk National Park**, with mangrove swamps, forests, and two islands. There is also a coral reef and lots of wildlife. You can take a half- or full-day boat tour to explore the area (about $25 for up to four people). You can also trek three to five hours (guide required) for just a few dollars. There is limited, basic accommodation at the entry station if you don't make a day-trip. The best way to get there is to hire a motorbike driver or a car and driver in Sihanoukville.

Local Transportation

Much of the area lends itself to walking, and you can also catch a ride with local moto operators for well under $1 (a few thousand Riel). If you really want to you can rent your own motorbike from many of the guesthouses for about $10 per day.

There are taxis that overcharge ($5 flat fee) to the beach.

You can hire a boat and pilot for part or all of a day and visit nearby islands.

■ Bokor Hill Station - Kampot

This is one of the few areas of Cambodia that is still largely covered in forest. If you are lucky (or not so lucky) you might see elephants, tigers, leopards, civets, gibbons, and countless birds. The French knew this area because it was much cooler than most of Cambodia (the elevation of over 1,000 m/3,000 feet helps). Beware of landmines if you must venture off the roads and tracks.

Getting There & Away

The base most people use is Kampot, then they hire a car or motorbike (and driver) and spend the day at Bokor, a trip of about 40 km (90 minutes) each way.

Where to Stay

Kampot is your best bet. There are a few guesthouses, none with impressive facilities. You might try:

$$ **Marco Polo Hotel**, ☎ 033-932314.

$ **Borey Bokor Hotel**, ☎ 033-932826.

Where to Eat

Most of the guesthouses have a simple restaurant attached. Otherwise your choices are limited. You might try:

- **Procham Mit**
- **Mittapheap**
- **The Little Garden Bar**

All are at or close to the riverfront.

Books & Websites

Books

Angkor, An Introduction to the Temples by Dawn Rooney. (1994, Passport).

Angkor, Heart of an Asian Empire by Bruno Dagens (Thames & Hudson).

The Splendors of Angkor Thom, by Michael Buckley.

Websites

Birdwatching

www.camacdonald.com/birding/asiavietnam.htm

Country Websites

❖ Cambodia-Specific

www.cambodia.org
www.worldinfozone.com/country.php?country=Cambodia
www.cia.gov/cia/publications/factbook/geos/cb.html
www.nationsonline.org/oneworld/cambodia.htm
www.angkorwat.org
www.aneki.com/Cambodia.html

❖ Laos-Specific

www.worldinfozone.com/country.php?country=Laos
www.aneki.com/Laos.html
www.muonglao.com
www.laosnews.net
www.cia.gov/cia/publications/factbook

❖ Vietnam-Specific

www.vietnamonline.net
www.worldinfozone.com/country.php?country=Vietnam
www.cia.gov/cia/publications/factbook/geos/vm.html
www.aneki.com/Vietnam.html
http://geography.about.com/library/maps/blvietnam.htm
www.vietnam-holidays.com/vietnam_holidays.asp

Cycling

www.veloasia.com

Eco-Travel

www.ecotravel.com
www.zeal.com/category/preview.jhtml?cid=220206
www.wildernessweb.com

General Travel Information

www.interpidtravel.com
www.tripadvisor.com
www.talesofasia.com
www.aworldawaytravel.com
www.indochinatravel.com
www.mekong.net
www.state.gov

Golf

www.vietnamgolfresorts.com

Health - General

www.mdtravelhealth.com
www.tripprep.com
www.cdc.gov
www.who.org
www.istm.org

Health - Travel Insurance

www.insuremytrip.com

Hotels

www.asia-hotels.com

Maps

www.itmb.com

Newspapers & Magazines

www.iht.com
www.cnn.com
www.saigon-news.com

Transportation (Air)

www.united.com
www.cheaptickets.com
www.expedia.com
www.orbitz.com
www.cheaptravelnetwork.com
www.vietnamair.com.vn
www.bangkokair.com
www.mekongexpress.com/laos/schedule/ttcentre.htm (Lao Aviation)
www.siemreapairways.com
www.presidentairways.com
www.silkair.com

Trekking

www.wildernesstravel.com
www.iexplore.com/qmap/South+and+South-
east+Asia/Hiking+/+Trekking+/+Walking
www.nationalgeographic.com/adventure/0210/trips_33_seasia.html
www.indepthadventures.com
http://gorp.away.com/gorp/location/asia/seasia/top_twenty17.htm

Visas

www.vietnamembassy-usa.org

Weather

www.weatherbug.com
www.weather.com
www.worldweather.com

Index

Accommodations, 35-38; Champasak, Laos, 226-227; Da Lat, Vietnam, 159-161; Danang, Vietnam, 140-142; Hanoi, Vietnam, 111-114; Ho Chi Minh City, Vietnam, 167, 169-170; Hoi An, Vietnam, 146; Hué, Vietnam, 133-134; Kampot, Cambodia, 313; Luang Prabang, Laos, 244-246; Mekong Delta, Vietnam, 178-179; Nha Trang, Vietnam, 152, 154; Pakse, Laos, 231-232; Phnom Penh, Cambodia, 279-281; Sa Pa, Vietnam, 128; Savannakhet, Laos, 223; Siem Reap/Angkor Wat, Cambodia, 292-293; Vang Vieng, Laos, 216; Vientiane, Laos, 204, 206-207; Vietnam, 108

Adoption racket, 90

Adventures, 4-5; Laos, 198-201, 252-262; Vietnam, 182-188

Allergies, 24

Altitude sickness, 184-185

American War of Aggression (Vietnam War), 92-96

Angkor Complex, Cambodia, 80, 294-307; around the area, 306-307; culture and lifestyle, 300; landmines, 298; main temples and sights, 296-299, 300-306; map, 303; poisonous snakes, 298; restoration, 299-300; souvenirs, 299; *see also* Siem Reap

Antibiotics, 28-29

ATMs, 9-10, 18

Bac Ha, Vietnam, 130

Bach Ma National Park, Vietnam, 143-144

Battambang, Cambodia, 80, 309-310

Beaches: Danang, Vietnam, 143; Hon Tam, Vietnam, 157; Sihanoukville, Cambodia, 310-312

Ben Tre, Vietnam, 178, 179, 181

Boating: Laos, 258-259; Mekong River (Cambodia), 288-289; Mekong River (Laos), 213-214, 250, 261-262; safety, 259

Bokeo, Laos, 219-220

Bokor Hill Station, Kampot, Cambodia, 312-313

Bolovens Plateau, Laos, 191

Business hours, 18

Cambodia, 263-313; about the country, 75-78, 263; adoption racket, 90; Angkor Wat, 80, 294-307; car rental, 279; climate, 276-277; culture and customs, 85-89; embassies, 13-14, 290; food, 84-85; getting there and getting around, 90-92, 289-290; highlights, 79-80, history, 81-83, 263-270; land, 3; language, 89; map, 75; medical concerns, 279; money matters, 18-19; sex trade, 89-90; suggested itineraries, 78-79; touring, 78-80; visas, 90

Canoeing and kayaking, Laos, 258-259

Can Tho, Vietnam, 179, 181

Car rental; driving, 6-7, 279

Cat Ba Island, Vietnam, 127

Caving (spelunking), Laos, 200, 249-250

Cell phones, 32

Champasak, Laos, 61, 189, 201, 226-231; accommodations, 226-227; day-trips from, 230-231; restaurants, 228; temple complex, 229-230
Chinese border, 42, 127
Cholera immunization, 28
Credit cards, safety, 10-11
Crime: drugs, 8; robbery, 8-9; shoe thefts, 7
Cu Chi Tunnels, Vietnam, 176
Customs: departure cards, 17; departure taxes, 17; embassies, 12-15; and immigration, 16-17; passport safety, 10; visas, 15-16
Cycling: itineraries, Vietnam, 186-188; Luang Prabang, Laos, 250; Mekong Delta, Vietnam, 180, 182-183; Vientiane, Laos, 214

Da Lat, Vietnam, 43, 46, 99, 158-164; accommodations, 159-161; day-trips from, 163; restaurants, 161; shopping, 161-162; sightseeing, 162-163
Danang, Vietnam, 46, 99, 139-144
Datanla Falls, Vietnam, 163
Dengue fever, 26
Departure cards, 17
Departure taxes, 17
Dining, see Restaurants
DMZ, Vietnam, 98
DPT (diphtheria, pertussis, tetanus), 27
Driving, 6-7, 279
Drugs, 8

Electrical appliances, 17, 32
Elephant trekking, Laos, 199, 256-258
Encephalitis, 26, 28

Fan Si Pan Mountain, Vietnam, 128, 129
Flora and fauna, 52, 144
Food: Cambodia, 84-85; Laos, 74; Vietnam, 55-56; see also Restaurants

Hai Phong, Vietnam, 42
Ha Long Bay, Vietnam, 42-43, 98, 127
Hanoi, Vietnam, 42, 97-98, 108-131; accommodations, 111-114; climate, 106-107; day-trips from, 127-131; embassies and consulates, 126; getting there and getting around, 109-111, 120-121, 125-126; history, 108-109; Internet/communications, 126; leaving, 131; map, 110; medical facilities, 126; nightlife, 117; restaurants, 114-116; shopping, 116-119; sightseeing, 121-125; tours, 119-120
HCMC (Saigon), see Ho Chi Minh City
Health and medical issues, 23-29; allergies, 24; antibiotics, 28-29; "Asian crud," 24; illnesses, 23-28; immunizations, 23, 27-28; jet-lag, 29; low-quality supplies, 32; medical facilities, 29, 126; mosquitoes, 25-26; pharmacies, 29; preventive measures, 24-25
Hepatitis vaccine, 27
Hiking, see Trekking and hiking
Hill tribes, Laos, 254-255
Ho An Lake, Vietnam, 42, 122
Ho Chi Minh City (HCMC), Vietnam, 43-44, 46-47, 99, 164-177; accommodations, 167, 169-170; climate, 104-105; consulates, 176; getting there and getting around, 165-166, 172-173, 176; history, 164-165;

Internet/communications, 177; map, 168; medical facilities, 177; nightlife, 171; restaurants, 170-171; shopping, 171; sightseeing, 173-176; tours, 172

Hoi An, Vietnam, 43, 46, 145-152; accommodations, 146; day-trips from, 150-151; map, 147; restaurants, 147; shopping, 98-99, 147-148, 150; sightseeing, 148-150

Hon Mieu, Vietnam, 157
Hon Tam, Vietnam, 157
Hon Tre, Vietnam, 157

Hué, Vietnam, 43, 98, 131-139; accommodations, 133-134; getting there and getting around, 132, 139; history, 131-132; Internet/communications, 139; map, 136; medical facilities, 139; nightlife, 134; restaurants, 134; sightseeing, 135-139; tours, 135

Illnesses, 23-28
Immigration and customs, 16-17
Immunizations, 23, 27-28
Indochina: accommodations, 35-38; adventures, 4-5; business hours, 18; cautions and advice, 6-11; climate and weather, 31; cultural activities, 5; customs, immigration and visas, 12-17; electrical appliances, 17; getting there and getting around, 30-31; health and medical issues, 23-29; information sources, 314-315; the land, 3-4; laundry, 19; money matters, 9-11, 18-19; packing tips, 31-35; recent past, 2-3; restaurants, 38; tours, 19-23; and Vietnam War, 92-96; why come here?, 4
Influenza immunization, 28

Internet/communications, 6

Jet-lag, 29
Jewelry, 11

Kampot, Cambodia, 312-313
Kampuchea, see Cambodia
Kayaking and canoeing, Laos, 258-259
Khmer Republic, see Cambodia
Killing Fields (Choueng Ek), Cambodia, 288

Landmines, 151, 298
Lao Cai, Vietnam, 127, 130
Laos, 189-262; about the country, 57-59, 189-193; adventures, 198-201, 252-262; arts and crafts, 72-73; climate, 198, 203; customs and culture, 63-64, 71-74; departure taxes, 17; embassies, 14-15, 215; food, 74; getting there and getting around, 68-71, 201-203; highlights, 61-62; hill tribes, 254-255; history, 64-67, 193-198; Internet/communications, 215; land, 4; map, 58; medical facilities, 215; money matters, 18-19, 215; Northern, 234-262, religion, 71-72, sightseeing, 203-204; suggested itineraries, 60; touring, 60-62, 260-261; visas, 67-68
Laundry, 19
Luang Prabang, Laos, 61, 235-252; accommodations, 244-246; day-trips from, 248-249; getting there and getting around, 238-241, 251; history, 235, 237-238; Internet & communications, 251; map, 236; money changers, 251; nightlife, 247; restaurants, 246-247; shopping, 247-248; sightseeing, 189-190, 201,

241-244; tours, 248; trekking, 251, 261; walking tour, 244

Malaria, 25-26
Maps: Angkor temples, Cambodia, 303; Cambodia, 75; Hanoi, Vietnam, 110; Ho Chi Minh City, Vietnam, 168; Hoi An, Vietnam, 147; Hué, Vietnam, 136; Laos, 58; Luang Prabang, Laos, 236; Mekong Delta, Vietnam, 178; Nha Trang, Vietnam, 153; Phnom Penh, Cambodia, 278; Sa Pa, Vietnam, 129; Vientiane, Laos, 205; Vietnam, 99; Vietnam regions, 51
Marble Mountains, Vietnam, 43, 46, 143
Medical concerns, 23-29; antibiotics, 28-29; facilities, 29, 126; illnesses, 23-28; immunizations, 23, 27-28; pharmacies, 29; preventive measures, 24-25
Mekong Delta, 61, 99-100, 177-182; accommodations, 178-179; cycling, 180, 182-183; map, 178; restaurants, 179; shopping, 180
Mekong River, 44, 61; boating (Cambodia), 288-289; boating (Laos), 213-214, 250, 261-262
Meningitis vaccination, 27
Mines, unexploded, 151, 298
Money matters, 18-19; ATMs, 9-10, 18; credit cards, 10-11; money pouch, 9; robbery, 8-9; US dollars, 18; vouchers, 11
Mosquitoes, 25-26
Motorcycle touring, Vietnam, 188
Mountain biking, Laos, 258
Mount Sapa, Vietnam, trekking, 184
Muang Ngoi, Laos, 259-260

Muang Sing, Laos, 190
My Son, Vietnam, 150-151
My Tho, Vietnam, 178, 179

Nha Trang, Vietnam, 43, 46, 99, 152-157; accommodations, 152, 154; map, 153; nightlife, 155; restaurants, 154-155; sightseeing, 156-157; tours, 155; watersports, 155
Nightlife: Hanoi, Vietnam, 117; Ho Chi Minh City, Vietnam, 171; Hué, Vietnam, 134; Luang Prabang, Laos, 247; Nha Trang, Vietnam, 155; Vientiane, Laos, 208
Northern Laos, 234-262; adventures, 252-262; Luang Prabang, 235-252

Oudong, Cambodia, 287-288
Oum Moung temple complex, Laos, 230-231

Packing tips, 31-35
Pakse, Laos, 231-234
Passports, safety, 10
Pharmacies, 29
Phnom Penh, Cambodia, 79, 277-290; accommodations, 279-281; airlines, 289-290; day-trips from, 287-289; embassies/consulates, 290; Internet/communications, 290; map, 278; medical concerns, 279, 290; restaurants, 282-283; sightseeing, 283-287
Plain of Jars, Laos, 61, 190-191, 220-221
Pneumonia immunization, 28
Polio shots, 27
Preah Sihanouk National Park, Cambodia, 312
Prenn Waterfall, Vietnam, 163

Rafting, Laos, 258-259

Red River Estuary and Delta, Vietnam, 130-131

Restaurants, 38; Da Lat, Vietnam, 161; Danang, Vietnam, 142; Hanoi, Vietnam, 114-116; Ho Chi Minh City, Vietnam, 170-171; Hoi An, Vietnam, 147; Hué, Vietnam, 134; Kampot, Cambodia, 313; Luang Prabang, Laos, 246-247; Mekong Delta, Vietnam, 179; Nha Trang, Vietnam, 154-155; Pakse, Laos, 232; Phnom Penh, Cambodia, 282-283; Sa Pa, Vietnam, 129; Savannakhet, Laos, 223; Siem Reap/Angkor Wat, Cambodia, 293-294; Vang Vieng, Laos, 217; Vientiane, Laos, 207-208

River safety, 259

Robbery, 8-9

Safety: ATMs, 9-10; boating, 259; credit cards, 10-11; discussing politics or religion, 88; drinking water, 7-8, 28; driving, 6-7; drugs, 8; extra baggage, 31; jewelry, 11; passport, 10; poisonous snakes, 298; robbery, 8-9; shoes, 7; unexploded ordnance, 151, 298; valuables, 10-11

Saigon, *see* Ho Chi Minh City

Sa Pa, Vietnam, 42, 127-130; accommodations, 128; map, 129; restaurants, 129; trekking, 183-184

Savannakhet, Laos, 191, 222-225

Sex trade, 89-90

Shoes, theft of, 7

Shopping: bargaining, 118; Da Lat, Vietnam, 161-162; Hanoi, Vietnam, 116-119; Ho Chi Minh City, Vietnam, 171; Hoi An, Vietnam, 98-99, 147-148, 150; Luang Prabang, Laos, 247-248; Mekong Delta floating markets, Vietnam, 180; opening hours, 18; Vientiane, Laos, 208-209

Siem Reap/Angkor Wat, Cambodia, 290-309; accommodations, 292-293; Angkor complex, 294-307; getting there and getting around, 291-292, 308; Internet/communications, 308; restaurants, 293-294; tours, 294

Sihanoukville, Cambodia, 310-312

Snakes, poisonous, 298

Spelunking (caving), Laos, 200, 249-250

Tetanus vaccination, 27

Thailand, departure taxes, 17

That Luang, Laos, 213

Tours, 19-23

Trekking and hiking: altitude sickness, 184-185; Fan Si Pan Mountain, Vietnam, 128, 129; Luang Prabang, Laos, 251, 261; Mount Sapa, Vietnam, 184; Northern Laos, 252-255, 261; Sa Pa, Vietnam, 183-184

Typhoid vaccination, 27

Unexploded ordnance (landmines), 151, 298

Valuables: jewelry, 11; safety, 10-11

Vang Vieng, Laos, 61, 191-192, 216-218

Vientiane, Laos, 192-193, 204-216; accommodations, 204, 206-207; day-trips from, 213; getting around, 209-212, 214; map, 205; nightlife, 208; restaurants, 207-208; shopping, 208-209; sightseeing, 212-213; tours, 209

Vietnam, 97-188; about the country, 39-41, 97-100; accommodations, 108; adventure travel, 182-188; climate, 52, 103-107; customs and culture, 51; DMZ, 98; embassies, 12-13; flora and fauna, 52, 144; food basics, 55-56; geography, 51-52; getting there and getting around, 44, 56-57, 100-103; government and economy, 52-53; highlights, 46-47; Hill Country, 99; history, 47-50; land, 3, 51-52; lifestyles, 53-55; map, 99; money matters, 18-19; Northwest Mountains, 97; packing tips, 107-108; regions (map), 51; suggested itineraries, 44-46; touring, 41-47; visas, 56

Vietnam War (American War of Aggression), 92-96

Vinh Long, Vietnam, 179

Visas, 15-16; Cambodia, 90; Laos, 67-68; Vietnam, 56

Vouchers, 11

Walking itineraries, Vietnam, 185-186

Water, drinking (DON'T!), 7-8, 28

Watersports, Nha Trang, Vietnam, 155

Weather, 31; Cambodia, 276-277; Laos, 198, 203; Vietnam, 103-107

Xieng Khoung, Laos, 220-222

Yellow fever immunization, 28